# JOHN KEBLE
# IN CONTEXT

Anthem Nineteenth Century Studies

Series editor: Robert Douglas-Fairhurst

Other titles in the series:

David Clifford and Laurence Roussillon, eds,
*Outsiders Looking In: The Rossettis Then and Now* (2004)

Simon James, *Unsettled Accounts:
Money and Narrative in the Novels of George Gissing* (2003)

Bharat Tandon, *Jane Austen and the Morality of Conversation* (2003)

# JOHN KEBLE IN CONTEXT

edited by
Kirstie Blair

Anthem Press
London

This edition first published by Anthem Press 2004

Anthem Press is an imprint of
Wimbledon Publishing Company
75–76 Blackfriars Road
London SE1 8HA
or
PO Box 9779, London SW19 7QA

This selection © Wimbledon Publishing Company 2004
Individual articles © individual contributors

The moral right of the authors to be identified as the authors of this work
has been asserted

All rights reserved. No part of this publication may be reproduced, stored in a retrieval system, or transmitted, in any form or by any means, without the prior permission in writing of Wimbledon Publishing Company, or as expressly permitted by law, or under terms agreed with the appropriate reprographics rights organization.

British Library Cataloguing in Publication Data
Data available

Library of Congress in Publication Data
A catalogue record has been applied for

1 3 5 7 9 10 8 6 4 2

ISBN 1 84331 146 1 (hbk)
ISBN 1 84331 147 X (pbk)

Typeset by Pentagon Graphics Pvt. Ltd., Chennai, India
Printed in India

# CONTENTS

*Acknowledgements*   vii

*Contributors*   viii

*Preface*
MICHAEL WHEELER   xi

Introduction   1
KIRSTIE BLAIR

**PART I. Reconsiderations: Keble's place in Tractarian politics and religion**

1. Keble's Creweian Oration of 1839: The Idea of a Christian University   19
   STEPHEN PRICKETT

2. 'The Duty of the State': Keble, the Tractarians and Establishment   33
   S. A. SKINNER

3. John Keble, National Apostasy, and the Myths of 14 July   47
   MARK CHAPMAN

4. John Keble and the Ethos of the Oxford Movement   59
   JAMES PEREIRO

**PART II. Reading Keble's Writings: The Poet and the Pastor**

5. Ways of Reading 1825: Leisure, Curiosity, and Morbid Eagerness   75
   WILLIAM MCKELVY

6. 'National Apostasy', *Tracts For The Times*, and *Plain Sermons*: Keble's Tractarian Prose   89
   ROBERT H. ELLISON

7. *Lyra Innocentium* (1846) and its Contexts   101
   J. R. WATSON

## PART III. Influence and Resistance: Literary Heirs and Successors

8. 'Healing relief...without detriment to modest reserve...':
   Keble, Women's Poetry and Victorian Cultural Theory 115
   EMMA FRANCIS

9. 'Her Silence Speaks': Keble's Female Heirs 125
   EMMA MASON

10. 'For rigorous teachers seized my youth': Thomas Arnold,
    John Keble and the Juvenilia of Arthur Hugh Clough and
    Matthew Arnold 143
    DANIEL KLINE

11. *In Memoriam* and *The Christian Year* 159
    MARION SHAW

12. 'A Handmaid to the Church': How John Keble Shaped
    the Career of Charlotte Yonge, the 'Novelist of the
    Oxford Movement' 175
    ELLEN JORDAN, CHARLOTTE MITCHELL AND
    HELEN SCHINSKE

# ACKNOWLEDGEMENTS

I am grateful to all the contributors for their work on this volume, and also to those who participated in the conference, in May 2003, from which this volume stems, but whose work is not represented here: Peter Groves, Esther Hu, Gavin Budge and all others who attended. Both the conference and this volume would not have been possible without the assistance of Keble College and the Oxford English Faculty. I am particularly indebted to the Principal of Keble College, Averil Cameron, and to the librarian, Margaret Sarosi.

I would also like to thank Emma Mason for her help and advice in preparing this volume; Robert Douglas-Fairhurst, for his valuable comments and criticism; and Elisabeth Jay, for fostering my interest in the Oxford Movement as a graduate student. I am also grateful to Tom Penn at Anthem Press for his interest in this project.

Kirstie Blair,<br>
Oxford, 2004

# CONTRIBUTORS

**Kirstie Blair** is a Supernumerary Fellow and Tutor in English at St Peter's College, Oxford, and prior to this was a Research Fellow and Tutor at Keble College. She has published work on Tennyson, George Eliot and Keble, and is currently completing her first book, *Victorian Poetry and the Culture of the Heart*, which will be published by Oxford University Press in 2005.

**Mark Chapman** is an Anglican Priest and Vice-Principal of Ripon College, Cuddesdon, Oxford, and a member of the Theology Faculty of Oxford University. He has written widely in the area of nineteenth- and twentieth-century theology and Church history. His books include *Ernst Troeltsch and Liberal Theology* (Oxford) and *The Coming Crisis* (Sheffield).

**Robert H. Ellison** is a Professor of English and Department Chair at East Texas Baptist University, where he has taught since 1995. His work on Victorian preaching includes *The Victorian Pulpit: Spoken and Written Sermons in Nineteenth-Century Britain* (Susquehanna, 1998) and an article on John Cumming published in *Victorian Literature and Culture* in 2003. His contribution to this volume will become part of his second book, tentatively entitled *Sermonizing Tractarians: The Preaching of the Authors of the 'Tracts for the Times'*.

**Emma Francis** is Lecturer in English at the University of Warwick. She is co-editor of *In a Queer Place: Sexuality and Belonging* (Ashgate, 2002) and has published essays on aspects of nineteenth-century British women's poetry. Her current research includes a monograph study *Women's Poetry and Women's Mission: British Women's Poetry and the Sexual Division of Culture, 1824–1894*.

**Ellen Jordan** holds a conjoint appointment in the School of Social Sciences at the University of Newcastle, Australia. Until recently her main area of research has been the history of women's work and the professions in nineteenth-century Britain, on which she has published a book and a number of articles. She is now developing an interest in High Anglican women of letters, in particular Anne Mozley and Charlotte Yonge, whose letters she is helping to edit.

**Daniel Kline** is a graduate student in the Department of English at Ohio State University, Columbus, Ohio. His research focuses on Victorian poetry and he is currently completing his doctoral dissertation on Victorian philology and the literary languages of Matthew Arnold and Arthur Hugh Clough. He has previously written on Matthew Arnold's *Sohrab and Rustum* in *Victorian Poetry*.

**William R. McKelvy**, Assistant Professor of English at Washington University, St. Louis, has published works on nineteenth-century figures ranging from Macaulay and Gladstone, to Tennyson and Eliot. He is currently finishing his first book, titled *The English Cult of Literature: Devoted Readers, 1770–1880*.

**Emma Mason** was recently appointed as Lecturer in Nineteenth-Century Poetry at the University of Warwick after a British Academy Postdoctoral Fellowship at Corpus Christi, Oxford. She is the author of *Women Poets of the Nineteenth-Century* (2004) and several articles on poetry and religion for *Victorian Literature and Culture*, *The Huntington Library Quarterly*, *The Journal of Victorian Culture*, *Romanticism on the Net* and *Victorian Poetry*. With Mark Knight, she is writing *Nineteenth-Century Religion and Literature: An Introduction* for Oxford University Press and her current project is a study of affection and Romantic lyric.

**Charlotte Mitchell** is a lecturer in the English department at University College London, and her main interest is nineteenth-century fiction. She co-authored *The Oxford Companion to Edwardian Fiction* (1997), and is one of the associate editors of the new *Oxford Dictionary of National Biography*. Currently she is editing a volume of short stories by Elizabeth Gaskell for the forthcoming complete edition, published by Pickering and Chatto. She has carried out much of the location research for the Yonge letters project, involving much badgering of surprised descendants of Yonge's correspondents.

**James Pereiro**, Chaplain of Grandpont House (Oxford), is an Associate Member of the Modern History Faculty at Oxford University. He holds degrees in History, Theology and Education, and has published extensively on ecclesiastical history of the nineteenth and twentieth centuries. His book *Cardinal Manning, An Intellectual Biography* (Oxford: Clarendon Press, 1998) has been published recently in Spanish.

**Stephen Prickett** is Margaret Root Brown Professor and Director of the Armstrong Browning Library at Baylor University, Texas. Previous appointments include the Regius Chair of English at the University of Glasgow, and the Chair of English at the Australian National University in Canberra. He is a Fellow of the Australian Academy of the Humanities, President of the George MacDonald Society, former Chairman of the U.K. Higher Education

Foundation, and former President of the European Society for the Study of Literature and Theology. His latest book, entitled *Narrative, Science and Religion: Fundamentalism versus Irony 1700–1999*, appeared with Cambridge University Press in 2002.

**Helen Erwin Schinske**, B.A. (Carleton College), M.Libr. (University of Washington) is a rare books librarian, book collector, and independent researcher who has been specializing in Yonge for about eight years. She is currently compiling a name-title index of the *Monthly Packet*. From 1990 to 1994 she was a cataloguer on the nineteenth-century American Children's Books Project at the American Antiquarian Society (Worcester, Mass.).

**Marion Shaw** is Emeritus Professor of English at Loughborough University. She has published on nineteenth-century literature, particularly on Tennyson, and is currently chair of the Tennyson Society Executive Committee. For several years until 1999 she was editor of the *Tennyson Research Bulletin*. She has also published on interwar women's writing, including a biography of Winifred Holtby, *The Clear Stream*, published in 1999. She is currently preparing an edition of Elizabeth Gaskell's *Sylvia's Lovers* for Chatto and Pickering and writing a study of general practitioners in the nineteenth century.

**Simon Skinner** is Fellow and Tutor in History at Balliol College and Lecturer in History at the University of Oxford. His *Tractarians and the 'Condition of England': the Social and Political thought of the Oxford Movement* is published by Oxford University Press (2004).

**J. R. Watson** is Emeritus Professor of English, University of Durham. He was educated at Oxford, where he won the Matthew Arnold Memorial Prize, and Glasgow, teaching at Glasgow and Leicester before going to Durham in 1978. He specialises in the Romantic and Victorian periods, with special interests in landscape and hymnology: his book *The English Hymn* (1997) was followed by *An Annotated Anthology of Hymns* (2002). In retirement he is attempting to edit a replacement for Julian's *Dictionary of Hymnology* (1892, 1907), a task which killed off several persons in the twentieth century.

**Michael Wheeler** was the founding Director of the Ruskin Programme and Ruskin Collection Project at Lancaster University, and then Director of Chawton House Library and Professor of English Literature at the University of Southampton. Now an independent scholar, he is also Director of the Gladstone Project, developing a unique residential library founded by England's most distinguished statesman. His publications include *Heaven, Hell and the Victorians* (Cambridge, 1994), and *Ruskin's God* (Cambridge, 1999). He is currently writing a book for CUP on the relationship between Catholicism and Protestantism in nineteenth-century English culture.

# PREFACE

## Michael Wheeler

John Henry Newman first set foot in Pome on 2 March 1833. Four days later, he and Hurrell Froude called on Nicholas Wiseman, then Rector of the English College, and were dismayed to learn that reunion with the Roman Communion would be impossible unless Anglicans fully accepted the Council of Trent. By 9 July, Newman was back in Oxford in time to hear, the following Sunday, the sermon which he came to regard as the 'start of the religious movement of 1833': John Keble's famous Assize Sermon on 'National Apostasy'. Eleven years earlier, when elected to a Fellowship at Oriel at the tender age of twenty-one, Newman had shaken hands with Keble, the 'first man in Oxford', and had 'felt so abashed and unworthy of the honour' done him, that he 'seemed desirous of quite sinking into the ground'.

Whereas Newman was an internationally renowned figure, rarely far from current religious controversies, Keble exercised his very considerable influence largely through *The Christian Year* and through personal contacts, both at Oxford and at Hursley, among his former pupils and colleagues. Whereas Newman felt that he was called to a single life, and spent his adulthood as a member of various male clerical societies, Keble was a married man and a country clergyman. Whereas Newman, at his busiest, was often on the move – hurrying up and down to London by coach and, later, train, enduring those frequent sea crossings to Dublin, and, as a Catholic, making more visits to Rome than he would have liked – one thinks of Keble moving about on foot, either crossing the quad or visiting the sick in his parish. He never visited Rome.

Newman's agonized relationship with Rome, before and after his conversion in 1845, has been discussed by numerous biographers and ecclesiastical historians. Much less has been said about Keble and Rome, not least because it is much less important in relation to Keble's religious and intellectual life. It is, however, illuminating. Keble's attitude towards Rome was shaped by his beliefs and opinions - on matters such as the apostolic succession and the doctrine of reserve – and by his worldview. Keble and his Roman Catholic contemporaries like Wiseman, we might say, lived in different worlds.

Yet Protestant cries of 'No Popery', which echoed through the early years of the nineteenth century, were after 1833 aimed at both Roman Catholics and Anglo-Catholics, sometimes in a confused and unfocused way. The Tractarians, also known as 'Puseyites', had, after all, challenged the Church of England to rediscover her historical identity as 'one Catholick and Apostolick Church'. Tractarians regarded themselves, not as 'Protestants' – a term reserved for Dissenters, in their view – but as 'Catholics'. Moving in a quite different direction from that of the older and more influential Evangelical movement, with its Protestant emphasis upon personal conversion and the authority of 'scripture', the Tractarians took great pains to raise the standard of Anglican public worship and private devotions, and tried to revive monastic traditions. The more extreme manifestations of these aims smacked of 'Popery', or 'papism', although those involved in the Anglo-Catholic revival saw it differently: their ideal was the beauty of holiness; their authority was grounded in tradition and the early Church; and their Catholicism was reformed. John Keble has been described as the 'patron saint' of the movement.

Conspiracy theories were rife, however. It was widely believed that Keble, Newman and Pusey, and their sometimes extreme ritualist followers, had a pact with the Pope and aimed to convert England to Roman Catholicism – a fear that seemed to be justified when Newman converted. Keble did not convert; indeed, in retrospect the very idea of his converting seems ludicrous. Two years after Newman and other friends had 'gone over', Keble published his *Sermons, Academical and Occasional* (Oxford: Parker, 1847). In the Preface, he reflected upon the 'safety' – a favourite word of his, here applied to salvation – of the Anglican who remained in the English fold and resisted the lure of Rome. 'The good Roman Catholic', he writes, 'is safe, by consent of both parties: not so the good English Catholic: therefore a prudent person will lose not time in ranging himself on the side of the former.' To a 'romantic imaginative mind', he adds, 'the Roman claims stand out in a very obvious manner, and the English deficiences are quite confessed and palpable'. So why stay? Keble's answer is prosaic and, more significantly, it is *homely*, in a way that is faintly reminiscent of George Herbert: 'to acquiesce in it, because it is providentially our own position, - to be dutiful and loyal amid the full consciousness of it, – savours of the same kind of generous contentment, as the not being ashamed of lowly parentage, nor unloving towards a dull monotonous home'. Earlier in the preface, Keble describes the Church of England, not as a home, but as a mother, arguing that it is an 'undutiful thing' for a good Anglican to 'doubt whether she be our real Mother, who has ever professed to be so'. Keble venerated his own father as an authority figure, and often cited his traditional views in the heady days of *Tracts for the Times*. His spiritual mother, however, was the Church of England, into which providence had placed him and whose claim to be his true mother could never be questioned. Once again, the contrast with Newman is telling. For Newman was to describe as the 'Mother of English Christianity' the city that Keble never visited – Rome.

Whereas a battalion of scholars has marched across the territory marked 'Newman' in modern times, and then marched back over it again, Keble scholars probably make up a couple of platoons, and some of them are reservists. When Kirstie Blair organized the conference at Keble College on which this book is based, some of the scattered few gathered together and enjoyed reinvestigating the life and career of this enormously influential, yet now grossly underestimated man. The collection of essays that Dr Blair has edited and introduced for a new generation of readers addresses some of the key questions about Keble in a lively and accessible way. She and her contributors deserve our thanks.

# INTRODUCTION

## Kirstie Blair

Writing in the 1930s, in one of the first twentieth-century biographies of John Keble, Kenneth Ingram looked forward prophetically to Keble's reputation in the modern age:

> They will either despise him as a man who worried intensely over technical issues which have no significance outside a narrow ecclesiastical sphere, or else they will pay him a romantic sentimental veneration, a devotion which is far too uncritical to have any relation to actual realities. (Ingram, 153)

With a few exceptions, Ingram's comment has been borne out by the historiography and literary criticism of Keble's life and works. There has been a dual tendency either to damn Keble with faint praise, recognising his strong beliefs while deprecating their objects, or to write a form of hagiography, glorifying his achievements for Anglicanism. One of the most significant twentieth-century works on Keble, for instance, Georgina Battiscombe's 1963 biography, is entitled *John Keble: A Study in Limitations*. While she acknowledges that some of Keble's 'limitations' – his conservatism, his traditionalism, his reluctance to engage with points of view opposite to his own – might have served as strengths, she also sees them as relegating him to lesser importance: her book describes someone who could have been great, had he not been so circumscribed by family, background and tradition (Battiscombe, *xviii–xix*). Owen Chadwick, in a review of Battiscombe's biography, took issue with this general predilection to criticize Keble for his failure to step forward as the true leader of the Oxford Movement:

> We must take Keble for himself, and not as a man unfitted to do what he is supposed to have done but never did. (Chadwick, 55)

This is a salutary warning, and one that has not always been heeded by critics and historians. Even when defending him and arguing for his significance, many writers have felt obliged to apologize for or castigate Keble for his arch-conservatism, his social views which were 'centuries out of date', and his backward ideas about poetry (Edgecombe, 55). To take only a small example of the latter, Sheridan Gilley, in an otherwise excellent article on Tractarian aesthetics, notes that the rhythm of Keble's poetry 'lacks the true romantic freedom', a comment which seems to define all poetry of the period which was not 'romantic' as false, and which implicitly assumes that Keble would or should have wanted to write like a Romantic poet (235). Much of this kind of criticism might be said to stem from two basic exasperations: firstly, that Keble, despite his popularity and prominence at the time, failed to produce the kind of work which would give him literary and political credibility in the next two centuries, and secondly, more specifically, that he failed to be John Henry Newman. This exasperation mirrors Newman's own. As he once complained to Pusey about Keble's poetic abilities, 'how can I draw out his literary merits, when he considers it his special office to edit, or to translate, or to discourse in a dead language, or to sing hymns?' (Rowell, 40). The disgust here can, of course, also be read as Newman's testimony to Keble's considerable poetic powers.

In his important essay on Keble, Newman combined praise of his talents with a certain amount of frustration, thus setting the stage for twentieth-century discussion. Even Chadwick, in defending Keble's limitations, heightens or exaggerates them, again with reference to Newman: 'Keble set Newman to work, but only as the perception of a sublime picture drives the apprehender to start painting' (55). To use the analogy of a painting implies that Keble was passive, static and fixed, rather than being dynamically involved in the literature, politics and religion of the period. It does not give any indication that Keble and Newman might have interacted as equals, forming their ideas through negotiation with each other and their wider circle. Yet if ultimately Newman has been judged as more significant to the literature and culture of the nineteenth century, it is far from clear that this was evident to him and his contemporaries at the time.

Despite the valuable work that has been done on Keble in the four decades since Battiscombe's biography, the view that Keble is essentially a minor figure, more significant in his failings than in his successes, still lingers. One of the aims of this volume is to challenge this view, by focusing predominantly on Keble's strengths, on what he represented, what he achieved, and how his achievements shaped his period. In understanding how Keble's life and work influenced his time, in ways which we have not fully appreciated, it is necessary to consider all facets of this work, and to think of Keble not primarily as a religious thinker, nor as a political thinker, nor as a poet alone, but as a combination of all these. Of course, for Keble there was no clear division between politics, religion and aesthetics. Peter Nockles comments that Keble and Newman 'would foresee and brand as "apostasy" our modern preoccupation with politics', recognising but deploring the increasing separation of sacred and secular affairs, which from their perspective should have been irretrievably linked (Nockles, 68). Similarly, Tractarian belief in 'the joint and mutually reinforcing activity of both religion and art' was fostered largely by Keble, and went on to colour the thinking of the next generation of artists and writers on Christianity (Tennyson, 23). The interdisciplinary nature of this volume, which contains essays by historians, theologians and literary critics, thus mirrors the interdisciplinarity of Keble's own writings. As the title, *John Keble in Context*, suggests, the contributors set out both to show how Keble's 'influence', a key word for discussions of his significance, acted on his historical, literary, political and theological contexts, and how his thoughts in turn were shaped by the contexts in which he wrote.

The facts of Keble's life, of who and what he was, are relatively straightforward, and on first glance unprepossessing. Born in Gloucestershire to a clergyman father, from a family of minor gentry, Keble grew up as part of a closely-knit family. He was educated at home, and demonstrated the value of this education when he won a scholarship to Corpus Christi College, Oxford in 1806, at the age of fourteen, following this up with a spectacular Double First and a Fellowship at Oriel College. Keble remained in Oxford as a College Tutor until 1823, when he made the decision to accept a curacy at Southrop, near his home town, and devote himself to parish duties and to the care of his elderly father and sisters. In 1825, shortly after he had found a niche for himself by starting a new post as the curate of Hursley, near Winchester, the death of his younger sister meant that he had again to return to the family home and assume the role of primary carer. It was at this point that he published his first volume of devotional verse, *The Christian Year*. Keble remained involved with Oxford affairs and was elected Professor of Poetry in 1832, which required him to give a series of Latin lectures, but fundamentally he remained at home until 1835, when his father's death freed him to take up the Hursley living again. Now married to his sister-in-law, Charlotte Clarke, he was the vicar of Hursley for three decades until his death in 1866.

It is easy to see why these facts seem to suggest a life of early promise which was then thrown away. But an alternative reading of Keble's life would cast him in quite a different light, pointing to his almost legendary status as a young graduate in Oxford: his reconception of the pastoral role of an Oxford tutor (which was to have significant impact on the drive to reform Oxford throughout the century), his influence over a group of young men, including Thomas Arnold, Edward Pusey, Hurrell Froude, Robert Wilberforce and John

Henry Newman, who were between them to have an immense effect on the Anglican Church and on Victorian society as a whole, and his constant and decisive involvement in debates which were shaking the foundations of Church and State. Keble's life as a country parson, moreover, was neither a defeat nor a withdrawal. Although he reputedly went through periods of doubt and despair (Newman censored all mentions of such moods when editing his letters), Keble never seems fundamentally to have questioned where his duties and inclinations lay, and always intended and indeed aspired to become a parish priest. Raymond Chapman has succinctly argued that 'Keble's success came from a full use of the opportunities which a country parish offered' (60), and in order to appreciate this it is necessary to see Hursley as one of the centres, the powerhouses, of the Oxford Movement, rather than marginal or at the periphery: a place where ideas were discussed and finessed, where Keble received constant streams of visitors, and from where he sent streams of letters, a place where his activities of writing, socializing, parish work and church-building created a community that, as J. R. Watson reminds us in this volume, was the ideal of the Church of England in miniature. From Hursley, Keble's influence expanded outwards to affect those who met and talked with him or were in some way allied with this community – Charlotte Yonge and her circle, as Ellen Jordan, Charlotte Mitchell and Helen Schinske note, provide a good example – and also those who only knew of Hursley second-hand, as the parish inhabited, or ruled, by one of the most famous personalities of the nineteenth century.

One reason why Keble's effect on his generation (and the succeeding generation) may have been underestimated is because so much of his influence, according to contemporary sources, depended on personality, and on private letters and conversations which have not been preserved. Keble did not always convert or convince through intellectual assent to his published works, but through feeling, through the affective force of his character – as in the well-known anecdote, reported by Pusey, of a waverer who was reassured in his Anglican beliefs simply by staying in Hursley for a fortnight. 'Keble did not say a word of controversy, but loved', Pusey told someone who enquired how this feat had been achieved (quoted in Griffin, 20). Many accounts attest to Keble's power of personality in terms which emphasize 'the vast *force* there was' behind his evident humility.[1] Contemporary writers had no doubt that this force existed: as Henry Wilberforce wrote to a friend about Thomas Arnold, 'I have heard that he expresses *a very low opinion of Keble's power!!!*' (Newsome, 165). This is intellectual power, intelligence, power of dispute, but also more generally power to shape and to convince. For Wilberforce, Arnold's denial of this was the final straw which demonstrated the ludicrousness of his position.

One obituary, in the *Literary Churchman*, notes that Keble possessed:

peculiar presence…so plain and simple, and yet so strong, it had a grasp upon you which you felt as if you could not shake off or trifle with: – so quiet, so unobtrusive, so self-repressing, and yet, for all its self-repressment, overflowing upon you, and influencing, and moulding you, as if by some subtle law of spiritual force.[2]

The language used here picks up on imagery (of flow, contained feeling, streams of influence) common in Keble's own poetry and prose. This is a striking account, which makes the most of the disparity between Keble's outward persona of a quiet, selfless, English country clergyman and the personality which infused that role with significance. As later writers have noted, it was precisely this disparity which caused him to seem such a significant figure for his century. Ingram sums this up nicely:

The very characteristics which, as he would have maintained, made him unsuitable for a leader made him a leader. His stability, his humility, his disinclination to court publicity and prominence, secured his position. (98–9)

In other words, Keble is not a prominent figure despite his refusal to lead the Oxford Movement and engage fully in its affairs, but because of this. His physical, geographical removal from the scene of the fiercest debates, and his primary concentration on parish life in the countryside, meant that he could provide a model for men and women who were not necessarily in sympathy with the aims of the movement he had helped to create. Keble was described in his lifetime and in obituaries as the epitome of a key aspect of the Victorian Dream, quietly and lovingly fulfilling all duties to family and neighbours in the sphere in which he had been placed; helping the poor and needy; devoting his life to what he himself famously described as 'the trival round, the common task' ('Morning', *The Christian Year*, l. 52); serving God, the English countryside and the established Church. Twenty-first century readers may not be particularly moved by Wordsworth's emotive evocation of 'those little, nameless, unremembered acts/ Of kindness and of love', and are inclined to feel frustration that George Eliot's Dorothea Brooke abandons her early ideal of founding a new community in favour of subsuming her life in another and working to influence politics through personality, yet there is no denying the attraction these renunciations held for nineteenth-century readers ('Tintern Abbey', lines 35–6; Eliot *passim*). Reading Keble's influence in this light, it is perhaps less anomalous that the *Oxford Undergraduate's Journal* should have declared in 1866 that:

The real truth seems to be that of the three leading men who worked together in the Oxford Movement, Mr Keble is the one whose influence has been the greatest.[3]

Such discussion of personal influence might again make it seem that Keble was innocently unconscious of his potential, a passive participant in the creation of his own image, and in the dissemination of his ideas. Yet clearly his choice to assume George Herbert's mantle as the epitome of the English country pastor was conscious, deliberate, and deeply political, suggesting at least one version of where Anglicanism should find its strengths and achievements. An example of this is provided by a series of articles apparently written by Keble for *The Penny Post*, in which a group of village inhabitants, comprising the schoolmaster, the minister, a saddler and his wife, consider various church issues through dialogues.[4] The didacticism and strong sense of natural class-divisions, and the emphasis on the honest workman, earnestly seeking to become a better Christian, now make these conversations seem highly implausible, but they do suggest a model in which all classes in a community will help each other to further their understanding of Christian, or rather Anglican, truths. This series of forgotten articles, as much as more famous works, highlights Keble's steady conservatism, and his refusal to countenance (or even to imagine) deviation from his principles. As he protested in the Assize Sermon of 1833, 'Under the guise of charity and toleration we are come almost to this pass; that no difference, in matters of faith, is to disqualify for our approbation and confidence, whether in public or domestic life' (Keble (1983),18). This rejection of toleration and deliberate attempt to exclude Dissenters, Roman Catholics and non-Christians is another of the main reasons why Keble now seems outdated, embarrassingly un-PC, but it is worth noting firstly, that as several contributors to this volume show, conservatism could sometimes lead to almost revolutionary and forward-looking policies, and secondly, that it was precisely through his refusal to countenance alternatives to one doctrine that Keble came to wield what power he had, and to ensure his community and communion would last. Whether or not Hursley actually resembled the orderly society of the *Penny Post* dialogues, it was the best forum for his beliefs, and perhaps the only one in which they could have been exercised to such effect.

Battiscombe has noted that in Oxford in the early 1820s there was already a strong perception that 'if ever there should be an occasion for taking sides the side which secured Keble's support would be in possession of a very considerable asset' (48). This held true throughout Keble's career. His involvement in the world of action and enterprise demonstrated that he made a valuable contribution to any cause whether or not he was directly engaged in debate. His participation in *Tracts for the Times*, for instance, though it caused less furore than that of Newman or Isaac Williams, helped to give the nascent Oxford Movement credibility and authority, given that he had been a respected Oxford figure for some years before the other main participants in the Movement arrived. Through his sermons, as Robert Ellison and others remind us, he reached a large audience of Oxford men, and when those sermons were published, a wide readership throughout the country. He was a regular contributor to periodicals, producing articles and reviews which frequently dealt extensively with vital political and theological issues: the question of disestablishment, as Simon Skinner notes, is a case in point. Later in his life, when the causes for which he had fought seemed to be waning, Keble's support for far-reaching projects, such as the Universities Mission to Central Africa, or his opposition, as in the Gorham judgement or the Matrimonial Causes Bill, still gave a boost to any campaign.[5] Even when he was not active in a cause, his allegiance to it, his name on a petition or letter, was of value. In addition, of course, Keble wrote and published a series of important scholarly and literary works, including a major and well-respected edition of Hooker, his lectures as Oxford Professor of Poetry, published in 1844 as *De poeticae vi medica*, and his poems themselves, including *The Christian Year* and its successor, *Lyra Innocentium*.

As this volume amply demonstrates, Keble's writings as a whole deserve serious study and re-evaluation, in order to show how they acted as key interventions in concerns of the day. Perhaps ironically, a possible explanation as to why his writings have seldom been accorded this value is because they were cast into the shade from the outset by the immense success of *The Christian Year*, and the subsequent focus on Keble as poet. One historian of Tractarianism writes that:

> Keble alone [i.e. without Newman, Froude and Pusey] would have been a Conservative county clergyman who wrote pleasing religious verse and came up to Oxford to vote against every reform. (Dawson, 12)

While this may be true with regard to Keble's political commitment, *The Christian Year*, placed in context, can hardly be dismissed as 'pleasing religious verse'. It made Keble into a celebrity author – as Watson trenchantly remarks, the initials 'J.K., Hursley' were 'the most famous initials and parish in early Victorian religion' – and he would have been known for it in his time even if the Oxford Movement, which did not begin to gain momentum until at least six years after its publication, had not existed.[6] Keble's volume of devotional poetry, designed as a companion text to the Book of Common Prayer, achieved a success he could never have predicted and was read in contexts which he could not have foreseen, and would not, in many cases, have welcomed. As an awareness of this success lurks behind many comments made in this volume, it is worth briefly noting some of its characteristics.

Looking back in the 1860s, the *Times* reported that the impact of *The Christian Year* on young men and women in the 1830s could be described as 'a positive possession', terms which suggest a kind of madness, and which imply that his poems materially worked on their readers, in the same way that his personality was said to work, seizing and changing them.[7] *The Christian Year's* near-legendary status as a publishing and reading phenomenon is attested to by the sheer number of anecdotes and accounts circulating about it in Victorian culture. A. P. Stanley, for example, reported that when four British travellers met on a Sunday in the Mount Sinai desert, three of them had brought *The Christian Year* (Stanley, 456). A minor Oxfordshire poet, J. M. Chapman, narrates this story, apparently from his own experience, in his ode to Keble:

> Three faithful friends, all lovers of their Church,
> Set forth to travel, and for health to search;
> Before they start, they all agreement make
> One favourite author each should with him take;
> A rest-day come, at breakfast all appear
> Each with his chosen book – 'The Christian Year'. (Chapman (1875), 14)

The anecdote is satisfying because we can so clearly predict the denouement. The appeal of *The Christian Year* stretched to America, where Keble's name was, according to the Bishop of New York, 'a favourite throughout our American Church'.[8] It also crossed denominations in England. In a sermon preached on Keble's death, one Dissenting minister forgave him his High-Church heresies on the grounds that *The Christian Year* demonstrated his true spirit:

> Many Dissenters praise the book, notwithstanding its High-church character. My ministerial acquaintance, almost to a man, speak of it as a beloved companion, and regard its author as one of their holiest helpers. (Williams, 12)

It was, moreover, allegedly read by all classes. In Margaret Oliphant's *Salem Chapel*, the wealthy young Lady Western buys handsome presentation copies for her parishioners in Masters, an upmarket Anglo-Catholic booksellers, but one writer in 1866 also assures us that 'you can go to any railway bookstall in the land and buy the 'Christian Year' for a shilling' (Oliphant, 61–3; Haweis, 174). While it may seem discomfiting to a modern critic to envisage a traveller choosing to read *The Christian Year* over *The Woman in White* or *Lady Audley's Secret*, the fact remains that huge numbers of Victorian readers did choose to read, reread, and, crucially, to use Keble's poems, whether as consolation, panacea or religious aid.

# INTRODUCTION

The ubiquitous mentions of *The Christian Year* in contemporary letters, memoirs and fiction have ensured that it is the one book authored by Keble to have received significant critical attention after his death, albeit that this attention is generally focused on the volume's influence on the literature of a later generation rather than the contexts surrounding *The Christian Year* itself. Valuable work has been published on *The Christian Year* and Christina Rossetti, Gerard Manley Hopkins, Matthew Arnold, and to a lesser degree, Alfred Tennyson, Arthur Hugh Clough, William Wordsworth and Samuel Taylor Coleridge.[9] In addition, attention to Keble's poetry has been backed up with attention to his statements on poetics, notably in his lectures as Oxford Professor of Poetry. These were rediscovered after M. H. Abrams praised them in *The Mirror and the Lamp* for their proto-Freudian emphasis on repression and sublimation (Abrams, 146–7; Shaw, 67). Later critics have expanded these ideas and have provided valuable accounts of how Keble's theories fit into a wider matrix of work on poetry and poetics in the period.[10] His writings on art can seem surprisingly modern, in their insistence on reader response rather than authorial intention, their sense of the arbitrariness of language and the difficulties of expression, and their interest in theorizing affect. Moreover, Keble as poet and critic is important because, as noted earlier, his work ensured that it is difficult to consider Tractarian theories of religion and politics without taking aesthetics into account, and vice versa. As J. C. Shairp commented, 'he gave the Oxford Movement poetry, and a poetical aspect' (238). Such remarks point us towards a more general understanding of how literature and Christianity were inseparable in the writing and reading practices of many Victorians.

The recent publication of a number of books on Victorian literature, history and religion suggests that critics are coming to the realization that this field has been relatively neglected, and as Keble necessarily looms large in any consideration of nineteenth-century Christianity, it might be expected that his works will receive increasing attention.[11] As the reassessment of popular works of literature by 'minor' writers continues to gain force, the cultural map of Victorian England is being redrawn to take account of texts which are no longer canonical. In this light not only Keble himself, but many writers whom he influenced, are emerging as topics of study and debate. The essays in this volume by Emma Francis and Emma Mason provide a case in point, showing how new explorations in the field of women's poetry and women's writing have contributed to a new understanding of Keble's role, particularly with regard to notions of affective poetics. In studies based on the late eighteenth and early nineteenth century, in addition, an interest in the discourse of emotion (a discourse of immense importance in Keble's writings and in Tractarian theory and practice), and in the ideological uses to which 'feeling' could be put, has led to reconsiderations of Keble's views. Positioned as he is in the crucial decades between 'Romanticism' and 'Victorianism', with Wordsworth and Coleridge on the one hand, and Tennyson and Browning on the other, Keble's statements on the uneasy relation between emotion and its expression not only affected the Tractarian position on such concepts but also served as a model for ways in which literature and religion were to develop throughout the nineteenth century.

In seeking to engage with areas of study which are just opening up, and to suggest that Keble is a key figure in these areas, these essays necessarily set his works in context, whether that context is political, social, theological, literary, biographical or all of these together. Indeed, in several essays it is less his works themselves than the contexts in which they operated which provide the driving force of the argument. Stephen Prickett opens the volume by setting a precedent for the discussion of forgotten or neglected texts by Keble: in this case his Creweian Oration of 1839, delivered at the ceremony for Wordsworth's honorary degree. Those present, besides Wordsworth, included Newman, John Ruskin, and a young Matthew Arnold and Arthur Hugh Clough (Gill, 19). Clearly this was an occasion of considerable significance. In retrieving the unpublished text of the speech, Prickett reveals that Keble's social vision may have been considerably more inclusive than it has seemed, as the oration points towards Keble's ideal of the university, and his hopes that the ideal could be extended through a wider educational network. In addition, Prickett's exposition of these views involves a broader reassessment of Keble's conservative attitudes to philanthropy and education, and to the concept of tradition itself, forcing us to question whether his allegiances were as straightforward as they may have seemed. The second essay, Simon Skinner's '"The duty of the state": Keble, the Tractarians, and establishment' also sets out to demolish the prevailing misconception that the Tractarians were uninterested in wider social questions, and deals with a crucial yet unremarked piece of writing by Keble, in this case his review of Gladstone's *The State in its Relations with the Church* (1838) in *The British Critic*. Skinner concentrates on the contested issue of Tractarian attitudes to disestablishment, arguing that despite his heated comments of the 1830s Keble never seriously rejected the idea of establishment itself, but rather 'resisted establishment on its current terms', terms which seemed to him to deny the clear superiority of the Church to the state.

The importance of these issues in historical scholarship, and their contested nature, can be seen by comparing Skinner's essay with Mark Chapman's 'John Keble, 'National Apostasy', and the Myths of 14 July'. Chapman, in contrast to Skinner, sees Keble's most heated comments on disestablishment as representative. He suggests that Keble's famed Assize Sermon implied 'a revolution in English political theory', precisely because it opened the door to disestablishment, and, while elaborating on Skinner's point that the doctrine of apostolicity meant that the Church was perceived as the superior party, argues that this doctrine also meant that the Church had an independent source of sovereignty, and could therefore survive alone. While he was never a conscious revolutionary, Keble, in this light, seems to have predicted the rise of pluralism. The fact that these two essays draw different conclusions from Keble's writing neatly demonstrates the complexity of Keble's negotiations with political and social ideas, and also shows the extent to which debate over his views is still very much an ongoing, vital concern for historians, given the implication of these views in the context of Church-State relations.

James Pereiro's 'Keble and the Concept of Ethos' might seem to move away from specific political and social debates to examine an ambiguous yet pervasive concept in Keble's writing and in Tractarianism as a whole. Yet the tenor of Keble's writings on *ethos*, as this essay decisively demonstrates, was strongly political in the widest sense of the word. Keble's use of *ethos* to indicate a certain mindset, a way of perceiving the world, gains its force, Pereiro argues, from Butler's *Analogy* and his argument that men could train themselves in virtue and thus develop what we might call a predilection for Christianity. The right *ethos*, comprising the right moral qualities and a dominant sense of truth and love, would directly lead to faith. The formation of this *ethos* then obviously becomes a crucial educational issue, on an individual and national level. Keble's laments about the state of the nation, in other words, are formulated as a sense that the dominant *ethos* of the country needs changed.

In the second part of the volume, the concern about the education and formation of a Christian, and about the Church's engagement with secular affairs, remains, although the focus shifts slightly towards investigations of Keble's place in the literature and culture of the period. William McKelvy turns to the reading culture of the day in his essay, 'Ways of Reading 1825: Leisure, Curiosity and Morbid Eagerness'. He argues persuasively that *The Christian Year* can be seen as an intervention in an ongoing debate about the purpose and value of reading. The clear designs that Keble's poems have on the reader should be seen in the context of this particular historical dispute. From this perspective, Keble's works, and those of other Tractarians, are attempts to uphold ideals of Christian reading, ideals increasingly challenged by secularism. Keble's tracts and sermons are obviously key reading material, and Robert Ellison gives a detailed account of their significance in the succeeding essay. In assessing these neglected prose writings, Ellison draws attention not simply to their content but to the significance of the tract and sermon genre, in relation to Tractarianism and as part of the wider publishing culture of the day.

J. R. Watson's essay is also concerned with how Keble's works were (and are) read, and more particularly with the construction of a child reader, or with the construction of an adult reader for children's literature. Both of these concerns are currently under critical investigation in the field of children's literature, and Watson demonstrates that they were equally current in the early-mid nineteenth century. He concentrates on Keble's volume of lyrics about children, *Lyra Innocentium*, setting it in the context of writing for and about children and suggesting that the value of these poems lies in their involvement in a wider set of concerns about how children could be educated in the Church. What Watson, Ellison and McKelvy have in common with each other (and indeed with most of the essays in the volume) is a concern less for criteria of literary merit than for the effect Keble's writings had, their participation in a network of contemporary discourses. All three essays are concerned with how and why these particular texts were read, and in the case of sermons, delivered, and whether they proved formative in the ways in which their author intended. Reading becomes a means of forming *ethos*, and a way of converting readers to the desired belief or point of view. The writings of Keble discussed in this section are not merely representative, but given his fame and the dissemination of his influence, perhaps the most representative of certain genres of writing which set out with these aims.

The final part of the volume opens out Keble's literary influence, tracing it both in his times and through later decades in the work of a diverse group of writers. The first two essays, by Emma Francis and Emma Mason, provide a valuable assessment of where Keble's works can be placed with regard to the strong tradition of nineteenth-century women's poetry. In locating Keble as a major theorist of expressive poetry, a tradition associated with women's writing both in the nineteenth century and in current criticism, they not only suggest that he may have been substantially more important to female writers than has been previously thought, but also point towards innovative readings of Tractarianism in relation to gender issues. The only women writers usually discussed in relation to Keble are Christina Rossetti, whose interest in his work is unquestioned, and Charlotte Yonge – and as Ellen Jordan *et al.* remind us, commentary on Yonge has been limited in scope. To set Keble in the context of women's poetry in general, therefore, and to argue that his writings were 'profoundly enabling for the woman poet', significantly expands the genres in regard to which he can be read.

Francis provides an overview of current critical theories on nineteenth-century women's poetry, and then turns to nineteenth-century theorists to see how their work contributed to the classification of women's poetry as expressive. Rather than positing a direct link between Keble and theorists of women's poetry such as M. A. Stodart, she sees Keble's lectures on poetry as a general contribution to the expressive tradition, a contribution which later writers would necessarily have taken into account. As both she and Mason note, the points of resemblance between Keble's poetic theories and commentaries on women's writing meant that they had immediate and personal application for female poets. Mason's essay takes these ideas and applies them specifically to poets such as Cecil Frances Alexander, Dora Greenwell and Adelaide Procter, all of whom had strong interests in Anglo-Catholicism. She argues that Keble's ideas about feeling and its containment are directly reflected in poetry which dwells on silence, reserve and regulated feeling, both in form and in content.

The next two essays turn to Keble's effect on his male successors. Daniel Kline continues the effort to extend Keble's influence into new intellectual and cultural contexts by demonstrating that his writings were operating as an influence not only in the sympathetic environment of Oxford, but in the somewhat hostile arena of Thomas Arnold's Rugby College, where the young poets Arthur Hugh Clough and Matthew Arnold formed their poetics in negotiation with Keble's model. Arnold and Clough, two poets who might be said to set the tone for the next Oxford generation of the 1840s and 1850s, were exposed to the contrasting views of Thomas Arnold and John Keble from the outset of their poetic careers, views which profoundly affected their views on poetry and poetic language. In considering their juvenilia – work which, again, has been very little discussed – Kline sheds new light on the subsequent development of these careers.

Marion Shaw, the only contributor to deal directly with *The Christian Year*, reassesses Keble's impact on one of the most well-known (and best-loved) religious poems of the century: Tennyson's *In Memoriam*. Shaw demonstrates, as does Kline, how Keble's influence flourished in an entirely different and possibly hostile intellectual environment: in this case Cambridge and the Apostolic circle. While *In Memoriam* emerges, from Shaw's account, as a poem with very different aims and ends, it nonetheless echoes Keble's lyrics in both form and content, reflecting upon the hymn tradition of which they formed a part, and playing with or evoking imagery and ideas from *The Christian Year* in its own reshaping of the traditions of religious verse.

Finally, Ellen Jordan, Charlotte Mitchell and Helen Schinske come to Charlotte Yonge, from a slightly different perspective to that of Francis and Mason on women's writing, but also one which attempts to rewrite Keble's legacy as enabling rather than disabling. Their essay, based on original primary material, contradicts work on Yonge which has tended to blame Keble for her conservatism, her traditional views of gender roles, and the moralistic outlook of her novels. As these critics point out, without the close proximity of the Keble household to her home, Yonge might never have been introduced to the 'intellectual and clerical social network' which provided the background for her novels and encouraged her in her literary career. In many ways, Yonge's immensely popular novels reveal the *ethos* of Hursley more than any other

Victorian text. Moreover, since Yonge herself acted as guide, mentor and critic to a circle of aspiring women writers, taking on the role which Keble had played for her, his ideas were further spread throughout her circle.

As a whole, these essays multiply the contexts in which Keble can and ought to be read. Whether relating his writings to his interests in a specific debate, discussing their effect on other writers of the period, or locating them as responses to his contemporaries and predecessors, they additionally constitute a valuable contribution to nineteenth-century studies in general. Taken together, they show the interrelations between various contexts, so that we can see how disputes over reading might relate to disputes over language, or how educational goals could be informed by political and social ambitions and could in turn inform the writing of poetry, how a sermon, a review, a speech might constitute a decisive intercession in a debate over politics and theology, and how poetic theories could raise broad questions of gender and authorial identity. And besides these textual interactions, these essays also demonstrate the significance of Keble's physical contexts: his geographical location in Hursley and Oxford, and his temporal location in a period of rapid upheaval and change. *John Keble in Context* presents a composite image of a writer who, far from being unconcerned or disengaged, was at the forefront of this change, and whose influence radiated outwards, not only to affect his fellow Tractarians but also to sway the thoughts of men and women of very different denominations and beliefs.

## Notes

[1] Review of J. T. Coleridge's memoir of Keble, *Literary Churchman*, February 7 1869. Collected in set of pamphlets on Keble's death, Bodleian Library, Oxford (G.Pamph. 2767). Further references to this collection cited as 'Bodleian'.

[2] *Literary Churchman*, February 7 1869 (Bodleian).

[3] Review of Coleridge's memoir, *Oxford Undergraduate's Journal* 46 (June 2 1869) (Bodleian).

[4] 'Notes on Church History', The Penny Post, I, 1–5. This series of anonymous articles was attributed to Keble by a letter published in the *Guardian*, April 1866 (Bodleian).

[5] On Keble's involvement with the African missions, see Faught 135–8. On his opposition to the Gorham Judgement, see Battiscombe 291–3, and to the first Divorce Bill, 315–16.

[6] Watson, below.

[7] *The Times*, 6 April 1866, 5.

[8] Letter from the Bishop of New York, *Guardian*, 23 April 1866 (Bodleian).

[9] Besides the work by Stedman and Scheinberg, mentioned in note 11, below, Arseneau's recent study of Rossetti and Johnson's and Ward's studies of Hopkins contain sigificant discussion of these poets with regard to Tractarianism and

Keble. See also my article on nineteenth-century poetry and The Christian Year (Blair 2003) and the forthcoming special issue of *Victorian Poetry* on 'Tractarian Poetics', to be edited by myself and Emma Mason.

[10] See Abrams 146–7, and Shaw 67, for a discussion of Keble's theories in this light.

[11] In fact, Keble is briefly discussed in several works published in the last few years, usually with regard to his poetic theories. See, for example, Scheinberg, especially 46–8, Stedman 174–5.

## Works Cited

'Obituary: John Keble', *The Times*, 6 April 1866.

Abrams, M. H., *The Mirror and the Lamp*, Oxford: Oxford University Press, 1953.

Arseneau, Mary, *Recovering Christina Rossetti: Female Community and Incarnational Poetics*, Basingstoke: Palgrave, 2004.

Battiscombe, Georgina, *John Keble: A Study in Limitations*, London: John Constable, 1963.

Blair, Kirstie, 'John Keble and the Rhythm of Faith', *Essays in Criticism*, 53 (2003): 129–50.

Chadwick, Owen, *The Spirit of the Oxford Movement: Tractarian Essays*, (new edn) Cambridge: Cambridge University Press, 1990.

Chapman, J. M., *Reminiscences of Three Oxford Worthies*, Oxford: James Parker, 1875.

Chapman, Raymond, *Faith and Revolt: Studies in the Literary Influence of the Oxford Movement*, London: Weidenfeld and Nicolson, 1970.

Dawson, Christopher, *The Spirit of the Oxford Movement and Newman's Place in History* (1933), Intro. Peter Nockles, biographical note Christina Stead, London: Saint Austin Press, 2001.

Edgecombe, Rodney Stenning, *Two Poets of the Oxford Movement: John Keble and John Henry Newman*, London: Associated University Presses, 1996.

Eliot, George, *Middlemarch*, ed. W. J. Harvey, Harmondsworth: Penguin, 1965.

Faught, C. Brad, *The Oxford Movement: A Thematic History of the Tractarians and Their Times*, University Park: Pennsylvania State University Press, 2003.

Gill, Stephen, *Wordsworth and the Victorians*, Oxford: Clarendon Press, 1998.

Gilley, Sheridan, 'John Keble and the Victorian Churching of Romanticism', *An Infinite Complexity: Essays in Romanticism*, ed. J. R. Watson, Edinburgh: Edinburgh University Press, 1983.

Griffin, John, *John Keble: Saint of Anglicanism*, Macon: Mercer University Press, 1987.

Haweis, H. R., *Poets in the Pulpit*, London: Sampson Low, 1880.

Ingram, Kenneth, *John Keble*, London: P. Allan, 1933.

Keble, John, *The Christian Year, Lyra Innocentium and Other Poems* (1827) Oxford: Oxford University Press, 1914.

— 'National Apostasy', Steventon: Rocket Press, 1983.

— 'Notes on Church History', *The Penny Post*, I (1851), London: J. H. Parker, 1851.

Ingram, Kenneth, *John Keble*, London: Philip Allan, 1933.

Johnson, Margaret, *Gerard Manley Hopkins and Tractarian Poetry*. Aldershot: Ashgate, 1997.

Newsome, David, *The Parting of Friends: The Wilberforces and Henry Manning*, 2nd edn, Grand Rapids: William B. Eerdmans, 1993.

Nockles, Peter, *The Oxford Movement in Context: Anglican High Churchmanship, 1760–1857*, Cambridge: Cambridge University Press, 1994.

Oliphant, Margaret, *Salem Chapel* (1863), Intro. Penelope Fitzgerald, London: Virago, 1986.

Rowell, Geoffrey, *The Vision Glorious: Themes and Personalities of the Catholic Revival in Anglicanism*, Oxford: Oxford University Press, 1983.

Scheinberg, Cynthia, *Women's Poetry and Victorian Religion: Jewish Identity and Christian Culture*, Cambridge: Cambridge University Press, 2002.

Shairp, J. C., 'Keble and "The Christian Year"' *North British Review* 45 (1866): 233–264.

Shaw, W. David, *The Lucid Veil: Poetic Truth in the Victorian Age*, Madison: University of Wisconsin Press, 1987.

Stanley, A. P., 'John Keble', *Macmillan's Magazine* 19 (1868): 455–464.

Stedman, Gesa, *Stemming the Torrent: Expression and Control in the Victorian Discourses on Emotions*, Aldershot: Ashgate, 2002.

Tennyson, G. B., *Victorian Devotional Poetry: The Tractarian Mode*, Cambridge MA: Harvard University Press, 1981.

Ward, Bernadette Waterman, *World as Word: Philosophical Theology in Gerard Manley Hopkins*. Washington D. C.: Catholic University of America.

Williams, Charles, *The Priest of the Most High God: A Sermon*, London: Elliot Stock, 1966.

Wordsworth, William, and S. T. Coleridge, *Lyrical Ballads* (1798), ed. R. L. Brett and A. R. Jones, 2nd edn, London: Routledge, 1991.

# PART 1

Reconsiderations: Keble's Place in Tractarian Politics and Religion

# 1

# KEBLE'S CREWEIAN ORATION OF 1839: THE IDEA OF A CHRISTIAN UNIVERSITY

## Stephen Prickett

The idea of tradition was central to the Tractarian idea of the Church. Keble's Oxford Assize Sermon of 1833 on 'National Apostasy' was not so much concerned with any immediate threat to the idea of Apostolic succession, as the discovery, triggered by the Catholic Emancipation act of 1828, that what he – and the minority of his fellow-clergy interested in such matters – had taken for granted was an independent ecclesiastical tradition, was in fact no such thing. It was subject to the will of a Parliament, which, if not exactly democratically elected, was catholic enough (with a small 'c') to include both nonconformists and a substantial number of the Irish variety with the large 'C'. From the Reformation in 1534 until the new Liberal reforming government of 1832 ecclesiastical disputes had been settled by Courts set up on an *ad hoc* basis by the sovereign, exercising the Royal Supremacy instituted by Henry VIII. Appeals from the Archbishop's Courts went to the Crown in Chancery, which, in turn, appointed a Court of Delegates which (in matters which did not 'touch the King') was supreme. In 1832, however, this royal prerogative was taken from the Crown and passed to a Judicial Committee of the Privy Council, of which only the Lord Chancellor himself was obliged to be a member of the Anglican Church (see Liddon, Preface, in Keble *v–vi*). As we all know, the problems inherent in this arrangement (which Keble had prophesied in 1833) came to a crisis in 1850 with the Gorham Case.

What was less noticed in these years of ecclesiastical and legal turmoil of the 1830s and 1840s was that the idea of 'tradition' was *itself* being radically questioned. Though it seems an obvious point, it is worth noting the inexorable progression by which what was initially an essentially legal dispute moved into a debate over the nature of the Church itself. The idea of tradition, which had begun largely as an assumption of the Apostolic Episcopal succession, rapidly involved not merely the Tracts themselves (with their own internal dynamic that was to lead many to Rome before Newman's eventual reception (or 'perversion') in 1845), but the interpretation of Church history implicit in such projects as the *Lives of the English Saints*, and the aesthetics of worship. All three elements of this tradition – Apostolic succession, Church history, and aesthetics – were widely caricatured and misunderstood, then as now. It is easy, for instance, to mock the author of the Life of St Neot who concluded, with an honesty even more commendable than his piety, '… and that is all, and, indeed, rather more than all that is known about the life of the blessed St Neot.' Yet there was behind such fervour a genuine thirst for a kind of historical truth about the Church that had been missing for generations – and which was, in the end, to affect the Catholic Church as much as its Protestant rival (see Prickett). Similarly, it is easy to mock Tractarian aesthetics as the 'smells and bells' of ritualists (nearly as much despised by Keble and Newman as by their Evangelical critics) without observing the significance of the fact that Keble and Newman were *both* poets. Keble was already famous as the author of *The Christian Year* (the best-selling poetry book of the century) well before the Assize Sermon of 1833, and any account of his thought that fails to stress the importance of *Tract no. 89*, or the Lectures on Poetry, *De Poeticae vi Medica*, published in 1844, but written between 1832 and 1841 when he was Oxford Professor of Poetry, misunderstands the degree to which the tradition of the Church had *always* been for Keble as much an aesthetic as a legal one.

What such a dichotomy still fails to account for, of course, is the relation of both to a third area of Church tradition: what is now called 'social policy'. The Tractarians hardly dominate most histories of nineteenth-century social reform. When the not inconsiderable role played by the Church is mentioned, it is the evangelicals, the Christian Socialists, and even the Catholics, led by the formidable figure of Manning, who tend to take pride of place. Pugin's *Contrasts* had been published in 1833, the same year as the Assize Sermon, and the whole thrust of his argument had been to show that aesthetics and charity went hand-in-hand in the Catholic tradition; whereas for Protestantism, worship and the Workhouse stood on opposite sides of the great divide between Church and State, for Catholicism the two had always flourished in tandem.

This is not to say that many of the Tractarians were not personally philanthropic, but rather that in many cases their vision of social reform tended to stop at *personal* philanthropy. For men whose minds were quick to think ecclesiastically on a national scale, it is noticeable that their social thought was usually parochial. An 1875 sermon of Pusey's captures both the best and the worst of Tractarian charity:

What shall we have to say to our Lord when he comes down to be our Judge – when we shall behold him whom our sins have pierced? 'True, Lord, I denied myself nothing for thee; the times were changed, and I could not but change with them. I ate and drank, for thou too didst eat and drank with the publicans and sinners. I did not give to the poor, but I paid what I was compelled to the poor-rate, of the height of which I complained. I did not take in little children in thy name, but they were provided for. They were sent, severed indeed from father and mother, to the poorhouse, to be taught or no about thee, as might be. I did not feed thee when hungry. Political economy forbade it; but I increased the labour market with the manufacture of my luxuries. I did not visit thee when sick, but the parish doctor looked in on his ill-paid rounds. I did not clothe thee when naked. I could not afford it, the rates were so high, but there was a workhouse for thee to go to. I did not take thee in as a stranger, but it was provided that thou mightest go to the casual ward. Had I known that it was thou' – and he shall say, Forasmuch as thou didst it not to one of the least of these, thou didst it not to me. (Carpenter 306)

In its recognition of the social role of the Gospel, this could rank with the best of the great nineteenth-century statements by Church leaders; but Pusey's words here were part of a campaign not for reforming the Poor Laws (which, after all, had been an object of liberal attack and derision since before Dickens' *Oliver Twist* twenty years before) but for promoting a revival of *private* charity. Pusey himself, of course, is beyond reproach personally: by far the wealthiest of the Tractarians, he gave away almost all his fortune in charitable enterprises of one kind or another. But in his inability to recognise that the relief of poverty might at least be as universal and well-organised as the other work of his beloved Church, he was typical of his movement. He was typical in another way. As the rhetoric of the sermon demanded, that list of modes of alleviating poverty and deprivation is, of course, openly scriptural. There is in it no mention of another form of poverty which, by the nineteenth century, was perhaps more disabling, and more difficult to deal with by piecemeal charity, than any of the listed scriptural ones: education, or in Basil Bernstein's telling phrase, 'cognitive poverty'. Among the twentieth-century charges thrown at the Oxford Movement, the elitism of its origins and its failure to address the problems of education have been among the most damaging. Thus S. C. Carpenter, writing sixty years ago in one of the early twentieth century's most thorough discussions of the social conscience of the Victorian Church, can sum up the origins of the Oxford Movement in these terms:

It is remarkable, and disappointing, that with so many signs of anti-Christ plain to be seen, irreligion and ignorance among the poor, irreligion and pride among the rich, vast areas of misery complacently regarded by the more comfortable as a thing inevitable, a penal system and a Poor Law full of cruelty, an almost complete lack of national education, Keble found National Apostasy in a point so purely ecclesiastical. (114)

Carpenter, of course, came from another tradition of Anglicanism not likely to be overly sympathetic to the ecclesiology of the Tractarians, but his point has some force, and by and large it has been taken as the judgement of history. In spite of heroic efforts by particular individuals or groups – including the work of Edward King in Lincoln (See Newton), Nathaniel Woodard of the Woodard Schools, and even the foundation of Keble College itself – on the evidence given by the leaders of the Movement themselves, the verdict has to be that they were more interested in liturgical and ecclesiastical reform than in social problems, including education. Or to put it another way, for them the resolution to social problems lay primarily in reform of the Church: the root from which everything else must grow. Here, for instance, is Liddon in one of the 1866 Bampton Lectures revealingly entitled 'Charity, a Product of Faith in Christ's Divinity':

> The hospital, in which the bed of anguish is soothed by the hand of science under the guidance of love; the penitentiary, where the victims of a selfish passion are raised to a new moral life by the care and delicacy of an unmercenary tenderness; the school, which gathers the ragged outcasts of our great cities, rescuing them from the ignorance and vice of which else they must be the prey; – what is the fountain-head of these blessed and practical results, but the truth of His Divinity, who has kindled man into charity by giving Himself for man? (Carpenter, 306–7)

An argument that apparently takes as its evidence for the divinity of Christ the 'care... delicacy' and 'tenderness' of the treatment of criminals in Victorian prisons would have been unlikely to make much headway with contemporary members of the Howard League for Prison Reform. Perhaps as telling, in its own way, is the vision of the role of charitable schools as rescuing the 'ragged outcasts of our great cities ... from ... ignorance and vice'. That given the right conditions, some of the ragged outcasts might find their way to university, though it was in fact already happening – as in the famous case of Joseph Wright, later to be Foundation Professor of Philology at Oxford – was still apparently unthinkable to ecclesiastics like Liddon, who seems to have been more in tune with the world of Hardy's *Jude the Obscure*. By implication, the divinity of Christ is the authority not for social change, or for the creation of a more just society, but for making the existing system more acceptable.

For a practical example of the non-ecclesiastical philanthropy of the Tractarians we can turn to Thomas Mozley's *Reminiscences*. Among its estates, Oriel College owned one at Wadley, near Faringdon, which in 1830 had been unoccupied for some years. In view of this, some labourers from a hamlet on the estate asked permission to have cottage gardens on the vacant land for their own cultivation. Their approach was however apparently couched in 'language which indicated a theoretical right rather than an appeal to benevolence'. 'This', Mozley tells us, 'promised some sport'. The Provost and senior fellows (including, we must suppose some prominent future Tractarians) rode out to confront this impudence. 'A labourer's best chance is wages,' they explained; 'his time and strength are due to his employer', and, rather oddly in view of the fact that they had only been asked for 'gardens': 'land above the scale of a garden is an encumbrance. Who is to pay rates and taxes upon it? What is to be done when the holders increase and multiply?' Hardly surprisingly, we are told that the dialogue was 'one-sided'. All the poor labourers could do was to 'repeat that they would like some land to do what they pleased with, and they had been told manors were for the poor as well as for the rich. Oriel College was a very great body ... it could do anything'. Anything, it seemed, except giving the men their gardens. A few years later one of the Fellows of the College devoted himself to building a pretty little church there. (Mozley, I, 200–1)

Certainly there was no need to look to the later Pusey or Liddon for evidence of this lack of interest in social as distinct from ecclesiastical reform. We have it, it seems, from the original first phase of the Movement in the words of Keble himself. On 12 June 1839 it was his role, as Professor of Poetry, to give the Creweian Oration at the Oxford Commemoration ceremony at which William Wordsworth was presented for an honorary degree. The account of this occasion is given by Keble's first biographer, J. T. Coleridge:

> The Oration commences with pointing out a close analogy between the Church and the University as institutions, and after tracing this out in several particulars, notices a supposed and very important failure of the analogy in respect to the poorer classes, to whom the gates of the latter are not practically open, nor instruction afforded. This failure the orator then proceeds to explain and neutralize so far as he is able... (248)

This passage, concluding with Keble's graceful tribute to Wordsworth himself as the poet of the poor, and its tumultuous reception, has become one of the most famous accounts of Keble's attitude not merely towards poverty, but in particular towards the virtual exclusion of the poor from higher education in general and Oxford in particular. Its ambiguity has been read as symptomatic of an ambiguity towards education and social privilege that was endemic in the Oxford Movement right from its beginnings.

\*\*\*

When, in 1992, Geoffrey Rowell very generously invited me to give the paper on Keble in a series of lectures in the Chapel of Keble College, Oxford, to mark the bi-centenary of Keble's birth (see Rowell, 1992), I decided to take another look at that Creweian Oration of 1839. It did not surprise me overmuch that Glasgow University library turned out not to have a copy; I was disappointed by what seemed to be Scottish parochialism when I discovered that there was no copy in the National Library of Scotland. By the time that I had ascertained that there was no copy in the British Library I began to wonder just what J.T. Coleridge's own source had been. In the end, of course, I did what I should have done much earlier: I phoned the librarian at Keble College who, after some investigations of his own, confirmed that the speech had not merely never been published, but that all we have of it is Keble's own lecture notes – all 21 pages of them – which he obligingly faxed to me that day. What I received was a series of sheets covered in the most illegible scrawl which, on close study, turned out to be not merely, as one might expect, in Latin, but in Keble's own private abbreviated form of Latin: not so much a continuous piece of prose, as a series of jottings from which he could speak. Here I must record my undying gratitude to my late colleague, Paul Jeffries-Powell of the Glasgow Department of Humanity who sat up all one night to produce from these notes a readable Latin text. The final stage of an English translation was then a comparatively simple matter. What emerged from this text was startling and, for me, quite unexpected.

In the first place it was now clear that J. T. Coleridge himself must have been the source of all previous references to this speech. Though in passing he refers to Dr Wordsworth's printing of it 'in the original' this seems only to refer to the paragraph directly concerned with William Wordsworth. For the rest we are apparently reliant either on Coleridge's own recollections of the occasion twenty-six years later, or on notes he had made at the time. Either way, his summary of its contents was selective to the point of being totally misleading. Keble had indeed noted that Oxford was in no sense open to the poor, but so far from proceeding to 'explain and neutralize' this failure, as Coleridge suggests, he had gone on to say something very much more pertinent:

> First, I pray you, recall and re-imagine what was the shape and figure of academic things, at the time when we began to enjoy a firm succession of records. There were more than thirty thousand Clerks: some attended to learning here, some wandered all over England, in such a condition of life, for the most part, that the phrase became

proverbial: Oxford means poor; while meantime aristocratic youths despised and detested all pursuits except soldiering.

Poverty, moreover, was never an accidental quality of Oxford in its early days. Keble then proceeds to cite page after page of evidence showing that poverty, and its concomitant, unworldliness, was actually an ideal of the founding patrons of the various colleges: as it were, part of the Platonic *idea* of Oxford. Here he is on the foundation of his own college:

> And I have a superstitious dread of leaving out at this point the name of the founder of Oriel; who of his piety made sure that this eloquent rule was sworn to, that none should be received into his number 'except the decent, the chaste, the lowly, and the needy'. No need for more: almost everybody bears witness that it was for the sake of the poor that they had these houses founded; right up to the time when the ceremonies of religion, and the whole spirit of literature and politics was changed, and the custom gradually grew up of allowing access to the Academy for the talented rich...

Once again, ecclesiology is paramount: the mediaeval idea of a university, centring on poverty and learning, was fatally undermined by the materialism of the Reformation. Nonetheless, Keble's roll-call of poverty, godliness, and good learning does not stop at the sixteenth century. Samuel Johnson, who 'was not so far removed from true piety and ancient faith' stands as a shining witness that even in the eighteenth century the old ideals had not been quite extinguished.

Significantly, there is absolutely no attempt whatsoever, in J.T. Coleridge's terms, to 'neutralize' the failure of nineteenth-century Oxford to open its doors to the poor. Immediately after the encomium to Wordsworth somewhat floridly translated and quoted by Coleridge, Keble returns to his main theme of the true calling of the University:

> So he who would pay his debt of gratitude, let him to the best of his ability defend that part especially of our discipline which is contained in a worthy and thrifty mode of life; let nothing profuse, nothing immoderate, nothing voluptuary be readily allowed to cross this threshold, within which dwell the poor; and in the tutelage of the poor are honoured the testaments of the dead.

That Alfred Dolittle might have been somewhat sceptical of this sentimentalized portrait of the 'deserving poor' is beside the point. As the following paragraphs make clear, Keble is not just paying lip-service to a lost ideal. Contained within the rhetoric of a peroration is a perfectly practical programme to realise this dream.

Therefore we will call such people back as best we can, and devote ourselves to ensuring that since the waters have been, as it were, divided, our Academy may share its blessings with the commonality and the tribe of the needy. I would wish there to go forth from this place men who shall lead colonies, so to speak, [planted] on every shore of our [native] Britain, nay, and of her provinces. Let the Academy join itself more closely with the views of those who, at this very moment, have by divine inspiration (for I shall speak boldly) formed the plan of propagating in each town not only elementary schools or places to learn a profitable trade, leaving aside the lecture-rooms of a wordy and empty philosophy, and creating those schools which nurture servants and children worthy of Holy Church.

At this very moment, I say, there have gone forth from the bosom of this Academy – and may they succeed and prosper – distinguished architects of this policy; and I pray that our Lord may favour their enterprise, and that he may bring it about, day by day, that this dear and kindly mother of ours may reflect the [true] image of his Church.

For Keble the time has come. Through poets like Wordsworth, the Reform Bill, and the whole process of early nineteenth-century social agitation that was yet to culminate in Chartism, the poor, like a new Israel, have been led out of bondage to the shores of the Red Sea. Social change has begun, and there is no return to the old order. The university must reform itself, in the first place by a system of scholarships to allow scholars from *any* class of society to attend it. But there is more to this than merely opening up Oxford. As Keble has already made clear, admitting the poor with a desire to learn has an inevitable concomitant: *excluding* the idle rich, who have no such desire. Oxford must be re-invigorated academically from top to bottom. Moreover, it is clear from that metaphor of 'colonies' that the Latin *Academia* is not simply to be translated by the word 'University' let alone by implication, 'Oxford University'. What he seems to mean by 'colonies' is nothing short of a nationwide system of provincial universities, presumably on the lines of newly-founded Durham University, and King's College, London, which will make the ideal of godliness and good learning available to all who really wanted it sufficiently to take the path of academic poverty. Even more interesting, perhaps, is the hint that Oxford might stand at the apex of such a national system – providing, in effect, what might nowadays be described as a 'graduate school'. He does not, of course, mention Cambridge – presumably already too far gone down the paths of secularism and the physical sciences to be within the scope of his proposal.

A marginal note to the manuscript in Keble's handwriting, possibly of later date – but not after 1843, when Wood died – clarifies the reference to the 'distinguished architects of this policy' who are named as 'Mr Acland, Mr Mathieson, Mr Wood and others'. Thomas Dyke Acland was the son of a reforming and philanthropic west- country MP, a graduate of Christ Church, who had been a Fellow of All Souls from 1831–39. His plans for such a national educational system reaching out from his university were to lead to the establishment of the Oxford Local Examinations syndicate in the 1850s. Gilbert Farquhar Graeme Mathieson had left Oxford without a degree, but after working for a while in the Opium trade (which he abandoned on moral grounds) he went on to become private secretary to the Chancellor of the Exchequer and finally Secretary to the Mint. With Acland and Wood he played a central role in the re-invigoration of the National Society for the Education of the Poor – the main educational arm of the Anglican Church. Samuel Wood, the brother of the Earl of Halifax, had been a pupil of both Keble and Newman at Oriel, and continued to work closely with them, as with Acland and Mathieson to promote Church schools.[1]

\*\*\*

Much of the detail of what Keble is advocating reflects the thinking of this group – though in visionary scope, and especially in his ideas for the reformation of Oxford itself, he reaches far beyond them. The years leading up to 1839 had produced a ferment of new educational ideas, and in April 1839, only two months before Keble's speech, the Whig Government under Lord John Russell had set up a Parliamentary Commission on Education which had both Acland and Gladstone among its members, and which was still sitting at the time of Keble's speech. Both were to incur great unpopularity with nonconformists and the more radical secularisers by their (successful) rearguard action to delay the findings of the Commission so that the Church could set up its own system of national education in advance of the government reforms – whose purpose had been to take education out of what it saw as potentially divisive sectarian control.

Though, since it was in Latin, it could hardly have been meant as a popular rallying call, Keble's Oration was clearly intended to give a force and direction to the social conscience of his University, and of the Oxford Movement, that the former never, and the latter hardly ever achieved. The intention was clearly to support the efforts of Acland and his associates to extend the influence and ethos of Oxford to a much wider circle: and, going beyond their immediate and practically limited objectives, to give a vision of plain living and high thinking that for Keble was essential to the original conception of what a university should be, and the direct equivalent for Oxford of the recovery of first principles that he wished to see in the Church. No matter that it was not immediately achievable; neither was his goal of a regenerated Church. One day indeed, in God's good time, there might flourish a Church of England, true to its ancient principles, and co-extensive with a national system of university education, also true to its ancient statutes, and bringing the benefits of university education, as Keble understood it, to all serious-minded scholars. In the meantime, the Oration was on record in much the same way as the Assize Sermon of 1833: a prophetic call for reform and a return to primitive purity. It provided a programme that, seen in hindsight, suddenly begins to draw together what might otherwise seem to be scattered, uncoordinated, and spasmodic attempts to improve not just primary, but secondary and university education on a national basis. Nathaniel Woodard's systematic attempt from 1847 onwards to found Church schools in every region of the country may have been a personal crusade, but it was also no more than Keble's ambitious programme had already laid down.

What went wrong? Why, if this were so, did the Oration fail to ignite his peers in the way the 1833 Sermon had? Why was it later so carefully edited as to make it lose all its revolutionary thrust? The short answer is almost certainly Newman. It was, by coincidence, the very next morning after that Commemoration, 13 June 1839, that Newman began reading about the Monophysites. 'It was during this course of this reading,' he tells us in the *Apologia*, 'that for the first time a doubt came upon me of the tenableness of Anglicanism' (108). The rest, as they say, is history.... Writing to Bishop Selwyn in December 1845, just after Newman's defection to Rome, Charles Marriott, sub-Dean of Oriel, commented 'There has been much talk of extending Education in Oxford. Had it been eighteen months ago, I could have raised money to found a college on strict principles. Now, people are so shaken that I do not think anything can be effected.' But history is not the story of inevitabilities. Another fortuitous tragedy had also distracted the energies of the Movement: less than three weeks before that Commemoration of 1839, on 26 May, Pusey's wife had died, and with her much of his personal energy and vitality. With both Pusey and Newman otherwise occupied, Keble's call to reform Oxford and the education system it represented scarcely stood a chance. Samuel Wood died tragically young in 1843. The crisis into which Newman was to plunge the Oxford Movement was to last for the whole of the 1840s, and the Movement that was finally to emerge as the High Church of the 1850s was, in some ways, a very different creature. Not merely had it lost Newman, its most charismatic leader, it had also lost Manning – perhaps the only one of the Tractarians to have any real understanding of or sympathy for the working class. Pusey was by then a shadow of his former self. Moreover, the world of the 1850s was also itself a very different place. Any faint chance there might have been of creating a reformed Anglican Oxford in 1839 was finally dispelled by the Royal Commission of 1851 that was effectively to secularize the institution and to hand control of it from the clergy to a new generation of career dons who were totally to transform it within a generation.

\*\*\*

How practical, in any case, was this idea of a university? What kind of institution would Keble and his fellow-Tractarians *actually* have produced if they had been able to realize their vision? The first thing to note is that despite the ostensible appeal to return to the middle ages, this was, like all appeals to tradition, a tactical reading of a disputed past for contemporary purposes. There is something unmistakably Victorian about the implicit social engineering behind this concept of a seamless and comprehensive national system from primary school to graduate school whose only criterion of entry was need – and a desire to learn. Keble says little about curriculum beyond indicating the study of theology and philosophy, but even from those references it is not unreasonable to assume that what we have here is, in effect, a first draft of the nexus of ideas that were to be given final articulate form in Newman's 1852 lectures on a new University of Dublin, published as *The Idea of a University*. But from Keble's *Lectures on Poetry*, published only five years after the Crewian Oration, in 1844, it is also a fair assumption that his curriculum would also have included one other very important element – the study of poetry. If on the one hand this recapitulates the education of Plato's philosopher kings outlined in *The Republic*, those same *Lectures* make it clear that this was no empty gesture towards the classical tradition. Keble's poetic canon had included not merely the English classics – Milton, Shakespeare, Spenser, etc. – but *living* poets, such as Wordsworth himself, whom he was honouring in this address. Perhaps even more surprisingly, it also included Byron and Shelley – notorious atheists, whose sexual antics had titillated the readers of a British press then, as now, always happy to relay scandal. There is no evidence that Keble shared any of Newman's interest in contemporary science.

More important than speculations on the curriculum, however, is what Keble does *not* say about his reformed Oxford. Firstly, it is ruthlessly sectarian. This is a point he would have hotly disputed, because for him the National Church could not, by definition, be *sectarian*. It was the other religious groups, Protestant and Catholic alike, who were 'non-conformist' and sectarian because they had rejected the broad cover of the National Church. The repeal of the Tests Acts, which had hitherto excluded nonconformists from Oxford and Cambridge, only came in the wake of the Royal Commission of 1851 – and was fiercely resisted by the Tractarians. Secondly, and associated with this, there is little evidence that Keble had ever understood the value of freedom of speech and open intellectual debate. As J. A. Froude observed, 'If you did not agree with him, there was something morally wrong with you.' 'There was no getting on with Keble,' said Tom Mozley, 'without entire agreement, that is submission... He very soon lost his temper in discussion.' (Mozley, I, 220)

When, for instance, it became clear that Thomas Arnold (a loyal fellow-member of the Church of England) disagreed with him theologically he terminated their friendship, and made it clear that his old friend was no longer welcome in his house – though, with typical scrupulousness, Arnold's son, Matthew, who was openly not even a Christian in Keble's sense, continued to be a welcome guest because he was Keble's godson.

In short, what Keble (along with many of his Oxford contemporaries, it must be said) never recognized was the degree to which the England of the 1830s was already a highly pluralistic society, where expectations of religious or philosophic conformity could never be assumed – and, in the wake of the 1832 Reform Bill, were totally unrealistic politically. Whether a non-sectarian Christian university which actively engaged with all the doubts, antagonisms, and complexities of the surrounding society would *ever* have been possible is, of course, still an open question.

But in view of this, the fate of Keble's address at the hands of J. T. Coleridge in 1868 takes on a different significance. Coleridge's Memoir is the first of a whole series of works that display the old unreformed Oxford in a golden haze of nostalgia. Its purpose is not to show a lost moment of opportunity, but to eulogize a vanished era. Money was already being raised to build the Oxford College that was to bear Keble's name. In a sense, Coleridge's book was less a biography than a hagiography - a fund-raiser for the memorial to a saint, not a plea for allowing the working-class into Oxford. By switching the focus of the address specifically to Wordsworth, Keble's biographer is able to make it seem that it was primarily the tribute of one poet to his master. Wordsworth's death in 1850 was yet another finality sealing off the present from that vanished past. The statement that Keble 'explains and neutralises' the 'supposed failure' of Oxford to admit the poorer classes is part of the process of gilding a past whose importance is already more symbolic than actual. In so doing, of course, he is, consciously or unconsciously, re-writing the history of the movement and making his hero less worldly, less socially aware, less prophetic than in fact he turns out to have been. It also prevents us from seeing what was a serious proposal for one of the boldest social and educational experiments of the last three hundred years. Finally, of course, it represents yet another example of inventing a tradition.

## Notes

[1] I am much indebted to James Pereiro's forthcoming article, 'Tractarians and National Education (1838–1843)' for details of the political background.

## Works Cited

Carpenter, S. C., *Church and People 1789–1889*, SPCK, 1933.

Coleridge, J. T., *Memoir of the Rev. John Keble*, Oxford: Parker, 1869.

Keble, John, *Difficulties in the Relations between Church and State* (1850), Preface by H. P., Liddon, Oxford: Parker, 1877.

Mozley, Thomas *Reminiscences, Chiefly of Oriel College and the Oxford Movement*, 3 vols, London: Longman, 1882.

Newman, John Henry, *Apologia pro vita Sua*, ed., M. J., Svaglic, Oxford: Oxford University Press, 1967.

— *The Idea of a University* (1852), 3$^{rd}$ edn, London: Pickering, 1873.

Newton, John A., *Search for a Saint: Edward King*, London: Epworth Press, 1977.

Prickett, Stephen *Romanticism and Religion: the Tradition of Coleridge and Wordsworth in the Victorian Church*, Cambridge: Cambridge University Press, 1976.

Rowell, Geoffrey, ed., *The English Religious Tradition and the Genius of Anglicanism*. Wantage: Ikon Press, 1992.

# 2

# 'THE DUTY OF THE STATE': KEBLE, THE TRACTARIANS AND ESTABLISHMENT

## S.A. Skinner

The neglect of John Keble's political thought which this essay asserts is not, perhaps, hard to explain. The familiar representation of Keble as the poet and pastor of the Tractarian movement, in quietist retreat from ecclesiastical politics at Hursley, is not easily reconciled with Keble the polemicist and political theorist, while the preoccupation of historians with the movement's theological and ecclesiological legacy has served to marginalise the very social and political commentary in which much of this thought is found. An especially important source for Tractarian political commentary is the *British Critic*, a quarterly periodical which was hijacked and thereafter edited by John Henry Newman in 1838; it was then rapidly established as the movement's house magazine, its reviews on contemporary affairs augmenting the theological contents of the incomparably better remembered *Tracts for the Times*.[1] Attention to this periodical material subverts the conventional construction of Tractarianism as an episode in Church history and the attendant historiographical commonplace that Tractarians had little interest in social questions; in fact, first-generation Tractarians directed a vigorous commentary upon the 'condition of England' question. The fulcrum of this commentary was a radical and aggressive model of clerical sovereignty – of which Keble, it is argued here, was Tractarianism's major theorist.

Attention to Keble's ideal of establishment is the more necessary given that historians, preoccupied with the movement's rhetoric at times of crisis, have tended to stereotype Tractarian attitudes to Church-State relations as instinctively disestablishmentarian. In reality, Tractarians effectively inverted what they took to be the traditional High-Church axiom that the material endowments of establishment were somehow indispensable to the Church's ministry, and instead emphasised that the influence of the Church was indispensable to the State in its government of temporal affairs. For all the anti-Erastian bravado, in practice this ultimately compelled Tractarians to go on contending for a high establishment ideal which transcended the ephemeral question of political establishment which has mesmerised historians. It is a neglected article by John Keble that constitutes the classic expression of this ideal.

Certainly, the conviction that the Church of England had been compromised by the Erastian pretensions of a liberal state sent up clouds of anti-establishment chaff. Keble himself had clearly anchored Tractarian protest to the reforms of 1828–9 when he wrote in the *British Critic* that 'Ever since the passing of the Catholic Relief Bill, perhaps we might say ever since the repeal of the Test and Corporation Acts, the stream of events seems to have tended…to the permanent elevation of the enemies of the Church in the State' (Keble (1839), 355). Parliament's admission of Dissenters and Roman Catholics had invalidated almost at a stroke Hooker's tranquillising theory of parliament as the lay synod of the Church, rendering parliament instead, as Keble put it, 'a body of laymen, any number of whom may be heretics' (Keble (1839), 387), and raising the spectre of 'profane intrusion' (Keble (1833), *v*) by 'an Infidel government' (Newman, *Letters & Diaries*, IV, 23 (JK to JHN, 8 August 1833)).[2] This widely documented apprehension[3] led to the Tractarians' emphasis on the independence of the Church from the State; on the derivation of its authority not from the 'accident' of national establishment but from the 'plain historical fact' – in the words of *Tract no. 1* (Newman (1833), 3) – of the apostolic succession.

The corollary of this emphasis was – obviously – to question the very desirability of sustaining establishment. At the time of Keble's sermon on 'National Apostasy', for example, when the threat of spoliation from the state seemed at its height (with the suppression of the Irish bishoprics proposed under the terms of the Irish Church Temporalities Bill), Keble could exclaim:

> I think we ought to be prepared to sacrifice any or all of our endowments sooner than sanction *it*. "Take every pound, shilling, and penny, and the curse of Sacrilege along with it, only let us make our own Bishops, and be governed by our own laws." This is the length I am prepared to go. (*L&D*, IV, 22 (JK to JHN, 8 August 1833)).[4]

Other Tractarians, on other occasions, were of course equally vehement that the task of preserving the spiritual integrity of the Church should not preclude disestablishment. Successive sources of Tractarian alarm at what Pusey, in the course of one, called the 'anti-Christian tyranny of the State' (Liddon, IV, 89 (EBP to JK, June 1864))[5] – the proposed Jerusalem bishopric in 1841, the Gorham judgment of 1850, the publication of *Essays and Reviews* ten years later, Gladstone's appointment of Frederick Temple to the see of Exeter in 1869 – all sustained in Tractarian thought the possibility of formal separation from the State. Such views, noisily espoused at times of crisis, have been regarded by historians as Tractarian watchwords on establishment. It is not only the soggy centenary literature which holds, as Desmond Morse-Boycott put it, that Tractarians 'cared little for the State connexion' (35): J. R. Griffin and J. R. Rowlands are among the modern commentators who regard anti-Erastianism as translating straightforwardly into anti-establishmentism.[6] George Herring's recent and historiographically informed survey text, *What was the Oxford movement?* of 2002, equally, argued for the 'implicit disestablishment view of the Tractarians' (30), while Mark Chapman's essay below, 'John Keble, "National Apostasy", and the Myths of 14 July', insists on the representativeness of Keble's disestablishmentarian exclamations.

It is argued here, however, that to infer Tractarians' attitudes to establishment from their moments of rhetorical brinkmanship is deeply misleading. For attention to Tractarian commentary outside the moments of political crisis permits a vital distinction: between the circumstantial problems posed by political establishment, and the much broader question of the ideal relationship between Church and State. Keble, as we shall see, was very careful to distinguish what he called the 'terms' from the 'grounds' of establishment: that is, between its contemporary and its ideal character. The 'terms', certainly, were in danger of imposing a State-Church; the 'grounds', however, were scripturally warranted and binding on kings and their ministers in proper submission within a Church-State. Tractarian expressions in favour of disestablishment, that is to say, did not imply any quietism on the Church's part or the feeling that the Church ought ideally to stand alone. On the contrary, they derived from a feeling that the 'terms' of union fell far short of the ideal; and that that ideal was better nourished in separatist protest than acquiescence in a debased form. Even in the case of those Tractarians who were the strongest inclined at times of crisis to go it alone, any alarmism was generally displaced by the conviction that the divinely ordained vehicle for the fulfilment of this responsibility was a political relationship between Church and State, and the fear that their separation would hopelessly disorientate the nation. It was in this very sense that Keble emphasised the fact of 'national apostasy' – that is, the abandonment by the nation of the Church (Keble (1833)); that Newman feared 'so deplorable a calamity as the unchristianizing of the State' (Newman (1872), 23) and held of disestablishment that 'the Nation would lose by it' (*L&D*, IV, 34 (JHN to Bowden, 31 January 1833)); and that Pusey warned Gladstone in 1849: 'The State has no guide but the

Church; and if it rejects that, it must flounder endlessly. I see not what standard it can substitute' (Liddon, III, 184 (EBP to Gladstone, 24 March 1849)). The apparent ambivalence in Tractarian attitudes to establishment, that is to say, was generally resolved in favour of the Church's responsibility to society. As Pusey concluded: 'The parting of the State from the Church is no light matter. To the State it is suicide' (Pusey (1850), 208).[7]

The definitive Tractarian expression of this wider conception of the relationship between Church and State, and the clearest acknowledgement of its advance on older High-Church justifications, was Keble's detailed review in the *British Critic* of William Gladstone's two-volume work of 1838, *The State in its Relations with the Church*. Keble had written to Newman early in 1839 noting that 'a good field for saying something useful in the B.C. is afforded by Gladstone's [book]'. 'It is excellently well-meant,' he added, 'but wants a little reconciling' with Tractarian views (Keble Papers 1.A:68 (JK to JHN, 31 March 1839)).[8] Keble intimated that he might undertake it himself, and the review finally appeared in the issue of October.[9] It is symptomatic of the *Critic*'s wider neglect by historians that scholars have only recently noticed the existence of Keble's long and revealing critique. The standard study of Gladstone's writings on establishment, for example, Alec Vidler's *The Orb and the Cross* (1945), made no use whatever of the piece and did not therefore situate Gladstone's argument in relation to the position of leading Tractarians. Yet Keble's treatment reportedly made a far deeper impression on Gladstone than Macaulay's famous salvo in the *Edinburgh Review* in the spring of 1839, which Keble dubbed 'facetious' (Keble (1839), 363). The simple response to William Thomas's recent grumble that 'No recent biographer of Gladstone makes any serious attempt to assess the effect of Macaulay's review on Gladstone's political convictions' (Thomas 238 n. 74) is probably that its impact was negligible – and certainly dwarfed by Keble's. One of Gladstone's earliest commentators records that 'the moment that he read Keble's words he recognized the truth he was in search of. The process of emancipation had begun' (Lathbury, I, 18; Brendon, 146). Among recent Gladstone scholars Colin Matthew has rightly argued that the review is one 'whose nuances are today of more interest than Macaulay's sledge-hammer blows' (Matthew, 65), while Perry Butler pronounces it 'undoubtedly the most impressive' (Butler, 86). Yet as Matthew added, Keble 'found Gladstone's book deficient in a number of Tractarian virtues' (Matthew, 65).

Foremost of these virtues, on Keble's model, was an idea of the Church as a kingdom which historically anteceded and functionally transcended the State. In the course of his lengthy interrogation of Gladstone – the article runs to some forty-two densely printed pages – Keble articulated a general theory of Church-State relations, extrapolated from scripture and confirmed by antiquity. The basis of the article was its rejection of any conception of establishment which was not predicated on the basis of the Church's clear supremacy; Keble therefore began by censuring such representations of the establishment as were conceived in marital terms. The Victorian context of such an analogy is obviously important: Keble demurred at representations of the Church as the wife of the State because to him they would plainly have connoted the Church's inferiority. The Church was not, he made clear, subordinate to the State as a wife was subordinate to her husband, for its 'relation to the State' was 'very unlike that whose duties are summed up in "love, service, cherishing and obedience."'[10]

Gladstone was acquitted of such 'lax and unworthy notions' as this, but his conception of Church and State in equal terms, Keble wrote, 'yet seems hardly to come up to our own view of the relations of Church and State'. He admonishingly noted that if Gladstone claimed to have rejected the term 'Alliance' for the title of his book, he had not altogether eschewed the spirit of it in his text, where 'it may perhaps have here and there communicated to his reasonings an unconscious tinge, we will not say of Erastianism, but of State as distinct from Church policy' (Keble (1839), 358–9).[11] Keble proceeded to assert an altogether loftier conception of the relationship than one predicated merely on terms of equality. As he put it, in a highly significant passage:

> To us, we confess, the word Incorporation, though Mr. Gladstone at once discards it, would have appeared in the abstract far preferable to Marriage, Alliance, Union, or any other like them: provided always that we understand it as the meaning of the terms requires, of the admission of any particular State, as of any particular individual, into the bosom of the Holy Universal Church: *reserving the superiority, according to the idea of a Corporation, to the body adopting, for the benefit of the member adopted.* (Keble (1839), 359)[12]

This theory of 'Incorporation' and this language of 'superiority' define the Tractarian Church-State model. If Gladstone's notion of 'Alliance' elevated the Church from the servitude implicit in any Victorian metaphor of matrimony, Keble's notion of 'Incorporation' elevated it yet further above the mere equality connoted by 'Alliance'.

In classifying Gladstone's 1838 model in such terms, moreover, Keble was enlisting it in the ranks of earlier Anglican theories of establishment which fell short of the incorporation ideal. As Peter Nockles and Stephen Taylor have pointed out in other contexts, this sort of conflation was wilfully insensitive to the nuances which divided writers such as Richard Hooker and William Warburton – let alone Thomas Chalmers, whose celebrated lectures of 1838 had provoked Gladstone's book in the first place.[13] Hooker's *Laws of Ecclesiastical Polity* (1594)[14] had assumed a natural and organic relationship between Church and State from which the contractual idioms of Warburton's *The Alliance between Church and State* (1736) notably departed. Taylor's work on Warburton has demonstrated that the *Alliance* was certainly not the definitive expression of Hanoverian attitudes to establishment that Tractarians chose to think it. Both Warburton's application of 'Lockean contractarianism to Church-State relations', and his denial 'that the civil magistrate had any concern with the truth of a religion', divided him even from most contemporary churchmen (Taylor 284–5). Nockles has duly argued that amongst Tractarians Froude and Newman were the most culpable of perpetuating 'a historical misrepresentation of Orthodox teaching on Church and State' (Nockles (1994), 55–6); clearly, though, in parodying orthodox theories of establishment as Warburtonian and Erastian, Keble was not immune from the polemical contagion.

What is important for us, however, is not the inaccuracy or injustice but rather the intention behind Tractarian (mis)representations of earlier High-Church positions. Edward Norman and, following him, Nockles, may be right to insist that orthodox apologetic typically followed Hooker and not Warburton: assuming, that is to say, 'the interdependence of Church and State, and not the dependence of the Church upon the State' (Norman, 33; Nockles (1994), 56–7). But Tractarians were not merely reasserting high Hookerian ideals without a proper acknowledgement of their debt to later High Churchmen for carrying the flame. They went further in emphasis than the symbiosis of which Hooker was the classic exponent: not merely rejecting the dependence of the Church upon the State, but asserting the dependence of the State upon the Church.

This suggests, for the sake of exposition, a three-tier model of the Tractarians' view of Anglican conceptions of establishment. The lowest, conceiving of the Church as a subsidiary of the State, was that of Locke and Warburton. The second, higher and more 'orthodox' position, conceiving of the Church as a partner of the State, was that of Filmer, Hooker – and, Keble insisted in his *Critic* review, Gladstone. Keble was asserting a third and still higher conception, however: that of the Church as superior to the State. Those historians who have argued that Tractarians parodied the Hanoverian High-Church position on establishment, in order to exaggerate the novelty of their own, are right to point out that in general pre-Tractarian High Churchmen were already occupying the ground of this middle tier, and not – as Tractarians often argued – Warburton's utilitarian lowlands. Keble's article, however, was emphatic that even this organic, relational emphasis was inadequate to the Church's proper office. If he caricatured past positions in order to clarify present ones, Keble nonetheless pulled together and systematised older elements of Anglican apologetic to scale new heights of clerical sovereignty on the question of establishment. This is emphatically not to say that Keble renounced a relational view of Church and State. On the contrary: he claimed that the very basis of the State's legitimacy was its function as an instrument of 'God's universal government'. The State was sanctified by its service to Christian polity. It was this high calling which distinguished it from other secular corporations, rendering it 'more sacred in its kind' (Keble (1839), 364–5), and which animated his warnings to 'public men' – such as young Gladstone – of the 'desecration of their calling ... should ever the service of the State in this country be authoritatively and formally separated from that of the Church' (Keble (1839), 371). Pusey, too, argued that this calling, rather than the Church's needs, was the foundation of temporal benefits: they served as a token of the righteousness of the State, and of the State's recognition of the fruits of incorporation (Pusey (1837), 22). Should the day come, Keble therefore wrote, when statesmen

> have no longer to accompany them in their most irksome and unsatisfactory toils, the consciousness that all is but part of the price of the continuance of so great a blessing as the presence of the Church in all parts of the realm: then, indeed, we may well believe that their calling may seem perfectly intolerable, their occupation quite gone. (Keble (1839), 371)

Keble's insistence on a theory 'antecedent to all experience' (Keble (1839), 372–3) – antecedent, that is, to the contemporary political preccupations which had framed earlier Anglican apologetic – was a summons back to basics. He claimed plainly that 'such a theory is found in Scripture'. That the Church-State relationship was 'divinely sanctioned' could be adduced from the bible 'as virtually containing the terms of the union in question' (Keble (1839), 366). Keble duly subjected Isaiah's famous declaration, that 'the especial office of kings and queens' was to serve as the Church's 'nursing fathers and mothers',[15] to detailed exegesis. His purpose was to demonstrate that this passage did not, as some had assumed, connote the dependency of the Church – 'as though the Church were a helpless infant in the arms of some Defender of the Faith' – but rather that monarchs 'are among her servants and attendants'. Kings and queens, Isaiah said, '"shall bow down to thee with their face toward the earth, and lick up the dust of thy feet"'; '"*kings shall minister unto thee*"'; and '"*the nation and kingdom that will not serve thee shall perish*"'. This was 'proved unquestionably by the fearful sanction annexed: perishing and utter wasting to the nation and kingdom that will not serve Zion' (Keble (1839), 374–5). That contemporary potentates fell short of these expectations comes as no surprise. Recent developments – Keble instanced 'certain late proceedings in the matter of Christian Education'[16] – compelled churchmen to 'turn back the mind's-eye' to days when 'the kings and rulers of the world' bowed to these injunctions. For the sovereign, he insisted, was 'a servant of the Church

… and bound to wait on and guard her bishops and priests', just as modern statesmen 'would well understand that in spiritual matters they were to execute the laws of Christ's Church, not impose laws upon her' (Keble (1839), 375–6).

This ideal of a Church-State, for which Keble asserted unequivocal biblical warrant, begged an obvious question. If the establishment was 'divinely sanctioned and grounded', if there could be discerned 'in His word clear indications of His will that the Church should be in a certain sense politically established' (Keble (1839), 366, 370), then why should the Church movement for which the *British Critic* authoritatively spoke have seemed so clamorous in undermining it? Keble certainly anticipated this point. He insisted that disquiet at 'the terms of the union', or 'the particular form in which the relation of Church and State appears in this country at present', ought not to be taken as renunciation of its 'grounds', or 'the abstract principle of establishment'. Affirmations of the Church's antecedence to the State did not therefore connote any ideal of independence from it. 'We have never met with', he maintained, 'we have never read of – any set of persons admitting the divine origin and paramount claims of the Apostolical Church, yet denying the obligation of the civil magistrate to enter into relations with it.' This is a striking passage, and one which emphatically confounds disestablishmentarian interpretations of the movement. For Tractarian criticism of the State's conduct, Keble emphasised, had at no point implied a rejection of the ideal of establishment itself: 'All the scruples and demurs that we have met with in such persons have had reference, not to that *principle* of incorporation, but to the *terms* of it in this or that particular instance.' Gladstone, Keble wrote, was therefore

> mistaken, if he thinks, as some of his expressions appear to imply, that any thing which has happened in the way of wrong done to the Church, or of unworthy compromise on the part of her defenders, has caused *such* religionists to doubt or deny the duty of the State to connect itself with the Church. They are perfectly aware of that duty, and of the danger of falling away from it. (Keble (1839), 365)

Keble's article insisted that 'both Church and State are (*though in several ways*) of divine appointment: that kings, as well as bishops, are *in a manner* representatives of Jesus Christ on earth' (Keble (1839), 365; my italics). These (italicised) caveats were, of course, critical: they emphasised the distinctness and superiority of the Church's authority, and preserved Keble's representation of the ideal relationship between Church and State from the ordinarily egalitarian model which he imputed to Gladstone and to earlier Anglican apologetic. The question of 'a certain relation between the Church and the State', therefore, was one not only of 'wisdom and rectitude' but of 'positive divine institution'; it was confirmed by 'the seal of the Almighty...the reasonings of wise men, and the natural feelings of religious men' (Keble (1839), 365).

Keble had stressed that misgiving at the 'terms' did not undermine commitment to the 'grounds' of union. Having repeatedly asserted the 'divine appointment' of the grounds, he proceeded to justify Tractarian criticism of its current terms. He first advanced, by natural extension of the principle of incorporation, the general right of the Church to upbraid the State and to question its handling of the union. This was an obvious attempt to legitimise Tractarian agitation. As he argued: 'one thoroughly imbued with ancient principles would find himself continually forced to qualify his adherence, under present circumstances, to the supporters of the connexion of Church and State in this kingdom' (Keble (1839), 367). Since it is expressions such as these which are invariably quoted by historians, it is unsurprising that the movement is generally regarded as sentimentally disestablishmentarian. Keble was emphatic, however, that Tractarians resisted establishment on its current terms, rather than the principle of establishment itself. If Froude is regarded as the most tenaciously anti-Erastian of the first-generation, this is at least partly because a disproportionate quantity of his thought is preserved in the form of private conjecture, but partly also because it was confined to the very period when fixation with the 'terms' of establishment was most understandable. Early death spared Froude the ultimate dilemma which Keble – whose private noises could be just as hysterically anti-Erastian as Froude's in the early 1830s[17] – was forced to resolve. Keble's insistence that churchmen be 'continually called to the disagreeable duty of protesting against the lax notions and irreverent proceedings of those with whom themselves are acting' was always made against the background of his earlier conviction that a Church-State axis was divinely ordained. As he put it, in a refrain which was an absolutely essential precondition of such warnings, and which was to remain the keynote for the remainder of his life: 'it is the part of resignation and obedience to go on' (Keble (1839), 366).

Of course, in the course of the article, Keble held out the notion that the circumstances of establishment might become so injurious to the Church that it would be compelled to repudiate formal union. In the most extreme hypothetical instance, of a State which might for example 'exclude from her councils the attached members of the Church', then plainly 'the State must be given up,' as 'it would be impossible for a good Christian to serve it'. But such an eventuality at no point implied the retreat of the Church from the world's affairs. The State can separate from the Church, but not the Church from civil society. Quite the contrary: the Church would simply be forced to assume those capacities previously held on trust by the State, the State having abdicated its high responsibility to the service of Christianity (Keble (1839), 372). It would therefore be misleading in the extreme to infer that Keble in particular or Tractarians in general were sentimentally anti-establishment; and that such a repudiation in some way connoted the retreat of the Church from the temporal sphere. K. A. Thompson has concluded on the basis of this very article that 'The Oxford Movement had little interest in a State which had become secularised' (Thompson, 38). But this is to confuse Keble's revulsion at the 'terms' with his insistence on the 'grounds': he argued that the scope of 'God's universal government' was infinite. Perry Butler, too, has noted rightly that Keble's piece was 'the authentic voice of the new High Churchmanship'; but, apparently in seeking to vindicate the Gladstonian ideal, Butler concluded that 'the more extreme Oxford men' thus seemed to be 'more concerned that the Church should be free than that the nation should be Christian' (Butler, 89). Yet this, again, is to misconstrue a difference over means: the end, Keble was quite emphatic, was the propagation of 'the truths and duties' of Christianity 'amongst the "dense masses"... to every creature in the vast wildernesses of London and our own manufacturing districts' (Keble (1839), 381).

Keble's thinking on establishment therefore merits close attention. His critique of Gladstone – meticulously assembled for wide public consumption and appearing in pages which Newman aggressively policed – has good claim to be regarded as the most sustained and theoretically trenchant expression of the Tractarian Church-State model. Its militancy is the more significant given that Keble is conventionally regarded as the most temperate and historically minded of leading Tractarians, and might therefore have been expected to be the least radical on the establishment question. Despite this, the article has received no scholarly assessment whatever, beyond mention in (Gladstonian) despatches. Yet behind the smokescreen sent up by Newman's argument that conversion was the logical working out of the early movement's rejection of establishment, and the justificatory rhetoric of the Gorham converts, Keble's ideal of 'Incorporation', this quasi-theocracy, represented the *echt* Tractarian position. Peter Nockles has demonstrated, for example, how much Pusey's 'positive view of a union of the two powers working together, of his intense belief in the ideal of a Christian State guided by the precepts of the Church', owed to Keble's influence (Nockles (1983), 290). For Pusey similarly asserted that 'the spiritual is higher than the civil Government': 'No one,' he said, 'could doubt of the superiority of things spiritual to things temporal, or that the office of a Bishop of Christ's flock was higher than that of a temporal sovereign' (Pusey (1837), 9, 27).

Tractarians therefore rejected contractual justifications of establishment which had been nourished by the revolutionary epoch, and which seemed to them to be based on the Church's propagation not of right doctrine but of propriety and good social order. In doing so they shifted the justification for patronage and endowment from broadly practical to narrowly spiritual grounds. Certainly, the Church might serve to underline the providential ordination of social rank, and to inculcate the habits of sobriety which made the tasks of secular government easier. But as Newman put it in a sermon of the 1830s, the 'main undertaking of a Christian Church' was not merely 'to make men good members of society, honest, upright, industrious and well-conducted', but to make them 'Saints' (Newman (1873) IV, 160).[18] On Keble's model, the Church of England was endowed because the State had historically recognised its enshrinement of the truth which might thus make its citizens saints. As Keble's language of 'Incorporation' made plain, it was the State, by this transaction, that was being adopted by a historically antecedent and functionally transcendent Church. It was this mechanism by which Tractarianism justified an extensive commentary on contemporary affairs which its historians, typically operating behind disciplinary partitions, have almost completely overlooked.[19] The caricature of Keble as the poet and pastor of Tractarianism has obscured the importance of his theoretical contributions to that commentary.

## Abbreviations

KP  Keble Papers, Keble College, Oxford.
L&D  *Letters and Diaries of John Henry Newman*, eds C. S. Dessain, T. Gornall, E. E. Kelly, I. T. Ker, and G. Tracey; Vols I–VIII, Oxford, 1978–99; XI–XXII, London, 1961–72; and XXIII–XXXI, Oxford, 1973–7.

## Notes

[1] For an assessment of the tractarian *British Critic* see Skinner, 1999.

[2] Hereafter *L&D*.

[3] See, for emphasis on the political and constitutional background to the movement, Brose 7–21; Chadwick I, 7–100; Thompson, *passim*; and Norman, *passim*.

[4] The words which immediately succeed this much-quoted declaration rather muffle its thunderous report: 'of course if we could get our liberty at an easier price, so much the better.'

[5] The occasion was the continuing controversy surrounding the publication of *Essays and Reviews* in 1860.

[6] See for the most obvious examples Griffin (1971), 167–75 esp. 169; *idem* (1973), 431–9; *idem* (1976), 47–56; and *idem* (1984); also Thompson 37–42; Rowlands, *passim*.

[7] That Pusey should have spoken of 'the parting of the State from the Church', rather than the customary reverse, is itself a typical expression of the Tractarians' conception of the church as a historically antecedent community. Frederick

Oakeley also described such a process as 'suicidal' to the state: see Oakeley, 24.

[8] Hereafter KP. Newman later wrote similarly of Gladstone's *Church Principles considered in their Results* (1840): 'Gladstone's book ... is doctrinaire, and (I think) somewhat self-confident, but it will do good': *L&D* VII, 470, (JHN to F. Rogers, 26 December 1840).

[9] See, for correspondence over the piece, KP 1.A:69 (JK to JHN, 22 April 1839); KP 1.A:74 (16 August 1839); KP 1.A:75 (7 September 1839); and KP K.14 (JK to T. Keble, 23 Sept 1839). Keble and Gladstone, of course, were to become regular correspondents. See KP K. 90, an assortment of letters from Gladstone to Keble which began in 1840 and continued until Keble's death in 1865.

[10] For a discussion of the common use of the marital metaphor in writing on church-state relations, see Vidler 94 n 2. See also, for further Tractarian examples, Bowden 43, 127–8; and Gresley 136.

[11] W. J. Copeland, writing two years previously in the *Critic*, had similarly protested that 'The word "*alliance*," and the word "*union*," ... both assume on the face of them the independent existence of the two bodies' (Copeland, 223).

[12] My italics. Although he discarded the term 'marriage', as explicitly connoting the inferiority of church (and wife), Keble himself subsequently employed the terms 'alliance' and 'union' in the course of the review, though on the conditions he had stated.

[13] 'Such a jumble of church, un-church, and anti-church principles as that excellent and eloquent man Dr. Chalmers has given us in his recent lectures,' Gladstone wrote to Henry Manning on 14 May 1838, 'no human being ever heard' (Butler 78). Gladstone further recalled Chalmers's impact in his *Autobiographica* of 1897: see Brooke and Sorenson, I, 42–3.

[14] Richard Hooker's (1554–1600) *Of the Lawes of Ecclesiasticall Politie* appeared over eight books, the first four of which were published in 1594, the fifth in 1597, and the last three posthumously in 1648 and 1662. Nockles has argued that Edmund Burke did much to infuse high-church thought with Hooker's ideal at the end of the eighteenth century (Nockles (1994), 63); but see for a rejection of this Hilton, 1, 27.

[15] Isaiah 22. 23: 'And kings shall be thy nursing fathers, and their queens thy nursing mothers'; Keble also adduced 60. 12.

[16] Tractarians had no shortage of anxieties in the realm of education: writing in early 1839, Keble would have had in mind Russell's proposal to extend education grants to dissenting and Roman Catholic schools outside the National Society and the British and Foreign Schools Society, between whom £20,000 had been annually (and unevenly) divided since the 1833 Factory Act, as well as to increase the grant to £30,000 and introduce civil inspection; and to establish teacher-training for 'Normal Schools' dispensing undenominational religious instruction. Russell jettisoned the Normal Schools on 4 June in response to clerical agitation, but retained plans for inspection and dissenting grants. Archbishop Howley sustained Anglican resistance, and under the 'Concordat' of 15 July 1840 the Church conceded the right of inspection in return for archiepiscopal veto over the inspectorate. See *Hansard*, 3rd ser., 45, cols. 274–80 (12 February 1839); Chadwick, I, 338–40.

[17] See, for early fusillades of separatist rhetoric, KP K.47:G-240 (JK to E. Churton,

21 February 1833): 'Any thing, to my mind, will be better for us, than going on in Union with a Whig State'; also KP K.62 (Froude to A. P. Perceval, 14 August 1833), which records that Keble 'thinks the Union of Church & State as it is now understood, actually sinful.'

[18] W. G. Ward may well have had this passage in mind when similarly proclaiming in his *Ideal* that the church's 'highest office is to train, not ordinary Christians, but those predestined to be Saints' (18).

[19] See Skinner, 2004, for a study of this social commentary.

## Works Cited

Bowden, J. W., *Thoughts on the Work of the Six Days of Creation*, ed. J. H. Newman, Oxford: J. H. Parker, 1845.

Brendon, P. *Hurrell Froude and the Oxford Movement*, London: Elek, 1974.

Brooke, J., and M. Sorenson, eds, *The Prime Ministers' Papers: W. E. Gladstone*, vol. I, *Autobiographica*, London: HMSO, 1971-2.

Brose, O. J., *Church and Parliament: the Reshaping of the Church of England 1828-1860*, London: Oxford University Press, 1959.

Butler, P. *Gladstone: Church, State, and Tractarianism. A Study of his Religious Ideas and Attitudes, 1809-1859*, Oxford: Oxford University Press, 1982.

Chadwick, W. O., *The Victorian Church*, 2 vols, London: A&C Black, 1966-70.

Copeland, W. J., 'Holden's *On Church Establishments*, Hook's *Sermons*, &c., Keble's *Sermon*' British Critic, XXII, 43 (July 1837).

Gladstone, W. E., *Correspondence on Church and Religion of William Ewart Gladstone*, ed. D. C. Lathbury, 2 vols, London: John Murray, 1910.

Gresley, W., *Sermons Preached at Brighton*, London, 1858.

Griffin, J. R. 'John Keble: Radical', *Anglican Theological Review* (hereafter ATR), 53 (June 1971): 167-75

— 'The Anglican Politics of John Henry Newman', ATR 55 (October 1973): 431-9.

— 'The Radical Phase of the Oxford Movement', *Journal of Ecclesiastical History*, 28, 1 (January 1976): 47-56.

— *The Oxford Movement: a Revision*, Edinburgh: Pentland Press, 1984.

Herring, G. *What was the Oxford Movement?* London and New York: Continuum, 2002.

Hilton, B. 'Apologia pro Vitis Veteriorum Hominum', *Journal of Ecclesiastical History*, 50 (1999): 117-30.

Keble, J. 'National Apostasy Considered in a Sermon Preached in St. Mary's, Oxford: Before His Majesty's Judges of Assize, on Sunday, July 14, 1833', Oxford: J. H. Parker, 1833.

— 'Gladstone – *The State in its Relations with the Church*', British Critic, XXVI, 52 (October 1839): 355-97.

Liddon, H. P., *The Life of Edward Bouverie Pusey*, ed. J. O. Johnston and R. J. Wilson, 4 vols, London: Longmans, 1893-7.

Macaulay, T. B. 'Church and State', *Edinburgh Review*, LXIV, (April-July 1839): 231-80.

Matthew, H. C. G., *Gladstone 1809–1874*, Oxford: Oxford University Press, 1986.

Morse-Boycott, D., *The Secret Story of the Oxford Movement*, London: Skeffington & Son, 1933.

Newman, J. H., *Tracts for the Times, No. 1, Thoughts on the Ministerial Commission. Respectfully Addressed to the Clergy, Ad Clerum*, Oxford: Rivingtons, 1833.

— *Discussions and Arguments on Various Subjects*. London: Basil Montagu Pickering, 1872.

— *Parochial and Plain Sermons*, 8 vols, London: Rivingtons, 1873.

Nockles, P. B., 'Pusey and the Question of Church and State', *Pusey Rediscovered*, ed. P. Butler, London: SPCK, 1983.

— *The Oxford Movement in Context: Anglican High Churchmanship, 1760–1857*, Cambridge: Cambridge University Press, 1994.

Norman, E. R., *Church and Society in England, 1770–1970: a Historical Study*, Oxford: Oxford University Press, 1976.

Oakeley, F., *Thoughts on Some of the Recommendations of the Ecclesiastical Commissioners, and on Popular Views of the Church. In a Letter to Sir Robert Harry Inglis, Bart. M.P. for the University of Oxford*, London, 1837.

Pusey, E. B., *Patience and Confidence the Strength of the Church. A Sermon preached on the Fifth of November, before the University of Oxford: at S. Mary's, and now published at the wish of many of its Members*, Oxford and London: J. H. Parker, J. H. and F. Rivington, 1837.

— *The Royal Supremacy not an Arbitrary Authority but limited by the Laws of the Church of which Kings are Members*, Oxford: J. H. Parker, 1850.

Rowlands, J. H. L., *Church, State and Society: the Attitudes of John Keble, Richard Hurrell Froude and John Henry Newman, 1827–1845*, Worthing: Churchman, 1989.

Skinner, S. A. 'Newman, the Tractarians and the British Critic', *Journal of Ecclesiastical History*, 50, (1999): 716–59.

— *Tractarians and the 'condition of England': the social and political thought of the Oxford Movement*. Oxford: Oxford University Press, 2004.

Taylor, S. J. C., 'William Warburton and the Alliance of Church and State', *Journal of Ecclesiastical History*, 43, (1992): 271–86.

Thomas, W. E. S., *The Quarrel of Macaulay and Croker: Politics and History in the Age of Reform*, Oxford: Oxford University Press, 2002.

Thompson, K. A., *Bureaucracy and Church Reform: the Organisational Response of the Church of England to Social Change, 1800–1965*, Oxford: Oxford University Press, 1970.

Vidler, A. R., *The Orb and the Cross: a Normative Study in the Relations of Church and State with Reference to Gladstone's Early Writings*, London: SPCK, 1945.

Warburton, W., *The Alliance between Church and State, or the Necessity and Equity of an Established Religion and a Test-Law Demonstrated, from the Essence and End of Civil Society, upon the Fundamental Principles of the Law of Nature and Nations*, London, 1736.

Ward, W. G., *Ideal of a Christian Church Considered in Comparison with Existing* Practice, Containing a Defence of Certain Articles in The British Critic in Reply to Remarks on them in Mr. Palmer's 'Narrative', London: James Toovey, 1844.

# 3

# JOHN KEBLE, 'NATIONAL APOSTASY' AND THE MYTHS OF 14 JULY

## Mark D. Chapman

'In times of revolution,' wrote Eric Hobsbawm, 'nothing is more powerful than the fall of symbols'. This is what made 14 July 1789 such an important date – it was not the release of a few prisoners that made it significant, so much as the symbolic force unleashed by the storming of the citadel. Within three weeks the 'social structure of French rural feudalism and the state machine of royal France lay in fragments' (Hobsbawm, 82). Now it would obviously be quite ludicrous to claim that the revolution inaugurated by Keble's Assize Sermon of 14 July 1833 was of the same character as the French Revolution. Indeed the Sermon itself was something of a non-event, and was hardly even noticed at the time. It took a while before Keble even thought of publishing it, and he sought his brother's approval beforehand. The only future Tractarian who seems to have said anything about it at the time was Palmer (letter to Thomas Keble, July 1833, in Martin, 37), and it was claimed by Dr Pusey's biographer that his copy of the published version of the sermon, even though it had been sent with the author's compliments, had never had the pages cut (Liddon, I, 276). More recently, Peter Nockles has suggested that the sermon was arguably more conservative in tone than one on a similar theme preached by H. J. Rose the previous year (Nockles (1994), 83). As a great revolutionary date, 14 July 1833 does not look very promising. Its elevation to symbolic status, to what Frank Cross called the 'myth of July 14, 1833' (Cross, 162), occurred only after Newman had published his *Apologia* where he famously wrote that he had always kept the date as the beginning of the 'religious movement of 1833' (Newman (1912), 42). One hundred and fifty years later, however, the myth was still intact: 14 July was kept as the day of the festival to celebrate the beginnings of the Oxford Movement, and a new version of the sermon was published in a limited edition (Keble (1983)).

In reading through the text of the Sermon it is difficult to see much that is explicitly revolutionary: there is certainly no exhortation to man the barricades. Using a text from I Samuel (12.23) Keble asks as to the symptoms by which one might judge whether a nation was 'becoming alienated from God and Christ' (Keble (1983), 14–15). He goes on to point to some parallels with the Old Testament and his own day. Just as the Israelites had failed in their duties as the people of God, he claimed, so 'in modern times, when liberties are to be taken, and the intrusive passions of men to be indulged, precedent and permission, or what sounds like them, may easily be found and quoted for everything' (Keble (1983), 17). He then goes on to outline the religious problems of his own age:

> Under the guise of charity and toleration we are come almost to this pass; that no difference, in matters of faith, is to disqualify for our approbation and confidence, whether in public or domestic life. Can we conceal it from ourselves, that every year the practice is becoming more common, of trusting men unreservedly in the most delicate and important matters, without one serious inquiry, whether they do not hold principles which make it impossible for them to be loyal to their Creator, Redeemer and Sanctifier (Keble (1983), 18).

The key word here, it seems to me, is 'toleration'. Against the notion of a Church under the control of a Parliament increasingly apostate on account of its tolerance and openness to non-churchmen, Keble and the other Tractarians sought refuge in ecclesiastical independence. Indeed Tractarianism, of which the Assize Sermon marked the symbolic start, was every bit as much a response to toleration as the Irish Temporalities Act itself.

Consequently there is some plausibility in seeing the Assize Sermon, or at least the constitutional reforms to which it was responding, as marking the beginnings of a revolution in English political theory. It would not be too much of an overstatement to suggest that the enfranchisement of non-conformists, Catholics and shopkeepers led to a reshaping of the doctrine of political sovereignty partly through the concept of apostolicity. In earlier Anglican theology the doctrine of apostolicity had usually been regarded as a supernatural bolster to the authority of the Church of England as an organic part of the wider society under the ultimate sovereignty of the monarch. It had seldom been claimed as an independent source of sovereignty over and against that of the State (See Chapman 2000, 474–503; and Nockles (1983), 44–103). With the Tractarian recourse to what they dubbed the 'Apostolical Church', however, it became the justification for the independent corporate existence of the Church. This is clear from the well-known words of the first Tract, published only a matter of months after the Assize Sermon, where Newman asked: 'should the government and country so far forget their God as to cast off the Church, to deprive it of its temporal honours and substance, *on what* will you rest the claim of respect and attention which you make upon your flocks?' (Newman (1833), p. 1).

Such a model meant that there was a real shift away from the ideology that had prevailed beforehand: although Keble's ideal political principle probably remained a unified vision of Church and State as two sides of a divinely ordered society, what Griffin calls his 'ancestral Protestantism' (Griffin (1987), 79),[1] he realised, at least for the period around the Assize Sermon and the first *Tracts*, that such a model was not simply under threat, but had been virtually destroyed by a parliament which could no longer be conceived as a lay synod of the Church of England. As Nockles notes, Keble could see the full implications of the constitutional reforms and was not simply imprisoned in an unrealistic preservation of the *ancien régime* (See Nockles (1994), 71 and Nockles (1996), esp. 85). Indeed, for Keble, at least in this period, it was clear that, as Paul Avis puts it, 'The ancient Anglican ideology of kings as the nursing fathers of the Church was a dead letter' (Avis, 160).

In a response to the Bishop of Leighlin and Merns in the *British Critic* of 1834, Keble wrote to the editor how:

> the late changes in the Constitution affect the rights of Parliament to legislate for the Church. Many considerate persons think, that the changes are so vital, so wrought into the very ground of the system, as to amount to a virtual breach of the terms of union between Church and State. So that, in their judgment, the governors of the Church are at liberty, whenever in their consciences they shall deem it most expedient, to decline submitting themselves to the ecclesiastical laws of the Parliament. For the two societies are no longer identical, according to the theory of Hooker and the practice of the days of Queen Elizabeth. (Keble (1869), 61)

Keble undoubtedly would have preferred something else, and after his appointment to Hursley it did not take long for him to take refuge again in Richard Hooker,[2] but at least in 1833 he was prepared for the worst, and that required a radical solution. As Newman wrote to Froude in July 1833: 'I have never till the last month or two thought Keble *would* go lengths: but I hope now he will. I think he is unchained' (Palmer, 5). Despite the fact that Keble had earlier been a shining example of High Church Anglicanism, the 'finest flower of the old High Church Tory tradition' (Dawson, 13; see also Church,

21) with a hatred of heresy and insubordination (see, for example, Mozley I, 441–2; II, 215), he was prepared to resort to radical solutions to resist what he called in a letter to J. T. Coleridge as early as 22 June 1827 'the "tyranny of liberalism"' (Griffin (1971), 171; see also Griffin (1976)). While there may have been few, if any, concessions to toleration on the part of Keble and the Tractarians themselves, all of whom remained inflexible on matters of doctrine, there was nevertheless a recognition that the Church needed to accept and respond to the fruits of toleration however unwillingly. Although it would be misleading to call Keble a political radical, as Griffin does,[3] there is a sense, possibly ironic, in which he prepared the way for a slow but inexorable move towards the independence of the Church and the freedom of religion in a pluralist State.

\*\*\*

As the senior figure of one of the most unlikely bands of revolutionaries of all time, Keble unwittingly prepared the way for the rise of English political pluralism. In a remarkable essay, 'The Politics of the Oxford Movement', written during the First World War, Harold Laski, at the time one of the leading political pluralists and a future Chairman of the Labour Party National Executive Committee, wrote that Tractarianism was a 'tremendous and brilliant plea for ecclesiastical freedom that is clearly born from the passionate sense of a corporate Church' (Laski, 94). What he called its 'unconscious theory of the State' was derived from the degree of liberty which had to be conferred on the different constituent groups which comprised the State. Since they were under threat from an increasingly non-Anglican parliament, both the Church of England and Oxford University (see Nockles (1997)), as the hitherto dominant institutions of the Establishment, were compelled to assert their corporate independence: 'In its essence,' Laski went on, 'Tractarianism is essentially a plea of the corporate body which is distinct from the State to a separate and free existence. It is a denial that the members of the Church are as its members no more than individuals, living under the all-inclusive sovereignty of the Crown' (Laski, 108–9).

For Keble, as for the pluralists, the dominant question was that of sovereignty: rolling back the power of the State became necessary when the reformed Parliament had begun to use its unbounded sovereignty to threaten the spiritual society. In response, the Church needed to erect barriers and defend itself through an alternative theory of sovereignty. It was thereby forced to question the absolute authority of Parliament over all corporations in the realm. The 'Apostolical' Church was thus not simply a theological theory but a bold political statement of the independent authority of the Church over and against the State: politics and ecclesiology were united in the defence of the Church, the concomitant of which was a nascent pluralist theory of the State. Laski wrote: 'It was a definition of the Church that the Tractarians attempted, and they found almost immediately that to define its ideality was to assert its exclusiveness. If it was created by God it could not be controlled by man; if it was erected by God, it was not subject to the ordinances of a man-created institution like the state' (Laski, 114).

The conservative defence of the Church against what he perceived as parliamentary profanation thus forced Keble to develop what might be termed a 'primitive pluralism'. Politics had moved too far down the road of liberalism to expect anything else: the right to exist as an independent corporation was as much as could be hoped for. In a letter of 31 March 1831 Keble wrote to J. T. Coleridge:

> What will be the effects of this new institution [i.e. the reformed Parliament] upon the Church of England? If this neighbourhood is at all a fair specimen of the middle-ranks, into whose hands it is even professed (is it not?) to throw the entire House of Commons I do not think the privileges of the establishment can possibly out-last another parliament....If the Church and State are to be untied, I do hope it will be before any attempt has been made to reform *us* by a Papysocratic Government. It would be a matter of great doubt for me how far I was to submit to Ecclesiastical Censures enacted by Lord Landsdowne, O'Connell, Hunt and Hume: even though the Bishops had not lost their votes. (Griffin (1971), 172)

Indeed, he even prophesied that English institutions would dissolve if 'shop-keeping orators [i.e. the newly enfranchised middle-classes]...are allowed to reform us at their will' (quoted in Griffin (1971), 172). The following year Keble wrote again to Coleridge, this time making a more explicit call for disestablishment: 'I am more and more inclined to think, that the sooner we come to an open separation from these people, the better for ourselves and our flocks: and this is some comfort as one watches the progress of Revolution in which the said separation will, I expect, be a very early step' (8 May 1832, in Griffin (1971), 172). Logically, this meant that an independent corporate identity for the Church – in other words, a separation from the State – seemed the only viable way forward for the protection of the Church. Indeed, as Hurrell Froude wrote to A. P. Perceval in the summer of 1833, 'Keble...thinks the Union of Church and State as it is now understood, actually sinful' (18 August 1833, in Griffin (1971), 170). This meant that unless the Church were to disestablish itself on its own terms in order to preserve its apostolic integrity, then the State would begin its work of demolition on the lines begun in Ireland. Not surprisingly this disestablishmentarian strand has become an important counter-current to the ideology of the 'National Church' which has run through the different strands of Anglo-Catholicism ever since.

It was only in such a way, according to Keble, that there could there be protection for the truths of the Church, as well as its apostolic structures and its liturgy. After July 1833 this led rapidly to the growth of the Oxford Movement. The plea for independence was coupled with the return to apostolicity and seriousness which accompanied the rediscovery of the absolute authority of the Church. Thus Keble remarked: 'We had rather be a Church in earnest separate from the State, than a counterfeit Church in professed Union with the State' (Keble (1877), 226). Shortly after preaching the Assize Sermon, Keble wrote to a friend outlining his aims for a group to defend the Church. The new association was to 'circulate primitive notions regarding the Apostolical Succession, & c.; and secondly the protection of the Prayer-book against profane innovation' (26 August 1833, in Coleridge I, 220). The external threat to the Church thereby elevated the life of the church and would lead to a renunciation of mere external conformity. Again this can be seen as stemming from the problem of toleration. There is consequently some truth in J. N. Figgis's observations in his classic defence of the independence of the Church in the pluralist State in *Churches in the Modern State*:

> From the Christian standpoint the great advantage of toleration is that it elevates automatically the life of the church. At this moment for every person we lose, who has dropped a merely conventional religion owing to the greater liberty, we gain in the intensity of the religious life of those we keep. And we gain too by this very hostility. The advantage of toleration is that it acts automatically on the purity of religious bodies and the reality of their faith; and, where complete, it produces a temper which, annealed in the fires of constant criticism, is analogous to that produced in persecution in the earlier days of the church (Figgis (1914), 119).

Persecution could lead to religious renewal and the preparedness for sacrifice: there may have been no lions in 1833 but there was undoubtedly a sense of danger (see Keble (1869), 46).

By focusing on the internal purity of the Church, Keble, who was one of the more anti-democratic thinkers of the nineteenth century,[4] paved the way for the future recognition of a plurality of different groups within the State, all of which were to be protected, but none of which was to be officially sponsored. Tractarianism thus marked a response to what might be called the legitimating of 'sectarianism' within the English Constitution: the removal of religious penalties forced pluralism on the State and a tendency towards disestablishment on the Church. Given the nature of the reformed Parliament, and however much one might clamour for something else, the truth was that the Church of England would be better off not as a national church, but as what Keble himself termed a 'sect'. Hence in the 'Advertisement' to the first published version of the Assize Sermon Keble could write:

> The Legislature of England and Ireland (*the members of which are not even bound to profess belief in the Atonement*), this body has virtually usurped the commission of those whom our Saviour entrusted with *at least one voice* in making ecclesiastical laws, on matters wholly or partially spiritual. The same Legislature has also ratified, to its full extent, this principle; – that the Apostolic Church is only to stand, in the eye of the State, *as one sect among many*, depending, for any pre-eminence she may still appear to retain, merely upon the accident of her having a strong party in the country. (Keble (1983), 11 (italics in original))

On such a sectarian model, because there was no longer any all-embracing unified vision of a society where Church and State could be regarded as two aspects of the one divinely constituted whole, it proved inevitable that there would be a diffusion and disintegration both in society and Church. As J. N. Figgis put it: 'It was the competing claims of religious bodies, and the inability of any single one to destroy the others, which finally secured liberty.' (Figgis (1914), 101). Thus all the Church could hope for in the modern world was that it should become one group among many, since it was no longer either possible or desirable to impose the will of one particular corporation on the whole. That was 'tenable in theory only on the puritan or medieval notion of a State, and in practice as absurd as the proposal of John Knox to punish adultery with death' (Figgis (1914), 123–4). As soon as there was liberty of conscience there could only ever be sects: although 'people dislike calling [the contemporary church] a sect or a denomination, it can be nothing else, so long as there are large numbers who repudiate all part or lot in it and in many cases detest its ideals' (Figgis (1912), 32). Figgis here enunciates the logic of Keble's position: in a situation where pluralism was practised, the authority claimed by the Church had to be redefined. Although there was inevitably a proclamation of an exclusive truth by any Church or sect, there was always the further presupposition of the possibility of other competing claims. This implied in turn a recognition of the limitations of the possibilities of the power of the Church:

> We cannot claim liberty for ourselves, while at the same time proposing to deny it to others. If we are to cry 'hands off' to the civil power in regard to such matters as marriage, doctrine, ritual, or the conditions of communion inside the church – and it is the necessary condition of

a free religious society that it should regulate these matters – then we must give up attempting to dictate the policy of the State in regard to the whole mass of its citizens (Figgis (1914), 112–13).

On this basis, in the years around 1833 Keble was thus able to contemplate a complete reversal of the Henrician and Elizabethan Settlements of Religion with their manifest Byzantine model of authority (albeit tempered by the notion of the Godly Prince) (see Laski, 22). Keble might have continued to pray for his rulers, but such rulers could no longer have sovereignty over the Church, at least in its spiritual affairs. He wrote to a friend a few days before the Assize Sermon:

> I shall be speaking the thoughts of a very large body of the Clergy of England: who feeling daily that it becomes more and more questionable in point of duty and impossible in point of fact, that we should continue in the same relation we are in at present to the government of the country, are naturally looking round on all fragments of the Church Apostolic…all Church-men, who are not Erastians (I trust a very considerable party) [will separate from the State] the schismatical body, remaining, at such cost, in union with the State (Letter to Mrs Pruen, 10 July 1833, in Griffin (1987), 81).

Thus against the national Church principle, and against the unbridled sovereignty of king-in-parliament, Keble wrote to Newman on 8 August 1833, even contemplating total disendowment:

> I cannot take the *Oath of Supremacy* in the sense that the legislature clearly now puts upon it. I cannot *accept* any curacy or office in the Church of England but I have not made up my mind that I am bound to resign what I have…If there is any chance of such a reaction as shall lead the state to mend what she has done, re-establish the ten bishops in Ireland, and make the nation pay the church rates, by all means let us wait for it…but if the *reaction* does not amount to a retraction of the Anti-Church *principles*, I think we ought to be prepared to sacrifice any or all of our endowments sooner than sanction it. 'Take every pound, shilling, and penny, and the curse of Sacrilege along with it – only let us make our own bishops, and be governed by our own laws'. This is the length I am prepared to go: but of course if we could get our liberty at an easier price, so much the better. (Ker and Gornall, 23)

Never prone to understatement, Harold Laski spoke of such an approach as the 'Guelfic attitude' to the State of the early Tractarians:

Marsilio of Padua's claim that the Church is no more than an institution within the State, was exactly the expression of the Whig Government's attitude. With him it would have said that the ecclesiastical sovereign was to be the body of the faithful, just as he would, with their approval, identify the faithful with the nation as a whole. (Laski, 114–15)

The Marsilian theory, which had been so important in the formation of the English Settlement from the 1530s, had been defeated by the fact of religious pluralism: 'The whole foundation of Tractarianism lies in the fact that [the identity of the faithful with the nation] had ceased to be the case' (Laski, 115).[5] Thus, as Nockles similarly suggests, the Oxford Movement was a 'response to the collapse of the *ancien régime* and heralded a new beginning' (Nockles (1996), 100).

\*\*\*

While it is important not to overstate the case and to stress the durability of the old model of Church and society, as well as the inconsistency in many of the Tractarians in the approach to political authority (and here I am in agreement with Peter Nockles), it is also crucial not to underestimate the importance of Keble and the early period of Tractarianism for the development of pluralist political theory. Keble's single-minded devotion to the independence of the Church pointed towards a model of Church and State which saw separation as both inevitable and desirable. Self-regulation was to be the way forward, which has important political repercussions even to the present day. It must be said, however, that both Church and State have yet to accept the Tractarian logic in its entirety. 'The tribunals of the State,' wrote Laski, will leave the Church, 'free to work out, as best she may, the grave and complex problems that confront her. ... And the state will understand that the degree of her freedom will be the measure of her progress. In the event the tragedies of Oxford will not have been in vain' (Laski, 119). Indeed, it might be suggested that both Church and State still have something to learn from the element of trust that this theory of independent authority implies.

## Notes

[1] See also Rowlands 27–77 and Gloyn 45–84. Simon Skinner in the present volume emphasises Keble's ideal of establishment and his 'quasi-theocracy'. The point of this chapter is to show how the Tractarian logic of apostolicity leads, however accidentally, towards pluralism, despite the ideals of the Tractarians themselves.

[2] See, for instance, the sermon on Church and State in Keble (1848), 149–72. On this see Rowlands 46–62.

[3] 'For a period of about six years Keble was a political Radical, as he understood

that term. That is, he looked forward to the separation of the Church of England from the State and every other lay controlling force, a gesture that he believed was the first object of the Radical party' (Griffin (1971), 169).

[4] For a fascinating linking of the principle of reserve in religion and the dislike of democracy see Keble (1912), I, 257.

[5] Keble himself noted this in 1834. See Keble (1869), 61.

## Works Cited

Avis, Paul, *Anglicanism and the Christian Church*, Edinburgh: T & T Clark, 1989.

Chapman, Mark D., 'The Politics of Episcopacy', *Anglican and Episcopal History*, 69 (2000): 474–503.

Church, R. W., *The Oxford Movement, Twelve Years 1833–1845*, London: Macmillan, 1891.

Coleridge, J. T., *A Memoir of the Rev. John Keble*, 2 vols, Oxford: Parker, 1970.

Cross, Frank, *John Henry Newman*, London: Philip Alan, 1933.

Dawson, Christopher, *The Spirit of the Oxford Movement*, London: Sheed and Ward, 1933.

Figgis, J. N., *Civilisation at the Cross Roads*, London: Longmans, 1912.

— *Churches in the Modern State*, London: Longmans, 1912.

Gloyn, Cyril K., *The Church in the Social Order: A Study of Anglican Social Theory from Coleridge to Maurice*, Forest Grove, Oregon: Pacific University, 1942.

Griffin, John R., 'John Keble, Radical', *Anglican Theological Review*, 53, (1971): 167–173.

— 'The Radical Phase of the Oxford Movement', *Journal of Ecclesiastical History*, 27, (1976): 47–56.

— *John Keble: Saint of Anglicanism*, Macon: Mercer University Press, 1977.

Hobsbawm, Eric, *The Age of Revolution*, London: Abacus, 1977.

Keble, John, *Sermons, Academical and Occasional*, Oxford: J. H. Parker, 1848.

— *The State in its Relations with the Church*, ed. Henry Liddon, Oxford: J. H. Parker, 1869.

— *Occasional Papers and Reviews*, Oxford: J. H. Parker, 1877.

— *Lectures on Poetry*, 2 vols, trans. Edward Kershaw Francis, Oxford: Oxford University Press, 1912.

— 'National Apostasy', Steventon: Rocket Press, 1983.

Ker, Ian and Thomas S. J. Gornall, eds, *The Letters and Diaries of John Henry Newman*, Vol. IV, Oxford: Clarendon Press, 1980.

Laski, H. J., *Authority in the Modern State*, New Haven: Yale University Press, 1919.

Liddon, H. P., *Life of Edward Bouverie Pusey*, 4 vols, London: Longmans, 1893.

Martin, Brian W., *John Keble: Priest, Professor and Poet*, London: Croom Helm, 1976.

Mozley, Anne, *Letters and Correspondence of Newman during his Life in the English Church, with a Brief Autobiography*, 2 vols, London: Longmans, 1890.

Newman, John Henry, *Thoughts on the Ministerial Commission, Respectfully Addressed to the Clergy*, London: Rivington, 1833.

— *Apologia pro Vita Sua*, London: Everyman, 1912.

Nockles, Peter, *The Oxford Movement in Context*, Cambridge: Cambridge University Press, 1994.
— 'Newman and Early Tractarian Politics' in V. Alan McClelland, ed., *By Whose Authority? Newman, Manning and the Magisterium*, Bath: Downside Abbey, 1996, 79–111.
'"Lost causes…and impossible loyalties": the Oxford Movement and the University', in M. G. Brock and M. C. Curthoys, eds, *The History of the University of Oxford*, vol. VI, Nineteenth Century, Part 1, Oxford: Oxford University Press, 1997, 195–267.
Palmer, W. P., *A Narrative of Events Connected with the Publication of the Tracts for the Times*, Oxford: J. H. Parker, 1989.
Rowlands, J. H. L., *Church, State and Society: The Attitudes of John Keble, Richard Hurrell Froude and John Henry Newman 1827–1845*, Worthing: Churchman, 1989.

# 4

# JOHN KEBLE AND THE ETHOS OF THE OXFORD MOVEMENT

## James Pereiro

The student of the Oxford Movement soon becomes familiar with the word *ethos*: it keeps appearing in the writings and correspondence of the Oxford Tractarians – particularly those of Keble, Froude and Newman – and it seems never to have been far from their lips. The well-known and often-quoted remarks of Isaac Williams and Thomas Mozley reinforce the impression that it encapsulated a concept of vital importance for Tractarianism. Keble, in Isaac Williams's words, 'in opposition to the Oriel or Whatelian [school], set *ethos* above intellect' (Williams (1892), 46); and Mozley, on his part, would affirm in his *Reminiscences*, that what 'Froude and others discovered continually was *ethos*, the dominant moral habit or proclivity' (Mozley, I, 211–12).[1] Being so present in their thoughts, and given the amount of scholarly attention focused on the Oxford Movement, it comes as a surprise that there should be such a dearth of studies on the subject.[2] Most scholars pass over the concept in the study and the interpretation of the Oxford Movement, as if the Tractarian idea of *ethos* had little or nothing to contribute to its understanding. If one were to seek reasons for this neglect, there can be but little doubt that, among them, John Taylor Coleridge's explanation of the idea of *ethos* in his *Memoir* of Keble made a considerable contribution to its trivialization. He considered that with Keble it 'imported certainly no intellectual quality, scarcely even any distinct moral one, but an habitual toning, or general colouring diffused over all man's moral qualities, giving the exercise of them a peculiar gentleness and grace' (Coleridge, 398).[3] These were deceptive words, and have in fact deceived many a scholar. It is the contention of this paper that, in the language of the Tractarians, *ethos* is a concept rich in consequences, involving a complex theory of knowledge – and of religious knowledge in particular – which deeply influenced the genesis and development of Tractarianism.

The concept of *ethos*, in its modern and Tractarian sense, was coined by Keble. However, as often happened with Oxford Movement ideas, the concept underwent considerable development in pre-Tractarian and Tractarian times. Froude and Newman – starting from Keble's original idea – contributed significantly to the development of the notion and the unfolding of its corollaries. Keble had forged the concept in Oxford, and two books included among those studied at Oxford – Aristotle's *Nicomachean Ethics* and Bishop Butler's *Analogy* – provided the materials he used to fashion it.[4] And Keble would always maintain that his concept of right ethos reflected the spirit of the University.

Butler, writing in the eighteenth century, had been primarily concerned with the defence of revelation from objections levelled at it by the deists. These, among other things, argued that if God had intended a revelation for the good of all men, it was unimaginable that he would have allowed most of humanity to remain in ignorance of it. Again, the argument went on, given the vital nature of that knowledge for man's salvation, it did stand to reason that God would not have left his revelation to rest upon doubtful evidence. Butler, in his response to these objections, delineated the general lines of a philosophy of religious knowledge which was to have great influence among the Tractarians. He relied on the argument from analogy to respond to the critics of revelation, and started by defining the concept of the analogy of nature in words borrowed from Origen: he who believes Scripture to proceed from him who is also the author of nature, might well expect to find the same sort of difficulties in his knowledge of revelation as he encounters when approaching nature (Butler, 9). Along those lines, Butler argued that the seeming lack of universality of revelation should not be an argument for incredulity: natural gifts are diversely distributed not only among different natures but even among individuals who share the same nature; therefore, there is no reason for wonder at the fact that revelation may have reached men in different degrees.

Butler probably felt that the second argument of the deists had greater force, and he dealt with it at length. They had argued that God could not have left his revelation to rest on doubtful evidence. Butler countered that the order of nature vastly exceeds in its complexity our powers of intellectual perception. As a result, we are unable to see the multiple connections which would explain realities and events which, although *a priori* seeming unreasonable to us, we are bound to accept as incontrovertible facts. The

> appearance of deficiencies and irregularities in nature is owing to its being a scheme but in part made known.... Now we see no more reason why the frame and course of nature should be such a scheme, than why Christianity should. And that the former is such a scheme, renders it credible, that the latter, upon supposition of its truth, may be so too (Butler, 248–9).

Butler considered it unreasonable to demand higher standards of proof and evidence in matters of religion than in matters of science or in the practical ordering of human life. The imperfection of the human intellect forces man to admit that, in most cases, he will have to be satisfied – both in his knowledge of nature and in that of revelation – with only probable knowledge, rather than certainty: 'probability is the very guide of life' (Butler, 5). Only the divine intellect, comprehending the whole of the natural and revealed dispensations, is able to have certain knowledge in every respect.

The vital question then was: how can man find his way to truth – particularly in respect of religious truth – in a maze of probable arguments? In his answer to this objection Butler took as his starting point the Aristotelian concept of *phronesis* or practical wisdom, as described in the *Nicomachean Ethics*. There Aristotle had affirmed that it is impossible to be practically wise – i.e., to discern the good to aim at and the means to achieve it – without being good: moral excellence confers a sort of instinct for goodness. Butler considered, with all Christian tradition, that God has granted man a perfectible nature, and that its potential for perfection is not confined to man's present earthly life: there is a future life which is to this one as manhood to youth. And man qualifies for that other life by developing his moral character in the practice of virtue: the improvement of one's human nature is achieved by the acquisition of sound habits resulting from the repetition of good actions. This is not a foregone conclusion. The present life is a state of discipline and probation, and man's resolve is tested by the disordered inclinations he experiences, calling on him to deviate from right. Besides, part of that probation consists in the very fact that the distinction between good and evil is not always perceived with absolute clarity. Man, however, is not left unprovided. Butler affirmed with Aristotle that virtue already achieved is – in its own measure – also a 'security against the danger which finite creatures are in, from the very nature or propension, or particular affections' (Butler, 122). Virtue strengthens the will in its search for good, and facilitates the perception of the path that leads to it.

Having followed Aristotle so far, Butler moved a step forward, taking the concept of practical wisdom or *phronesis* well beyond the confines Aristotle had set for it. In Butler's hands, without losing its ethical character, moral goodness acquired a more intellectual dimension. Doubtfulness in respect of the evidence of Christian revelation is, according to Butler, an element in man's probation. And he regarded probable knowledge as being perfectly adapted to the state of probation in which man has been established on this earth. In that respect, he even admitted the possibility that God, with that aim of probation in mind, might have withheld some truths which, had they been laid before us, might have facilitated our apprehension of revelation. This, however, by the very nature of the case, would be unknown to man. In man's present circumstances, different moral tempers would behave differently in respect to the evidences of revelation. Neglect in examining them generally implies one form or another of depravity: lack of interest, a desire that those things may be proved not true, passion, prejudice, and so on. On the other hand, a virtuous moral temper would pay active and careful consideration to the evidences of revelation. It would be more inclined to give religion its assent, and follow conviction by obedience to revealed precepts. For Butler, speculative difficulties play a role similar to moral temptations. Virtue, once more, is the reliable guide in doubt, helping the individual this time to weigh rightly the probability of divine revelation. A higher degree of virtue would be accompanied by a clearer perception of truth. Butler felt that it 'is a real imperfection in the moral character, not to be influenced in practice by a lower degree of evidence when discerned, as it is in the understanding, not to discern it' (Butler, 290).

Butler had used the argument from analogy to defend Christianity against unbelief. Keble, for his part, would develop it further, applying the same argument to the maintenance of orthodoxy against heresy, to the practical guidance of individual consciences among the contrasting claims of the different denominations within Christianity or among parties and schools within a particular Church. He was conscious of marching into territory uncharted by Butler but he thought that Butler's doctrine had not closed the door to this particular use of the analogy (Keble (1847), vi–viii).[5] And Keble considered his ideas a useful and timely development of the theory in the *Analogy*, given that in their days intellectual temptation and doubt were more common than previously.[6]

Already in 1814, Keble had suggested the importance of criticism for discovering the laws of the human mind, and, in particular, the connections between the intellectual and moral faculties (Keble (1814), 588). But it is in his sermons of the early 1820s that we find the clearest and best-developed study of his new application of the analogy of nature, supported by a different set of arguments from those used by Butler. The latter had argued with the deist who rejected revelation, and therefore used arguments drawn from human reason; Keble spoke or wrote for those who accepted revelation, and, consequently, made use of the witness of Holy Scripture. And Scripture, to his mind, confirmed Butler's theory and his own. Among the scriptural texts he quoted, two were particularly useful in support of his theory. One was taken from the Psalms: 'I have more understanding than all my teachers; for Thy testimonies are my meditation. I understand more than the ancients; because I kept Thy precepts' (Psalm 119. 99–100). The other quoted words of Christ: 'a good will to do His Will shall know of the doctrine if it is from God' (John 7. 17).[7] From these, and similar scriptural texts, he concluded that moral rectitude, honest attention and thoughtfulness, with the assistance of the Holy Spirit, are not only necessary, but sufficient...to guide us into all truths really important to our final welfare; not only to make us virtuous rather than vicious, but also to make us Christians rather than Infidels, orthodox Christians rather than Heretics, and conforming Christians rather than Schismatics (Keble (1847a), 4).

The inspired writers considered orthodox faith associated with sound morality; truth and duty were unfailing tests of each other (Keble (1847c), 44–5).

As far as Keble was concerned, moral qualities were of greater importance than intellectual ones when analysing the truth of religious propositions. The reason was his conviction that, in matters of revealed truth, the moral sense is empowered to correct the errors of the intellect, and to supply its imperfections. A person experienced in the life of virtue, and desirous to do good, would have a sort of instinct for truth, making him or her more able to detect the bent of a particular doctrine (Keble (1847), xvii; (1847c), 64). This not only corresponded to the nature of things but also played a particular role within the plan of God's providence: 'it has been God's will to constitute uprightness, rather than ability, judge of the truth on the highest of all subjects, as a means to put down spiritual pride' (Keble (1847b), 42).[8] On the other hand, as St Paul had written to Timothy, 'evil men and seducers shall wax worse and worse, deceiving and being deceived' (II Timothy 3. 13). Keble thought that there is a sort of blinding power in moral disease, leading man along an inexorable descent from error into further error; a sliding into heterodoxy which could only be arrested by spiritual conversion (Keble (1847d), 102).

Keble went on to establish

as a kind of canon of sacred criticism, that, in disputed cases, that interpretation of God's works and ways which approves itself most entirely to the sober and devout spirit, stands in general a fairer chance of being the true interpretation, than what has the suffrage of minds ingenious and original but deficient in those moral requisites' (Keble (1847a), 14).

If that offered a guarantee on the part of the interpreter, Keble also provided a criterion – based on his concept of *ethos* – for judging the interpretations in themselves: the doctrinal view or interpretation of Scripture tending to deepen faith, and promote holiness, humility, etc., is safer than that which lowers the standard of morality, engenders spiritual pride and the like; this latter one cannot be of God (Keble, (1847c), 62–3). He supplied further scriptural texts in support of these general criteria, which, he felt, were much the same thing as the Aristotelian concept of practical wisdom (*phronesis*), although, with

Butler, he had transferred Aristotle's *phronesis* to the realm of intellectual knowledge. Keble used the term *ethos* to refer to this moral disposition or character and, in his early *Lectures on Poetry* (started in 1832), described it as a stable disposition, not just a passing impulse but the result of a lifetime searching after virtue (Keble (1912), I, 75).[9]

Following Butler, Keble considered that man's knowledge is, for the most part, based on probable arguments. Within that scheme of human knowledge, he conceived moral rectitude as a light guiding man to find his way to truth, through the maze of possible answers offered to him; the right moral temper would provide sure guidance to identify truth among sometimes conflicting probabilities (Keble (1847), xvi). This principle, already suggested by Butler, was not only suited to, but almost demanded by the general theory, in order to give firmness and certitude to human knowledge of revealed truth. In this way, Keble's theory, according to Newman, conferred on knowledge based on probability a degree of certainty that it does not have of itself: the firmness of assent to religious doctrines is not derived from mere probability but, fundamentally, from the power of faith and love which serve as sure guides in determining where truth lies (Newman (1913), 19).[10] Keble saw the search for truth as a spiralling ascending movement: moral rectitude influences discovery of truth; truth discovered should commit the person vitally; this commitment, in turn, would bring with it a clearer perception of revealed truth, and so on. As a result, Keble – as Isaac Williams had said – set *ethos* above intellect, but he did so, among other things, for intellect's sake.[11]

Keble considered that God, the author of both reason and revelation, had conformed the latter to the permanent laws of human knowledge. The many-layered richness of Holy Scripture was well adapted to the ethical process of discovering truth. Christ's divinity implies that the least of his words and actions is charged with heavenly and mysterious meaning, has eternal and infinite associations and consequences. The deepest meaning of the Gospel can only be understood by those who are in close communion with Christ. On this count, Keble defended a mystical interpretation of Holy Scripture against those who only admitted a literal approach. A mystical interpretation, as its critics had remarked, might not be free from dangers, but Keble thought that this was so with all ways of communicating divine truth. The remedy is to strengthen the eyes of the intellect by means of repentance, devotion and self-denial, so as to make them able to stand the light of divine truth. Then, the assiduous study of Holy Scripture, together with the devout observances of the Fathers, will make man gain by degrees their perceptive eye and enable him to discern their first principles. Intellectual acuteness and industry, on the other hand, if not accompanied by that moral training, would be equivalent to the blind leading the blind. And experience showed that pouring scorn on the Fathers' mystical interpretation of Scripture, and reducing it to the merely critical and historical, had been in some well-known cases a step towards Arianism and other doctrinal errors. The poor and unlearned, who feared God and led pure lives, were for the most part better prepared to receive those divine lights than men of great learning and cultivation (Keble (1841), 134–6; (1847a), 17).

It followed that when it came to determine the primary aim of education, in its broader and truest sense, Keble saw it as the formation of a right *ethos*. Within this process, he thought that poetry played a central role. Indeed, writing in 1814, he described as poetry's mission 'the awakening of some moral or religious feeling, not by direct instruction (that is the office of morality or theology)' but by a process of imaginative associations (Keble (1814), 579). He considered religion and poetry closely related. God has used poetical language to communicate himself to man, employing symbolical associations – whether poetical, moral or mystical – to reveal a world beyond sense perception. Besides, in Keble's mind, poetry has a power of healing and restoring overburdened and passionate minds, and therefore, the more deeply a feeling penetrates human affections, the more permanently it influences them, the closer its relation with poetry. As it happens, man finds in divine revelation the deepest and most transforming feeling, and it naturally follows that poetry and religion are meant to advance each other. Poetry offers religion a means to express high realities, otherwise inexpressible, while religion offers poetry a lofty field of sentiment to work upon (Keble (1912), II, 478–84). The true poet is the one who uses ideas and language calculated to raise religious and moral associations: presenting something absent, awakening longings, making man feel his own dignity and a desire to better something still imperfect, detaching him from earthly affections and lifting him nearer to what he once was (Keble (1814), 581, 585).[12] Even the great pagan poets could not but be interpreters of the mysteries of nature, helping to restore a unified vision and experience of life. In so doing, they had prepared men to welcome the revealed doctrines of Christianity, and Keble highly recommended their study (Keble (1912), II, 470, 475, 477).

Keble went even further in claiming that history showed how religious revivals tended to be preceded by a change of tone in the immediately preceding poets. They had led the way, and had prepared men to accept a more serious and holier creed (Keble (1912), II, 473). By way of example, he mentioned the poetical revival of the late Elizabethan period. It produced poets like Spenser and Shakespeare, whose tone and temper had unconsciously prepared the religious revival in the reign of Charles I (Keble (1912), II, 479). And Keble, with Newman and Froude, thought that something similar had happened in Great Britain with the appearance of poets like Scott, Coleridge, Wordsworth and others. Their poetry, their personal shortcomings notwithstanding, had heralded, and prepared, the arrival of a new religious revival. They had reflected in their poetry the glory of God in his creation. Wordsworth, Keble said in his 1838 Creweian Oration, had exhibited 'the manner, the pursuits, and the feeling, religious and traditional, of the poor, – I will not say in favourable light merely, but in a light which glows with the rays of heaven' (Coleridge, 261). His poetry had infused in his readers those emotions which were most conducive to a religious revival. Scott's feeling for the chivalry and feudal life of past ages, imbued with a deep sense of honour and fidelity, as well as the strong bond of blood and of the clan, had a similar effect, and exerted a great influence on his age. It had prejudiced people in favour of ancient institutions, and the chivalrous tone of his writings had shaped the feelings of many who had reacted against the utilitarian temper of the times (Keble (1838), 438).

Keble could, however, criticise them both at the same time as he recognized their contribution as true poets to this revival. He tried to distance himself publicly from Wordsworth in 1815 when reviewing two books by the poet. Keble admired Wordsworth's talents but he did not subscribe all the tenets of his poetical system. He criticised Wordsworth's 'theories and eccentricities', his vision of poetic sensibility giving access to a higher realm inaccessible to mere humans, or his use of poetry to convey metaphysical ideas (Keble (1815), 225).[13] Many years after, he was even doubtful about whether he should dedicate to Wordsworth his lectures on poetry, given the unorthodoxy of some of the poet's tenets. As in the case of Sir Walter Scott, the *ethos* was right (the Catholic one), but both of them laboured under the disadvantages of the system in which they had been raised, and the prevailing tone of their time and place. They had both, however, risen above it by means of good sense and right instinct. And Keble could only wonder what their reaction would have been if the complete Catholic system had been fully and fairly presented to their minds. He thought that they would have welcomed it (Keble (1815), 474).

Froude absorbed the concept of *ethos* from Keble and made it central to his vision of the intellectual and religious life, developing at length the relationship between character and opinions, both in general and in the religious sphere In 1827 he jotted down some of his thoughts about the connexion between right faith and right practice, and *vice versa*, claiming that opinions are essentially consistent with particular characters, and that in a double sense: a temper of mind or character would tend to generate a certain set of opinions, and, conversely, a given set of opinions would tend to shape mind and character in a particular way. Froude, however, avoided all thought of psychological determinism: men were not born either Platonists or Aristotelians, heretical or orthodox believers. Character for Froude is defined morally, being as such in a constant state of formation and flux, and the alternative moral phases of the individual would have their corresponding effects on his opinions. Froude saw the development of character as controlled by a very sensitive tiller, holding or altering the course of moral progress at the touch of every moral decision. An almost imperceptible departure from the previously plotted course, if not corrected, could show itself later as having had momentous consequences. He concluded by repeating that opinions are essentially homogeneous with particular characters: a man who is morally good will have a right faith, while heresy would be the intellectual fruit of a vicious *ethos*. Froude did not, however, apply the principle too strictly, and partly exonerated those in error, particularly those whose opinions – while they were engaged in the search for truth – were still in process of formation (Froude, 'Connexion', 114–17).

This theory helped Froude answer a question pressing upon him. He had at first been puzzled by the damnatory clauses of the Athanasian Creed: he could not understand how opinions, of themselves, could be the object of God's wrath. Froude had also to contend with St Paul, who had clearly affirmed that errors of opinion, as well as of practice, made men unfit for the kingdom of Heaven. The new ideas about the influence of a particular *ethos* on the intellectual life offered Froude the elements for reaching a solution. He rehearsed the argument *ab initio*. Men deserved reward or punishment on the basis of the choices made in the exercise of their free will: they cannot be responsible for events or opinions over which they have no control. Therefore, if liberty of choice is implied in the idea of punishment or reward, the condemned opinion must involve something moral, either in its cause or in its effect. Froude concluded that, if men are to be punished or rewarded also for their beliefs (as the Athanasian Creed professes), this can only be in so far as these are accepted and held under the influence of man's will, and consequently the will's character cannot but play a decisive rôle in this process. Man is, therefore, responsible for his faith to the degree that he is responsible for his character. This line of argument, however, was not without its difficulties: it is a fact that man originally tends to accept religious truth – and also natural truths – on the authority of those who instruct him, and it is not easy in some cases (in others, perhaps, impossible) to rise above the errors or prejudices inculcated in early life. Froude, however, thought that the time arrives for all when one becomes responsible for adhering to error, and this implies that there must be some means by which truth is gradually open to man. When confronted by it, he is called to make his decision: either to become responsible for the errors transmitted by his instructors, or to accept the new truth now presented to him (Froude (1838b), 114–17).[14] Newman, along the same lines, would link these ideas with another element of Butler's general theory. Divine truth is revealed for our probation. Were man to enjoy absolute proof and certainty of the revealed truth presented to him, he would not be left any room for choice: the truth in question would impose itself on the mind, and there would be no merit in believing, no room for praise or blame. As it is, given that 'probabilities have no definite ascertained value, and are reducible to no scientific standard, what are such to the individual, depends on his moral temper' (Newman (1872), 200). Froude, commenting on Pascal's famous 'wager', had suggested in 1835 an interesting corollary to the general theory. The safest course, in truth or practice, is not always to be found in what is most probable: it may be safe to risk little if there is a small probability of a great gain; it may not be safe to risk much – i.e. eternal life – even when the probability of that happening is small (Froude (1839c), 379–80).

Man, unfortunately, does not start as a *tabula rasa*. As result of his sinfulness – beginning with original sin – man grows blind to God's revelations, and it is man's work to remove that blindness by persevering in good habits (Froude (1838e), 86). Froude would claim in one of his sermons that, without the discipline of loving and fearing God, man cannot even know him: it is by doing God's will that man shall gradually understand the doctrine God taught us about himself (Froude (1838c), 83, 93). People assume that familiarity with the words necessarily implies familiarity with the ideas they contain. This is not always the case. Froude distinguished between the knowledge of the fact, and the knowledge that truly affects the life of the person to his or her advantage: the latter depends on the habitual religious convictions of the individual in question (Froude (1838d), 49). A disposition to a life of ease and pleasure will indispose the person to understand and welcome God's word, and he or she must remain in ignorance, although familiar with the words of revelation.

Froude stressed the powerful 'influence of habit in moulding our opinions, and the consequent probability that every evil habit we may have contracted, consciously or unconsciously, from the day of our birth till the present hour, has in its degree perverted our judgement '(Froude (1839c), 359). It could be said, therefore, that there are as many different prejudices and opinions as there are different turns of mind, resulting from different moral histories. People, whether they are conscious of it or not, are likely to be prejudiced in some degree in the examination of evidences, inclined to underrate and neglect some while overrating and emphasizing others. The fact that they may not be conscious of those prejudices only makes the influence more pervasive and determining (Froude (1839a), 34–5). On the basis of this theory, Froude criticized the Protestant principle of private judgement. He ridiculed those who thought that they would not be prejudiced in their interpretation of Scripture:

> Such people are under a great delusion, let them try ever so much, they neither think for themselves nor interpret for themselves. ... Their notions, their feelings, their associations, are not their own. They have picked them up from others, or from opposing others. ... The views of their times are most dogmatic commentators, and will intrude at every instant or

unprejudiced thought, unperceived and unsuspected. (Froude (1839a), 88).

Keble's 1833 sermon on 'National Apostasy', later considered the first shot in the campaign of the Oxford Movement, did not merely denounce a particular measure being contemplated by Parliament (the suppression of some Irish bishoprics); his main criticism was aimed at the dominant national *ethos*. Its symptoms or characteristics, as Keble described them, were: growing indifference, following the rule of public opinion rather than the rule of truth, impatience under pastoral authority, etc. A nation led by this prevailing temper would go from bad to worse, abandoning the law of the Gospel through accommodations with evil, sometimes on the plea of toleration, at other times on that of State security or of sympathy with popular feeling, and similar others (Keble, 1833). A few years later, when comparing the liberal, indulgent and utilitarian ethics of the times with what was to be found in the Primitive Church, he remarked that the discrepancies between the two ages were the result of a difference as to first principles (moral temper or *ethos*) rather than being attributable to accidental or temporary circumstances (Keble (1841), 10).

Froude echoed Keble's words, and denounced the religious condition of the country: indifference to sacred things – amounting sometimes to contempt – accompanied by a veneer of empty artificial respect; and a clergy anxious to make the country appear Christian after it had ceased to be so (Froude (1839b), 273–4; (1838f), 186–7). The danger the Tractarians foresaw and dreaded was that the day might come when the State, without destroying the establishment, would corrupt it, constructing, 'under the pretence of the convenience of a profession of religion', a national religion, which the State would then proceed to use for its own purposes (Copeland, II, 18).

Keble's 'National Apostasy' was the first public stir of Tractarian religious and political agitation, and it set in motion, or rather accelerated, a chain of intellectual and doctrinal developments. The Tractarians wanted to restore the Church to its proper place in the life of the country, renewing its spiritual influence by restoring Catholic doctrine and practice. They intended at first only to reinstate and present afresh the old neglected truths of the Church of England; but their intellectual momentum impelled them to throw out new conclusions and advance novel theories. The concept of *ethos* was among those to develop further as years went by. Keble had taken Butler's ideas a step further, and conceived *ethos* as a light helping man to find religious truth among a variety of possible answers, and to discern it from error. Froude was to further refine Keble's concept, and Newman would add new dimensions to it. It is to the latter's writings that one must turn for a fuller perception of what the Tractarians came to understand by *ethos* and its dynamism, but this is beyond the purpose and the scope of the present study. Keble had opened up a rich seam of thought. Those who had discovered it under his influence will continue working it.

## Notes

1. Mozley himself, on occasion of his election as a Fellow of Oriel, was described by Newman as possessed of an admirable *ethos* (Newman to S. Rickards, 28 Apr. 1829, *LD*, II, 139).
2. The concept does not even appear as a separate entry in L. N. Crumb (1988 and 1993).
3. Later biographies of Keble have tended to ignore or gloss over the subject; see for example W. Lock (1893), G. Battiscombe (1963) and J. R. Griffin (1987). The only scholar who has made a cursory and rather unsatisfactory incursion into the subject seems to have been W. A. Beek (1959).
4. Keble seems to have become familiar with the ideas of the *Analogy* during his earlier education at Fairford, well before his Oxford studies.
5. Although the sermons were published more than twenty years after their delivery, and may have been revised for publication, there is no real reason to doubt their substantial identity with the original text.
6. Froude may have been the first among the Tractarians to express this idea in writing, even though he owed it to Keble: 'These thoughts are indeed cast by Bishop Butler in a mould more immediately suited to the doubts of the Deist than a Christian: but by very slight alterations here and there of words obviously immaterial to the argument, it will be found that they apply with equal force, and carry equal satisfaction, to those who doubt how much they shall accept for revelation, as to those who doubt about accepting any at all' ('Essay' 83).
7. These words of Scripture were a banner for the Tractarians. Frederick Oakeley used the same text of St John, and gave it a similar interpretation (Oakeley, *viii*). Isaac Williams also quoted those words in his tracts on reserve, writing in *Tract 87*: 'the senses of Scripture are revealed only to good men' ((1840), 37; see also (1838), 36).
8. His ideas were in dramatic contrast with the atmosphere at the time in the Oriel common room, which, it was said, stank of logic.
9. He considered that right *ethos* was a fundamental characteristic of true poetry. Froude had mentioned to Newman Keble's intention of connecting in his lectures high *ethos* with poetical feeling (Froude to Newman, 11 August 1830, *LD*, II, 260).
10. Newman would, however, consider Keble's concept deficient as a general theory of knowledge: Keble achieved no more than a 'loving guess', no more than a '*practical* certainty.'
11. Stephen Prickett considers that Butler reinforced in Keble ideas which he had received first from Wordsworth (108). The results of the present study suggest, on the contrary, that Wordsworth and Coleridge only reinforced ideas which Keble had already elaborated from his reading of Butler. Keble said as much, and it is interesting to note how his concept of the role of imagination was already well developed in his review of Copleston's lectures on poetry. This appeared in the *British Critic* in 1814, three years before the publication of Coleridge's *Biographia Literaria* (Keble, 'Praelectiones', 577–88). Keble's insistence on the

associational character of poetry seems to owe much to David Hartley, through the medium of Butler.

12   Poetry in general, and sacred poetry in particular, to be successful in this respect should be the expression of the general tone and feeling of the poet (Keble, 'Sacred Poetry' 217, 219, 220).

13   He thought that the true merit of a poet does not consist in possessing sensibilities 'different or more intense than those of other people, but in the talent of awakening in their minds the particular feelings and emotions with which the various objects of his art are naturally associated' (Keble (1815), 225). Again, in Keble's view, poetry is not an adequate vehicle for instruction: the poet teaches by association, using sign and gesture not to impart religious doctrine but to describe the effect that those doctrines have upon the human heart and mind ('Praelectiones', 579, 586; 'Sacred Poetry', 221).

14   'Anathemas', 117–18; 'Essay', 107.

## Works Cited

Battiscombe, Georgina *John Keble, A Study in Limitations*, London: Constable, 1963.

Beek, W.A., *John Keble's Literary and Religious Contribution to the Oxford Movement*, Nijmegen: Academic Centrale, 1959.

Butler, Joseph, *The Analogy of Religion Natural and Revealed to the Constitution and Course of Nature*, W.E. Gladstone, ed., Oxford: Clarendon Press, 1896.

Coleridge, J. T., *A Memoir of the Rev. John Keble*, 3rd edn, Oxford and London: Parker, 1870.

Copeland, W. J., *Narrative of the Oxford Movement* (MS), 2 notebooks, Copeland Papers, Pusey House, Oxford.

Crumb, L. N., *The Oxford Movement and its Leaders: A Bibliography of Secondary and lesser Primary Sources*, Metuchen, NJ: Scarecrow Press, 1988.

— *The Oxford Movement and its Leaders: Supplement*, Metuchen, NJ: Scarecrow Press, 1993.

Froude, R. H., *Remains of the late Richard Hurrell Froude*, J.H. Newman and J. Keble, eds, Part 1, 2 vols, London: Rivington, 1838.

— *Remains of the Late Richard Hurrell Froude*, J.H. Newman and J. Keble eds., Part 2, 2 vols, Coventry: H. Mozley, 1839.

— 'On the Anathemas in the Athanasian Creed' (16 July 1827), *Remains*, 1, I, 117–19, 1838a.

— 'On the Connexion between a right Faith and right Practice; on the *ethos* of Heresy' (16 July 1827), *Remains*, 1, I, 114—17, 1838b.

— 'Knowledge of God attainable by first acting on it' (c.1830), *Remains*, 1, II, 82—93, 1838c.

— 'Knowledge useless except for the serious minded' (Easter Monday, 1830), *Remains*, 1, II, 42—57, 1838d.

— 'Occasional Thoughts' (1826), *Remains*, 1, I, 85—6, 1838e.

— 'Religious Indifference', *Remains*, 1, II, 185—98, 1838f.

— 'Essay on Rationalism, as shown in the interpretation of Scripture' (c.1834), *Remains*, 2, I, 1—164, 1839a

— 'Remarks on Church Discipline', *Remains*, 2, I, 270–314, 1839b.

- — 'Remarks upon the Principles to be observed in interpreting Scripture' (1835), *Remains*, 2, I, 357—83, 1839c.

Griffin, J. R., *John Keble: Saint of Anglicanism,* Macon: Mercer University Press, 1987.

Keble, John, 'National Apostasy Considered in a Sermon, Preached in St. Mary's Oxford before Her Majesty's Judges of Assize, on July 14, 1833', Oxford: Parker, 1833.

- — *Lectures on Poetry,* 2$^{nd}$ ed., 2 vols, Oxford: Clarendon Press, 1912. (First edition (Latin) 1844).
- — 'Memoirs of the Life of Sir Walter Scott by J.G. Lockhart', *British Critic* (October 1838), 423—82.
- — 'On the Mysticism attributed to the Early Fathers of the Church', *Tracts for the Times, no. 89,* London: Rivington, 1841.
- — 'Poems by William Wordsworth', *Quarterly Review,* XXVII, (October 1815), 201—25.
- — 'Praelectiones Academicae Oxonii habitae ab Edwardo Copleston', *British Critic* (June 1814), 577–88.
- — 'Sacred Poetry', *Quarterly Review,* 32, 63 (June 1825), 211—32.
- — *Sermons Academical and Occasional,* Oxford & London: Parker and Rivington, 1847.
- — 'Favour shown to Implicit Faith' (1822), *Sermons,* 1—23, 1847a.
- — 'Implicit Faith Recognised by Reason', *Sermons,* 24—42, 1847c.
- — 'Implicit Faith Reconciled with Free Enquiry' (1822 or 1823), *Sermons,* 43—75, 1847b.
- — 'Iniquity abounding', *Sermons,* 76–104, 1847d.

Lock, W., *John Keble. A Biography.* London: Methuen, 1893.

Mozley, Thomas, *Reminiscences, Chiefly of Oriel College and the Oxford Movement,* 4$^{th}$ edn, 2 vols, London: Longmans, Green, 1882.

Newman, J. H., *Apologia pro Vita Sua,* London: Longmans, Green, 1813 (First edn 1864).

- — 'Faith and Reason contrasted as Habits of Mind' (6 January 1839), *Fifteen Sermons preached before the University of Oxford,* 3$^{rd}$ edn, London: Longmans, Green and Co., 1872 (First edn 1843).
- — *Letters and Diaries of John Henry Newman,* ed. I. Ker and T. Gornall, II, Oxford: Clarendon Press, 1979.

Oakeley, Frederick, *Sermons preached Chiefly in the Royal Chapel at Whitehall,* Oxford: Parker, 1839.

Prickett, Stephen, *Romanticism and Religion: The Tradition of Coleridge and Wordsworth in the Victorian Church,* Cambridge: Cambridge University Press, 1976.

Williams, Isaac, *Autobiography of Isaac Williams,* G. Prevost, ed., London: Longmans, Green, 1892.

- — 'On Reserve in communicating Religious Knowledge', *Tracts for the Times, no.80,* London: Rivington, 1838.
- — 'On Reserve in communicating Religious Knowledge' *Tracts for the Times, no.87,* London: Rivington, 1840.

# PART II

# Reading Keble's Writings: The Poet and the Pastor

# 5

# WAYS OF READING 1825: LEISURE, CURIOSITY AND MORBID EAGERNESS

## William McKelvy

One is tempted to collect into a book, rather small, the poetic gems strewn throughout *The Christian Year*. There are unforgettable similes – 'Like sailors shipwreck'd in their dreams' – and grand epiphanies – 'He watch'd till knowledge came / Upon his soul like a flame' – and idyllic retreats where 'The secret lore of rural things' calls to us 'in this crowded loneliness,' 'the ever-moving myriads' swayed 'in this loud stunning tide / Of human care and crime' (Keble (1841), 188, 158, 345–6). And there are excursions to lands of lotos where 'Bright maidens and unfailing vines' tend to desire, as well as moments of recoil from these idle dreams, revealed to be 'Poor fragments all of this low earth' (77). Then there are the fitting memorials to an unrelenting despair: 'We in the midst of ruins live' – 'Such thoughts, the wreck of Paradise' (197, 211).[1]

In order to attract readers in this twenty-first century, what we would want to avoid are the vast stretches of theology in which these relics of the imagination are buried. This book I propose only as a provocative travesty, for as Kirstie Blair has most recently reminded us (2003), Keble's aesthetic and poetic accomplishments are in fact abundant. But there is value in thinking about *The Christian Year* as a book that needs to be saved for the present time through the making of another book: it was in this complex situation that *The Christian Year* came to be both a bestseller and an ambiguous commentary upon the contemporary agency of the book it set out to recommend. In these 'times of much leisure and unbounded curiosity,' as Keble wrote in his Advertisement, 'when excitement of every kind is sought after with a morbid eagerness,' readers had forgotten 'the merit of our Liturgy' and its 'provision' for 'a sound rule of faith' and 'a sober standard of feeling in matters of practical religion' (Keble (1841), v). And to recall the usefulness of this liturgy, Keble produced a poetic cycle that, as G. B. Tennyson has demonstrated in detail, 'parallels the Book of Common Prayer throughout' (Tennyson, 75). Originating in the Prayer Book, *The Christian Year* likewise directs readers there as a destination, its 'object' being to assist the reader, as Keble wrote, 'in bringing his own thoughts and feelings into more entire unison with those recommended and exemplified in the Prayer Book' (v–vi).

It is because *The Christian Year* has such a beginning and such an intended end that any attempt to extract the poetry from the theology seems foolhardy. Indeed, the proper context for a scholarly reading of the poetry must remain theological. More specifically, it ought to be read in terms of the theology associated with the Oxford Movement or what I will, for convenience, call Tractarianism. With all this conceded, however, I want to invert the traditional scheme for understanding the production and subsequent reception of *The Christian Year*. For while it has been demonstrated both how Tractarian theology can account for *The Christian Year* and how *The Christian Year* was a vehicle for Tractarian theology, we have largely forgotten how *The Christian Year* and its theology were born in a wider debate that had theologized reading itself. Before describing this new theological discourse about reading, it is important to acknowledge that reading and religion – as well as literacy and heresy – had long been deeply involved topics. And the debates about reading in the late 1820s arose out of previously established discourses that could both express and challenge the nation's deeply ingrained Protestant ideology of the book. Nevertheless, I want to argue that in 1825 three distinct chapters in the history of reading – what I call Broughamism, the threat from Germany and Milton's heresy – were publicly clarified in the British Isles. And the context for the unprecedented popularity of Keble's famously reticent book was a convergence of religious and political history with the history of the reading nation on a scale that was itself unprecedented. Although *The Christian Year* would not be published until 1827, my argument suggests why 1825 was the crucial year when its author was persuaded to publish his poems and abandon his prior commitment to posthumous publication. As Keble wrote to J. T. Coleridge in March of that year: 'I will tell you a secret; which is that after all my backwardness (which I suppose was chiefly affectation) on such subjects, I am in a fair way to commence *author*' (Coleridge, I, 117). As we shall see, the birth of such an author in 1825 was not simply the expression of Keble's well-documented spirituality.

\* \* \*

Broughamism was the name that John Henry Newman gave in 1841 to the age's faith in the power of reading to redeem the lower and middle orders (Newman (1999), 544). Coming from Newman's satire *The Tamworth Reading*

*Room*, the label was an insult bestowed on the Tory leader Robert Peel for his adoption of the values of the Whig politician and man of letters Henry Brougham.[2] Though resonant to Newman's audience in the 1840s, Broughamism had become a public agenda to espouse or oppose sometime in the spring of 1825 when Brougham, then MP for Winchilsea and co-editor of the *Edinburgh Review*, had used his influence and remarkable energy to establish himself as the major national patron of the Mechanics Institutes movement, the Society for the Diffusion of Useful Knowledge and what would become London University.[3] And while Broughamism was, for Newman at least, a derogatory label for a kind of materialism, Broughamism also was, from the start, potent and controversial because it had inescapable theological dimensions. Take for example Francis Jeffrey's 1825 review of *Practical Observations upon the Education of the People*, the best-selling tract in which Brougham outlined the mission of the Mechanics Institutes. A 'review' of a pamphlet based on an article published in the previous number, Jeffrey's real task was further advertisement for his liberal co-worker's views, and to that end he gave a fine example of Broughamism, claiming that,

> Since the time when the Scriptures were first printed and circulated in the common tongue, there has been no such benefit conferred on the great body of the people, as seems now to be held out to them in the institutions which it is the business of this little work to recommend and explain. (Jeffrey, 508)

'We have only to add,' Jeffrey grandly closes, 'that the work is very short, and very cheap' (510). The bathetic plunge here to the 'very short, and very cheap' was just the kind of turn exploited by satirists of Broughamism, but Brougham and his allies were invited to speak in ways that gave scriptural qualities to cheap tracts because all previous attempts to educate the people on a national scale – all attempts to establish a national readership – had been frustrated by religiously inspired barriers erected, at different times, by both Dissenting and Establishment forces. Broughamism's aggressive gestures of sacralization, in other words, were often responses to the theological arguments used to prevent both the establishment of national primary education and the opening of advanced degrees beyond the terms of Anglican control. Only after long witnessing this frustrating history did Brougham redouble his faith in books themselves as objects imagined to be freed from socially retarding sectarian strife. '[T]he education of the people,' he wrote in 1826, 'is chiefly to be accomplished by reading; ... the main reliance, therefore, of all who desire the improvement of the body of the people, must ever be on books' (Brougham, 197). Brougham's gospel of improvement *was* the mass production and diffusion of an affordable commodity. Consumers of print were both the means and the ends of Broughamism. And, as Brougham frankly admitted, affordable works had also to be short to be of use in the lives of working people. Likewise, Brougham's support for a non-residential University in London was founded on a faith in the efficacy of diffusing knowledge in forms affordable and accessible to the middle classes. The institution was structured as a matter of economy that would open the university experience to a layer of society that could not afford the estimated three hundred pounds per year required to maintain a gentleman scholar at either Oxford or Cambridge.

Most adherents of Broughamism asserted the piety of their reliance on books. Their commitment to the printed word was represented as an extension of a history of modern enlightenment that began with the Reformation, and Brougham himself repeatedly endorsed the study of Scripture – without note or comment. But determined critics of Broughamism saw it as a concerted agenda to usurp ecclesiastical authority; and in the Church's place, Brougham was offering the compensatory institution of reading itself, a gesture summarized by his commitment to reading Scripture without the assistance of Church formularies. Similarly, while England's ancient residential Universities (theoretically) cultivated gentlemen through a series of pastoral relationships, Brougham's vision of a university featured students copying lectures, retiring to their own dispersed lodgings, and preparing for exams with books and a growing list of cram materials. The clergy was at the core of the ancient residential universities, where colleges were headed by priests and home to celibate Fellows, most of them required to take holy orders. For the new version of higher learning, there was a faith in print and in the individual reader.

Of course neither the history of modern British educational reform nor the history of the philanthropic dissemination of improving reading material begins with Brougham or these three institutions – the Mechanics Institutes, the Society for the Diffusion of Useful Knowledge and London University – that became prominent or initially took shape in 1825. What rendered Broughamism into an identifiable cultural and political programme was a result of Brougham's notorious energy, his position as a privileged speaker and a privileged writer, and his ability to turn public speech and public writing into mutually supporting acts of promotion. In his 1825 portrait of Brougham, William Hazlitt pointed to this aspect of his frenetic public life:

> In the midst of an Election contest he comes out to address the populace, and goes back to his study to finish an article for the *Edinburgh Review*; sometimes indeed wedging three or four articles (in the shape of *refaccimentos* of his own pamphlets or speeches in parliament) into a single number. Such indeed is the activity of his mind that it appears to require neither repose, nor any other stimulus than a delight in its own experience. (Hazlitt, 139)

Not merely an advocate for the flow of what Carlyle would describe as 'that huge froth-ocean of Printed Speech we loosely call Literature' (Carlyle, 163–4), Brougham was the feverishly active agent in the diffusion of his own views about the redemptive value of cheaply reproduced speech. And he more than any other single figure was responsible for making the nation at large produce so much printed material about an activity – reading itself – that was pursued in common by school-age children of all classes, skilled workers, the middle classes and the professional and propertied classes.

\* \* \*

If Broughamism names a controversy about an expression of faith in books, 'the threat from Germany' names a controversy about a scholarly creed, reportedly foreign, that held that all ancient books, both the 'sacred' and 'profane,' had to be read in the same manner.[4] In the June 1825 issue of the *Quarterly Review*, the first important notice of this threat came in an essay by the Oxford educated clergyman Thomas Arnold introducing British readers to Barthold Niebuhr, whose *History of Rome* had first been published in German in 1811. Niebuhr argued that early Roman history – recounted in works by Livy and others – was a mixture of reliable history and myth. By calling attention to this divide, he made the critic's first task the identification of mythical narratives. Once identified, they were given an historical interpretation based on available external evidence. In the process of denying the historicity of narratives by Livy, Niebuhr compared them to Greek poetical narratives as well as Scriptural narratives. Most controversially of all, he compared Mosaic genealogies to mythical dynasties of the Greeks; and he suggested that the division of the life of Moses into three equal parts, like the Gospel genealogies of Christ, was a numerical symmetry typical of primitive myths. Despite these positions, Arnold cautioned against any 'sweeping charge of "German folly and infidelity"', and he hailed Niebuhr's work as the expression of an 'inquiring' yet faithful historical mind (Arnold, 86–7).

Several other works and events of 1825 signaled the awareness of a new school of historical interpretation that had two hallmarks: it levelled the epistemology of 'revealed' texts with those of purely human origin, and it had a distinctive Teutonic character. At Cambridge, the Reverend Hugh James Rose condemned German rationalism in lectures published as *The State of the Protestant Religion in Germany*; while Connop Thirlwall, a fellow at Trinity soon to take orders, translated into English a key work of German biblical criticism, Friedrich Schleiermacher's *Über die Schriften des Lukas. Ein kritischer Versuch* (1817). Anonymously published as *A Critical Essay on the Gospel of St Luke*, Thirlwall's book included a long introduction from his own hand summarizing various theories of the origins of the Gospels, theories which were, as he put it, 'equally and decidedly irreconcilable with that doctrine of inspiration once universally prevalent in the Christian Church' (Thirlwall, xi). The same year Thirlwall, Rose and Arnold were either attacking, defending or promoting German historical criticism, the young E. B. Pusey traveled from Oxford to Göttingen, and he would go on to study at Bonn as well as Berlin where he came to know Schleiermacher. When he returned to England from the second of two extended periods of foreign study, Pusey published *An Historical Enquiry into the Probable Causes of the Rationalist Character lately Predominant in the Theology of Germany* (1828), a book that defended pious versions of historical criticism and faulted Rose for lumping together all German critics into one category. Despite these complicated intentions, Pusey's book was received as an apology for rationalism. Rose was perturbed and replied with *A Letter to the Lord Bishop of London, in reply to Mr. Pusey's work on the Causes of Rationalism in Germany* (1829), and a second, enlarged edition of his 1825 work (slightly retitled as) *The State of Protestantism in Germany* (1829). Pusey, now on the defensive and accused of holding rationalist tendencies himself, replied with *An Historical Enquiry into the Causes of the Rationalist Character lately Predominant in the Theology of Germany. Part II* (1830).[5]

Pusey, Rose and their reviewers were beginning a protracted debate about the significance and causes of the criticism associated with Germany, one that explicitly spanned classical and biblical philology and coincided with the publication, starting in 1828, of an English translation of Niebuhr's *Roman History*. This debate about historical criticism in the late 1820s and after had important features that distinguish it from a longer history of theological controversy that stretched back through the eighteenth century to the philosophical attacks on revealed religion. First, it was primarily an intramural battle fought by Anglicans, most of them ordained priests, rather than a struggle between the Church and external assailants. Secondly, this debate took place during the 'constitutional revolution' of 1828 to 1832 which undermined the Anglican hold on political and cultural power. Some leaders of a new dogmatic party in the Church were convinced that recently imported critical tendencies were reacting dangerously with the traditional agents of Whiggery. Newman, who had closely observed the debate between Rose and Pusey, recalled that Rose

> had been the first to give warning ... of the perils to England which lay in the biblical and theological speculations of Germany. The Reform agitation followed, and the Whig government came into power; and he anticipated in their distribution of Church patronage the authoritative introduction of liberal opinions into the country. He feared that by the Whig party a door would be opened in England to the most grievous of heresies, which never could be closed again. (Newman, *Apologia*, 45)

Eventually, the theorization of this threat was powerful enough to compel the delineation of an earlier Germanic source for all the trouble: Friedrich August Wolf, whose *Prolegomena ad Homerum* (1795) had denied Homer's solitary authorship of the *Iliad* and the *Odyssey*. Starting in the late 1820s, Wolf was on his way to becoming one of the century's grand heresiarchs, and Niebuhr, who had briefly studied under Wolf, was being hailed as either his most influential or pernicious heir (Grafton et al., 28). The increased attention to Wolf as a scholarly villain or hero in a narrative involving the classics, Scripture and the state of the nation reminds us just how little anxious attention was paid to Wolf's theories during the first two decades of their publication. The threat from Germany simply did not exist in English minds until the late 1820s, and before then the nationalized source of theologically subversive free-thought was France. For those most anxious about the new Teutonic threat, the fact that a socially corrosive theological liberalism had two German classicists – Wolf and Niebuhr – at its roots suggested that the source of theological error was a habit of reading itself. That this problem spread out from the geographic homeland of Protestantism raised the idea that it was the Protestant faith in the individual reader's private judgment that was the cause of the problem.

\* \* \*

As Broughamism and the threat from Germany were making self-consciously modern varieties of reading into rallying cries for political and religious parties, a resonant illustration of the consequences of unmediated Bible reading was made public in the summer of 1825 in Charles Richard Sumner's edition of John Milton's long-lost treatise on Christian doctrine. The newly recovered manuscript had been, by Royal command, translated by a well-placed clergyman; and its publication as *A Treatise on Christian Doctrine: Compiled from the Holy Scriptures Alone* was intended to be an event that would bind together more surely the nation's religious and literary foundations. But, as the publication of what turned out to be Milton's heresy called forth over fifty critical reviews in the following year, the event proved to be the century's most concentrated, vociferous collision between the doctrines of orthodox Protestantism and a cult of national literary veneration.[6]

Milton began his treatise by completely identifying reformed religion – and its pure doctrines – with the independent Bible reader, and this dedication to discovering a 'personal belief of his own,' through the reading of one book alone, the Protestant Bible, culminates with a remarkable plea to readers to judge his conclusions by no authority other than the one they are founded on. '[N]either adopt my sentiments, nor reject them,' he says as he closes the introductory epistle, 'unless every doubt has been removed from your belief by the clear testimony of revelation' (Milton, I, 10). Such dedication to the *sola scriptura* principle was not cause for scandal. But, for most observers, when Milton sat down to read his Bible without note or comment, he clearly rose up a heretic, endorsing a wide range of heterodox positions including a denial of the orthodox Trinity. Milton's religious and political views had of course long been the object of scrutiny and debate, apology and accusation. But even Samuel Johnson, a good hater of Milton's politics, had pronounced the poet 'to have been untainted by any heretical peculiarity of opinion' (Mineka, 116). And the English public sphere from 1688 onward was in theory and practice construed to tolerate Milton's most glaring dissent from establishment principles, his anti-episcopacy. The religiously tolerant Protestant Monarchy was based on the assumption of a peaceful cohabitation between the established Church and orthodox Protestant sects, all of them non-episcopal. Milton's confirmed Arianism, however, was a form of theological dissent of another order, and it directly pleased only the relatively small Unitarian communities.

In some ways, publication of the *Treatise* was most awkward for orthodox dissent, those confessions that had long venerated Milton for both his poetry and his theology. Thus, in periodicals such as the *Evangelical*, *Methodist* and *Congregationalist* magazines and the *Eclectic Review*, 'bitter sorrow and regret' were the most common reactions (Mineka, 120). From the perspective of the establishment periodicals, those like the *Edinburgh Review*, the *Quarterly Review*, *Blackwoods*, and their more overtly religious counterparts, the *British Critic* and the *Quarterly Theological Review*, the disclosure of Milton's heresy was, on the face of it, less disturbing. The poet had always been, to varying degrees, either a theo-political rebel, according to conventional Tory wisdom, or tainted with an excessive Puritan zeal, according to the standard Whig correction. A quintessentially moderate response to the new Milton of 1825 came in the *Quarterly Review* of October from the clerical man of letters Henry Hart Milman, who was then in the midst of his term as Professor of Poetry at Oxford. Milman admitted that Milton commenced his study on sound Protestant principles, but in Milman's forgiving portrait of the poet's error, Milton's reading of the Bible was undone by its peculiar intensity. While Milton discovered his religion in heroically diligent scriptural study, he had forgotten that the Gospel had been originally preached to the unlettered (Milman, 445–6). In the end, Milman subordinated Milton's theological opinions to a more important celebration of his literary immortality. Describing an inevitable future when the English of Shakespeare and Milton should 'become extinct in the vicissitudes of ages,' Milman insisted that 'the perpetual and devotional study' of their 'untranslatable' poetry would be the surest vehicle for preserving the beauties of the language (456–7).

Milman was sympathetic to the historical criticism at the heart of the threat from Germany, and he would go on to cause controversy himself with a

Niebuhrian interpretation of the Old Testament in his *History of the Jews* (1829), a work eventually withdrawn by its publisher John Murray. This scholarly inclination along with his literary accommodation of Milton's theological errors explain why Milman – despite his continued association with the *Quarterly* – has been placed within an influential group of 'liberal Anglican' ecclesiastics that included Thomas Arnold, Richard Whately, Renn Dickson Hampden, Connop Thirlwall and others (Brent, 139–41). A more strident Toryism, however, was what many readers expected to see on the pages of the *Quarterly*. One such reader in 1825 upset at the kindly disposition shown towards Milton was Richard Hurrell Froude, who was, as he wrote to his fellow clergyman John Keble, horrified 'at finding [Milton]...styled "the great religious poet of the Christian world."' To Froude the portrayal of Milton was out of the *Quarterly*'s character, particularly given the fact that the previous June number had included an article that expressed the position that 'it was to be regretted that even a person of Milton's talent should have undertaken a religious subject.' '[D]isgusted at this gross inconsistency,' Froude claimed he 'could not read the [Milman] review through' (Froude, I, 188). Froude's disgust recalls that there was a Church party, like the Unitarian community, small but influential, that was ready to welcome the publication of *De Doctrina* because it confirmed their own marginalized theological position. For readers like Froude, always glad to gain 'a better right to hate Milton' (I, 177), the treatise was useful for proving how the exalted notion of the Protestant reader did indeed lead to heresy.[7]

\* \* \*

Froude's disgust also provides evidence that, for some readers at least, as far as the *Quarterly* maintained a coherent position on Milton in 1825, that position was shored up by Keble, for he was the author of the June article, 'Sacred Poetry,' that had rendered Milman's piece grossly inconsistent. Once Froude discovered Keble's authorship, he was doubly surprised given Keble's 'aversion to reviews' and the fact that this one 'did not come up to' Keble's 'standard of aversion to Milton' (I, 190). Noting this double aversion was a shrewd tribute to his former tutor, for 'Sacred Poetry' is an essay about a complicated form of authorship that coordinates a denigration of Milton with a disdain for a contemporary literary sphere dominated by eager readers, opinionated critics and writers seeking the approval of both.

'Sacred Poetry' begins by pretending to review one 'little volume' of religious verse, Josiah Conder's *Star in the East* (1824). Even so, the opening paragraph speaks in an idiom that links the contentious topic of widespread reading, the periodical industry of 'criticism,' and theological debate:

> There are many circumstances about this little volume, which tend powerfully to disarm criticism. In the first place, it is, for the most part, of a *sacred* character: taken up with those subjects, which least of all admit with propriety, either in the author or critic, the exercise of intellectual subtlety. For the *practical* tendency, indeed, of such compositions, both are most deeply responsible; the author who publishes, and the critic who undertakes to recommend or to censure them. But if they appear to be written with any degree of sincerity and earnestness, we naturally shrink from treating them merely as literary efforts. To interrupt the current of a reader's sympathy in such a case, by critical objections, is not merely to deprive him of a little harmless pleasure. It is to disturb him almost in a devotional exercise. (Keble (1825), 211–2)

Over and above his local concerns here, Keble registers the central complaint of the dogmatic revival of the 1820s: things of a sacred character in general, things such as Scripture, the Church and its priesthood, were being irreverently handled by censorious criticism and intellectual subtlety. And this trend was summarily embodied by the dual claim that Scripture ought to be read like any other book and that the individual reader, not any profession of faith, was the key to biblical interpretation. These concerns lead to Keble's elaboration of a form of literary exchange involving authorless books and critically disarmed readers. For the book under review, as Keble put it,

> ... bears internal evidence, for the most part, of not having been written to meet the eye of the world. It is in vain to say, that this claim on the critic's favour is nullified by publication. The author may give it up, and yet the work may retain it. We may still feel that we have no right to judge severely of what was not, at first, intended to come before our judgment at all. This of course applies only to those compositions, which indicate, by something within themselves, this freedom from the pretension of authorship. (212)

Keble goes on to demonstrate the superiority of Edmund Spenser's allegorical mode over Milton's direct treatment of sacred subjects in an argument that aims to show how Spenser, not Milton, is England's preeminent sacred poet. And it has been shown how Keble's high valuation of Spenser's 'veiled' method is related to the Tractarian doctrine of Reserve and mystical modes of biblical interpretation that Keble would famously define and defend in *Tract no. 89* ('On the Mysticism Attributed to the Early Fathers of the Church') published in 1840. For good reasons then, 'Sacred Poetry' has been widely read as a theological manifesto, with its valorization of 'indirect' poetics represented as an early glimmer of essential Tractarian hermeneutic principles (Tennyson

66–7, 105–9; Shaw 67–74). But the endorsement of allegories and typologies in 'Sacred Poetry' primarily stems from Keble's identification of these modes as a needed therapy for contemporary writers and readers. More important than his comparative evaluation of Spenser and Milton was Keble's formulation of a mode of authorship allied to a kind of reading that escaped the pernicious effects of an intellectual pride that was, at once, embodied in modern print culture, most particularly its periodical reviews, the historical tendencies of Protestantism, and the timeless temptations of 'the Author of Evil himself' (Keble (1825), 229). Explaining how the nation's greatest sacred poet had adopted an allegorical discipline, Keble urged his own readers to avoid becoming unrestrained and self-sufficient.

Keble's 'Sacred Poetry', in other words, does not simply illustrate the otherworldly character of its retiring author by way of his attraction to mystical hermeneutics. Tractarian theology certainly has a valid Patristic (and thus antiquated) genealogy, but the allure of these ancient doctrines in the 1820s and after was paradoxically modern in its close attention to the age's impassioned debates about reading. In these 'times of much leisure and unbounded curiosity,' as Keble wrote in his Advertisement to *The Christian Year*, 'when excitement of every kind is sought after with a morbid eagerness' (Keble (1841), v), readers needed appropriately therapeutic experiences. For these reasons, it is useful to recall how Keble's poetics were 'rediscovered' by literary critics in the 1950s. M. H. Abrams, for example, sought to make Keble accessible by giving him credit for anticipating Freudian views on therapeutic narratives (Abrams, 145–8). G. B. Tennyson in his essential 1981 study *Victorian Devotional Poetry* stressed how this appropriation seems beside the point. It was, in any case, anachronistic, and Tennyson set about to describe Keble and the larger enterprise of Tractarian aesthetics in their own right. With this task in mind, and in concordance with Stephen Prickett's *Romanticism and Religion* (1976), Tennyson argued that the 'assumptions of Romanticism' and 'Romantic theory' provided 'a necessary background to the understanding of Tractarian poetics' (Tennyson, 13). An interdisciplinary history of the practice and representation of reading now allow us to reaffirm the older therapeutic model, albeit on terms other than those embraced by Abrams. For Tractarianism, like many of the creative and critical assumptions of Romanticism, was derived from specific anxieties about reading and certain kinds of readers.[8] Keble, to be sure, formulated his poetics in response to the reading crisis that has been briefly contextualized here. And if *The Christian Year* is, as G. B. Tennyson put it, 'the first and in many ways the most important fruit of Tractarian aesthetic practice' (Tennyson, 35), such fruit was initially so tempting to so many because of Broughamism, the threat from Germany and Milton's heresy.

It was only the palpability of a crisis in the Protestant ideology of the book that persuaded Keble to make his poems public. In doing so he embarked on one of the century's most intriguing spectacles of literary fame, one conducted behind an official veil of anonymity and a steadfast refusal to have his name put to any edition of *The Christian Year* during his lifetime. A book that insisted on its freedom from the pretensions of authorship, *The Christian Year* proved to be a compelling alternative to the fashionable literary annuals that rose to prominence along with it in the late 1820s. While secular annuals attracted buyers with the literary novelties of each year, *The Christian Year*, like the Anglican liturgical calendar, was simply repeated. The book's title offered readers the promise that *The Christian Year* – unlike the fickle productions of restless poets – did not simply pass away, but returned again and again by virtue of its divine, rather than human, derivation. And in these terms, the unchanging date of the Advertisement – 'May 30th, 1827' – came to be the signature line for a book that had no named author. Hardly frozen in time, however, Keble's book was the central poetic gesture in a larger literary campaign conducted by a powerful author who sought to diffuse specific reading practices during an era of crisis and transition.

## Notes

[1] The poems quoted are 'Tuesday in Whitsun-Week', '2nd Sunday after Easter', 'St. Matthew', '6th Sunday after Epiphany', '1st Sunday after Trinity', and '4th Sunday after Trinity'. There is no scholarly edition of *The Christian Year*, which was first published in June of 1827 and had an important history of revisions. In this essay, I quote from a copy formerly owned by Keble's godchild, Matthew Arnold, who, like Keble before him, would hold the Oxford chair in Poetry. This 21st edition from 1841 also marks a pivotal year in the Anglo-Catholic revival.

[2] Newman's original letters to the *Times*, signed 'Catholicus,' are reproduced with useful information, including a report of Peel's original speech, in the *Letters and Diaries*, 8, 525–61.

[3] For the best recent work on Brougham's status within an expanding, politicized print culture, see Christie 1999 and 2002. For the details about Brougham's involvement with the three institutions cited here, see Ford and Stewart. Brougham also makes frequent appearances throughout Altick's classic study.

[4] The second chapter of Crowther's study (40–65), entitled 'The Threat from Germany,' is a useful introduction to the Anglican reception of German scholarship in the 1840s and after. But its conclusion, that 'many of the clergy' were first introduced to German scholarship in the 1860s (64), is no longer convincing. All influential Anglican ecclesiastics by the 1830s had a good sense of the potential significance of German historicism.

[5] Taking stock of Pusey's early career is a key step to overcoming the myth (see n. 4 above) that Anglican theology during the 1820s and 1830s was innocent of the methods and presumptions of the higher criticism. On Pusey in particular, see the classic Victorian account of his brush with theological liberalism in Liddon, I, 70–114, 146–77 and the more recent work by Matthew, Frappell and Forrester (211–31).

[6] For the history of the recovery, initial publication and reception, see Kelley (3–10) and Mineka.

[7] For a fascinating account of the Tractarian antipathy for Milton, see Gill (75–8) and the description there of Frederick William Faber's successful campaign to have William Wordsworth tone down a poetic moment of Miltonic veneration.

[8] For the best recent study of early nineteenth-century authorship's engagement with readerships, see Newlyn. Before then, Klancher brought a good deal of attention to the topic.

## Works Cited

Abrams, M. H., *The Mirror and the Lamp: Romantic Theory and the Critical Tradition*, New York: Oxford University Press, 1953.

Altick, Richard Daniel, *The English Common Reader: a Social History of the Mass Reading Public, 1800–1900*, 2nd edn, foreword by Jonathan Rose, Columbus: Ohio State University Press, 1998.

Arnold, Thomas, 'Early Roman History', *Quarterly Review*, 32, (June 1825): 67–92.

Blair, Kirstie, 'John Keble and the Rhythm of Faith', *Essays in Criticism*, 53.2 (April 2003): 129–50.

Brent, Richard, *Liberal Anglican Politics: Whiggery, Religion, and Reform, 1830–1841*, New York: Oxford University Press, 1987.

Brougham, Henry, 'Diffusion of Knowledge', *Edinburgh Review*, 45 (Dec. 1826), 189–99.

Carlyle, Thomas, *On Heroes, Hero-Worship and the Heroic in History* (1841), Carl Niemeyer, ed., Lincoln: University of Nebraska Press, 1966.

Christie, William, 'State Patronage and the Romantic Writer: Henry Taylor's Modest Proposal', *Authorship, Commerce, and the Public: Scenes of Writing, 1750–1850*, E. J. Clery, Caroline Franklin, Peter Garside, eds, New York: Palgrave, 2002.

— 'Going Public: Print Lords Byron and Brougham', *Studies in Romanticism*, 38.3 (1999): 443–75.

Coleridge, J. T., *A Memoir of the Rev. John Keble, M.A., late Vicar of Hursley*, 2nd edn, 2 vols, Oxford and London: James Parker, 1869.

Crowther, M. A., *Church Embattled: Religious Controversy in mid-Victorian England*, Hamden, Connecticut: Archon Books, 1970.

Ford, Trowbridge, *Henry Brougham and His World: A Biography*, Chichester: B. Rose, 1995.

Forrester, David, *Young Doctor Pusey: a Study in Development*, Oxford: Mowbray, 1989.

Frappell, Leighton, 'Science in the Service of Orthodoxy: the Early Intellectual Development of E. B. Pusey', *Pusey Rediscovered*, Perry Butler, ed., Oxford: SPCK, 1983, 1–33.

Froude, Richard Hurrell, *Remains of the late Reverend Richard Hurrell Froude*, Part I, 2 vols, London: Rivington, 1838.

Gill, Stephen Charles, *Wordsworth and the Victorians*, Oxford: Clarendon Press, 1998.

Grafton, Anthony, Glenn W. Most and James E. G. Zetzel, 'Introduction' to Friedrich August Wolf, *Prolegomena ad Homerum*, Princeton: Princeton University Press, 1985, 3–35.

Hazlitt, William, *The Spirit of the Age*, Vol. XI of *Complete Works of William Hazlitt*, P. P. Howe, ed., London: J. M. Dent, 1932.

Jeffrey, Francis, 'Education of the People', *Edinburgh Review*, 41 (January 1825): 508–10.

Keble, John, 'Sacred Poetry', *Quarterly Review*, 32 (June 1825): 211–32.

— *The Christian Year: Thoughts in Verse for the Sundays and Holydays – Throughout the Year*, 21$^{st}$ edn, Oxford: J. H. Parker, 1841.

Kelley, Maurice, 'Introduction' to *Complete Prose Work of John Milton*, Vol. VI, New Haven: Yale University Press, 1973, 3–116.

Klancher, Jon P., *The Making of English Reading Audiences, 1790–1832*, Madison: University of Wisconsin Press, 1987.

Liddon, Henry Parry, *Life of Edward Bouverie Pusey*, 4 vols, 4$^{th}$ edn, London: Longmans, Green, 1894–98.

Matthew, H. C. G., 'Edward Bouverie Pusey: from Scholar to Tractarian', *Journal of Theological Studies*, 32 (1981): 101–24.

Milman, Henry, Hart 'Milton on Christian Doctrine', *Quarterly Review*, 32 (October 1825): 442–57.

Milton, John, *A Treatise on Christian Doctrine: Compiled from the Holy Scriptures Alone*, 2 vols, Boston: Cummings, Hillard and Co., 1825.

Mineka, Francis Edward, 'The Critical Reception of Milton's De Doctrina Christiana', *Studies in English*, 23, Austin: University of Texas Press, 1943, 115–47.

Newlyn, Lucy, *Reading, Writing, and Romanticism: the Anxiety of Reception*, Oxford: Oxford University Press, 2000.

Newman, John Henry, *The Letters and Diaries of John Henry Newman*, Vol. 8, Gerard Tracey, ed., Oxford: Clarendon Press, 1999.

— *Apologia Pro Vita Sua*, Martin J. Svaglic, ed., Oxford: Clarendon Press, 1967.

Prickett, Stephen, *Romanticism and Religion: the tradition of Coleridge and Wordsworth in the Victorian Church*, Cambridge: Cambridge University Press, 1976.

Rose, Revered Hugh James, *The State of the Protestant Religion in Germany; in a series of discourses; preached before the University of Cambridge*. Cambridge: J. Deighton & Sons, 1825.

— *The State of Protestantism in Germany, Described; in a series of discourses; preached before the University of Cambridge*. Second edition, enlarged, with an appendix. London and Cambridge: C. J. G. & F. Rivington and J. & J. Deighton, 1829.

— *A Letter to the Lord Bishop of London, in reply to Mr. Pusey's work on the Causes of Rationalism in Germany*. London and Cambridge: C. J. G. & F. Rivington and J. &. J. Deighton, 1829.

Shaw, W. David, *The Lucid Veil: Poetic Truth in the Victorian Age*, London: Athlone, 1987.

Stewart, Robert Mackenzie, *Henry Brougham, 1778–1868: His Public Career*, London: Bodley Head, 1986.

Tennyson, G. B., *Victorian Devotional Poetry: The Tractarian Mode*, Cambridge, Mass.: Harvard University Press, 1981.

Thirlwall, Connop, 'Introduction by the Translator', *A Critical Essay on the Gospel of St Luke*, by Frederick Schleiermacher (1825), Terrence N. Tice, ed., Lewiston: E. Mellen Press, 1993.

# 6

# 'NATIONAL APOSTASY', *TRACTS FOR THE TIMES* AND *PLAIN SERMONS*: JOHN KEBLE'S TRACTARIAN PROSE

## Robert H. Ellison

For nearly two hundred years, John Keble's reputation has rested largely on his poetry. Scholars have, of course, given some attention to other subjects – his role in the Oxford Movement; his relationships with Newman, Pusey, Williams and Froude; his pastoral work at Hursley, and so on – but it is probably safe to say that he is best known as a contributor to *Lyra Apostolica*, the author of *Lyra Innocentium* and especially as the man who gave the world *The Christian Year*.

I am not at all suggesting that Keble's poetry ought not to be studied, but I do believe that there is an aspect of Keble's work that has not been adequately considered. Keble himself commented on this in an 1858 letter to John Taylor Coleridge: 'I wish', he wrote, 'people would *consider* my prose as well as *like* my verses' (Coleridge, 480). By this time, *The Christian Year* had gone through nineteen editions and sold in excess of 60,000 copies (Beek, 183), but his canon of approximately forty prose works – mostly pamphlets and individual sermons, but also a few longer works on poetry and religion and multi-volume editions of the Fathers, Richard Hooker and Thomas Wilson – had received relatively little attention. The situation has not changed a great deal since then; as far as I am aware, we still do not have any extensive examinations of Keble's essays, tracts and sermons.

In this paper, I will offer at least the beginnings of the consideration Keble may have had in mind. I cannot, of course, discuss his entire canon, so I will focus on the works most closely associated with his Tractarian years: 'National Apostasy', his eight *Tracts for the Times* and his contributions to a little-known, ten-volume series entitled *Plain Sermons, by Contributors to the 'Tracts for the*

*Times'*. The subtitle identifies this collection as a companion to the *Tracts*, as does the Advertisement, which indicates that the sermons are intended to 'show that the subjects treated of in the 'Tracts' were not set forth as mere parts of ideal systems...but are rather urged as truths of immediate and essential importance, bearing more or less directly on our every day behaviour' (2). Taken together, these works help provide a sense of the range of Keble's ideas and expressions as a theologian and a preacher.

The best-known example of Keble's prose is 'National Apostasy', the Assize Sermon he preached in St Mary's church on 14 July 1833. Its structure and style are similar to his other sermons. J. T. Coleridge once described Keble's parochial discourses as 'truly Christian sermons, opening out the Scripture, full of citations from it, going directly to the heart that would open to receive it; affectionate, earnest, true, and high; but very simple, very unadorned' (Coleridge, 496). The same can be said of 'National Apostasy'. Keble asserts that, contrary to some popular opinion, the Old Testament has lost none of its relevance in the Christian age, and that the story of Samuel is especially instructive for Victorian Britain, a nation which, like ancient Israel, had committed the great sin of supposing that it 'may do well enough, as such, without God, and without His Church' (Keble (1931), 7). His exposition is replete with allusions to and citations from I and II Samuel, and he quotes a few passages from several other books as well. It is not, however, a complicated theological treatise. The style is simple and conversational, accessible to anyone who heard or read the sermon. It calls to mind the assessment of the parishioner who, when asked whether he thought Keble a great preacher, replied, 'Well, I don't know what a great preacher is...but he always made us understand him' (Lock, 193).

Most importantly, Keble emphasizes practical application, the *raison d'etre* of the Victorian sermon.[1] He is concerned not only with the theoretical, outlining the 'symptoms' that indicate when a nation is 'becoming alienated from God and Christ', but also with the practical, setting forth 'the particular duties of sincere Christians' living in 'a time of such dire calamity' (Keble (1931), 9). These duties are twofold: constant 'intercession' for 'the State, and all who are in authority', followed by public and private 'remonstrance' with those who are leading the country astray (19, 20). Christians who act in such a manner, Keble says, are sure to be rewarded: they are assured that, 'sooner or later, [theirs] will be the winning side, and that the victory will be complete, universal, eternal' (24).

The form of the sermon is familiar, but the occasion and audience, and therefore the content, are somewhat atypical. Like other Assize Sermons, the preaching of 'National Apostasy' was a religio-political event: it was a response to recent Erastian developments, based upon an Old Testament text, preached from the University pulpit, for an audience of His Majesty's judges. The *Tracts*, on the other hand, speak to the clergy and laity about matters of Apostolic faith, not the current crisis in the Victorian state, and the *Sermons* are parochial addresses marking not the beginning of a judicial term, but rather confirmations, church consecrations and major and minor dates in the Christian year. It is therefore not surprising that the political content we find in 'National Apostasy' is largely absent from these works.[2]

What, then, *do* we find in Keble's *Tracts for the Times* and *Plain Sermons?* One of the first things we notice about Keble's tracts is their variety of form. Two (*Nos. 4* and *13*) are brief essays; one (*No. 89*) is a 186-page theological treatise; four (*Nos. 52, 54, 57* and *60*) are sermons; and one (*No. 40*) is a dialogue between an unnamed narrator and a man named Richard Nelson. In each case, however, as we would expect, these documents all promote some essential doctrines of the Oxford Movement. Apostolic Succession, the first tenet mentioned in the Advertisement to Volume 1 of the *Tracts*, is also the subject of Keble's first tract, *Adherence to the Apostolical Succession the Safest Course*. It is the safest course because it is the most Scriptural: Christ himself instituted the succession at the Last Supper, so He is 'likely to be well pleased with those who do their best…to keep as near to His apostles as they can' (Keble (1838a), 4). Adherence to this succession is, in fact, not just safe, but essential, because only the Apostolic Church can truly administer the Sacraments. If ministers are not invested with Apostolic authority, they 'cannot be sure that [their] hands convey the [Eucharistic] sacrifice'; they cannot be sure that their parishioners are truly 'partakers of the Body and Blood of Christ' (2). Churchmen should, therefore, stop being 'cold and indifferent' to this doctrine, and should start boldly 'assert[ing] the authority of the Bishops and Pastors of the Church' (1, 5). They should also warn Dissenters of their error, impressing upon them the 'plain truth' that 'by separating themselves from our communion, they separate themselves…from THE ONLY CHURCH IN THIS REALM WHICH HAS A RIGHT TO BE QUITE SURE THAT SHE HAS THE LORD'S BODY TO GIVE TO HIS PEOPLE' (5).

The notes Keble sounds here echo throughout his other tracts. As he defended the Church's authority in Sacramental matters in *Tract no. 4*, he defends her authority in liturgical matters in *Tract no. 13*. Keble reminds those who would revise the Sunday Lessons in the Prayer Book, changing the selections from the Old Testament and adding selections from the New, that Archbishop Parker and others had '*some special* rule of selection in their minds' when they arranged the lessons, and that the Church shows a certain 'wisdom and kindness' in 'ordering' certain passages to be read at certain times (Keble (1838c), 7, 8). It is, therefore, 'very improper to deal with them as if they had been taken at random, or might fitly be changed at will', and Keble warns that any such changes would not be beneficial, but would rather be unwarranted concessions to an 'irreverent presumptuous age' (7, 11).

The subjects of the four saint's day sermons lend themselves to additional calls for 'Adherence to the Apostolical Succession'. The last of the four – Number 60, for St Philip and St James – does not explicitly mention the Succession, but it does call for proper regard for the Apostles from whom it derives. Keble's text is I Cor. 16. 21 – '*If any man love not the* LORD JESUS CHRIST, *let him be Anathema*' (Keble (1839i), 1). He argues that the love Paul has in mind is not just warm feelings or 'sincerity of heart', but also adherence to the doctrines 'first preached by the Apostles' (5). If anyone were to 'swerve from [this] platform of Apostolical doctrine', he would, Keble says, be subject to the 'Apostolic censure' mentioned in his text (5).

The other three sermons deal more explicitly with the Apostolic Succession itself. In the first, for St Matthias' Day, Keble asserts that Jesus 'purposely abstained from nominating St Matthias [as Judas' successor] in His life-time, in order that Christians in all times might understand that the ordained successors of the Apostles are as truly Bishops under Him, as ever the Apostles were themselves' (Keble (1839g), 3). The second sermon commemorates 'the Annunciation of the Blessed Virgin Mary', but Keble's thoughts quickly move from Mary's annunciation to Christ's incarnation, a doctrine which owes its preservation over the centuries 'to the chain of rightly-ordained Bishops, connecting our times with the time of its first promulgation' (Keble (1839h), 3). This is the case, in fact, with all matters of the faith, for a close 'connexion naturally subsists between sound doctrine and apostolical succession in the ministry' (11). Finally, the link between doctrine and the apostolic system is also the focus of the sermon for St Mark's Day. The text is Ephesians 4. 14, '*That we henceforth be no more children, tossed to and fro, and carried about with every wind of doctrine*' (Keble (1839j), 1). Many winds – Lutheran, Reformed, Presbyterian, Congregational, Baptist, Unitarian, Rationalist, Latitudinarian, even Roman – were blowing in Keble's day, and he traces them all to a single source: disparaging of 'the heavenly gifts, conveyed to us by the SPIRIT OF CHRIST through His Apostles', whom He had commissioned to safeguard 'the foundations of our faith' and to see that '*unity of doctrine*' was preserved (2, 3, 14).

Dissent and the Sacraments are also the focus of Number 40, the third of the 'Richard Nelson' tracts.[3] Nelson is troubled because his nephew, Philip Carey, wishes to marry a woman who has never been baptized into the Church of England. Concerned that the 'Church's blessing' cannot 'go along with such an union' (Keble (1838b), 3), Nelson does everything he can to prevent, or at least delay, the wedding. After he finds Philip and the woman's father unreceptive to his warnings about 'the sin and the peril' of living outside of 'Christian marriage', he calls on Philip's mother and tries to convince her that 'wilfully to remain unbaptized is a more grievous sin than the generality of Dissenters...imagine' (5, 10). He even talks with the young woman herself, warning her that if she were to die in her unbaptized state, she would be denied a Christian burial because she had not 'entered into the Church and Kingdom of God' (13). The narrator 'heartily approve[s] of [Nelson's] principles' and ends the conversation by assuring him that his efforts to uphold the Church's authority will not be in vain. 'Take this Scripture home for your comfort', he says, 'that if a man humbly "cast his bread upon the waters," – if he trust his Maker with it in earnest, he shall "find it after many days"' (4, 15).

Keble takes a somewhat different, but no less Tractarian, approach in his last tract, Number 89, *On the Mysticism Attributed to the Early Fathers of the Church*. As the title indicates, the issue here is hermeneutics, not the Sacraments, the liturgy, or Dissent, and the authorities to whom he refers are not the Apostles, but the men of the early Patristic Age who interpreted their teaching. The form of this *Tract* is very different from the others as well. The earlier tracts were short; *No. 89* runs to 186 pages. The earlier ones, with the exception of *No. 52*, are addressed *Ad Populum*; *No. 89* is written for the clergy. In keeping with their intended audiences, the style and argument of the earlier tracts are relatively simple and straightforward, referring often to the Scriptures but assuming little knowledge of biblical languages or early Church authorities. *Tract no. 89*, on the other hand, presents a complex scholarly argument that the Victorian layman probably would not have found accessible. It consists of seven major sections, each of which is further broken down into between 10 and 29 subdivisions. As the subject matter demands, Keble frequently draws upon the works of a long list of the Fathers – Ambrose, Augustine, Basil, Clement of Alexandria, Ignatius, Irenaeus, Jerome, Justin, Origen and Tertullian; his quotes from these figures and the Bible often appear, with no translation provided, in the original Latin and Greek.

In this *Tract*, Keble examines the current notion that 'the Fathers were Mystics, and need not be regarded at all' (Keble (1841), 3). The first half of the phrase is certainly true, as we see in Keble's many examples of symbolic or allegorical interpretations of the Scriptures and the natural world. Some, such as the view that both the sun and the ram Abraham sacrificed in Isaac's place are types of Christ (60, 155), are familiar and straightforward, and therefore rather unobjectionable. Others, however, like Augustine's assertion that 'the five loaves' Jesus multiplied 'are understood to be the five books of Moses' or the idea that 'every rod ... or staff, or sceptre' mentioned in the Old Testament is 'a designed emblem of the Cross' (24, 121), may seem overly imaginative or somewhat forced. One of the more extreme examples of mystical interpretation, which Keble himself admits may seem 'extravagant' to many of his readers, is a Christological interpretation of 318, the number of men Abraham circumcised in Genesis 17. According to an ancient commentary, Abraham performed 'a spiritual and typical action', for the letters that correspond to the ten and the eight are 'a cypher of the sacred Name', while Tau, the alphabetical symbol for 300, is a symbol of the Cross (17–18).

Keble's quarrel, then, is with the second half of the phrase, the idea that the Fathers 'need not be regarded at all' (3). Many saw their interpretations as fanciful, even fraudulent, but Keble regards their approach as perfectly valid – more valid, in fact, than the hermeneutics of his own day. It is valid, Keble asserts, because the mystical method of interpretation 'would appear to be amply authorized by the Scripture itself', and the Fathers are able to suggest symbolic or allegorical readings without doing violence to the 'historical and literal meaning' of the texts (70, 131). The problem, therefore, is not with the early centuries, but rather with the nineteenth. Too many Victorians, Keble asserts, showed a 'want of steady attention and reverential industry' in spiritual matters; when they did study the Scriptures, they were so enamored with 'common sense and practical utility' that they had become blind to the spiritual realities hidden there (4, 39). If his readers would see the sacred texts as the Fathers saw them, they might realize that interpretations 'which might seem at first glance overstrained, fantastic, or unnatural, might turn out in the end to be portions of true Christian wisdom' (6). In short, Keble argues that 'we have much more to learn from the Fathers, than to apologize for in them'; when it comes to biblical interpretation, it is 'at least possible...that the ancients may have been in the right, and we in the wrong' (10, 72).

Much of what I have suggested about Keble's *Tracts for the Times* can also be said of his *Plain Sermons*. The form of the sermons is more homogenous than that of the tracts – they are all six- to ten-page pastoral orations/essays – but they exhibit a similar variety of content. His one hundred and thirty-nine discourses were preached on many different occasions, they are drawn from texts from throughout the Old and New Testaments and they address subjects ranging from biblical characters to the Apostles and martyrs to the final judgment and the Last Days.

The sermons also deal with the same doctrines Keble emphasizes in his tracts. References to the Apostolic Succession appear in several of the sermons, and a passage in one entitled 'Christian Ministers, Tokens of Christ's Presence' sounds as if it could have come directly from *Tract no. 4*. 'Our spiritual life', Keble writes, 'entirely depends on a real, though mysterious, union with [Christ]; to which union the ministration of the Apostles, or of others ordained through them, is, ordinarily speaking, quite necessary' (Keble (1840a), 126). He places a similar emphasis on the Sacraments, asserting that baptism conveys 'Regeneration, Justification, [and] the beginning of Sanctification' and warning that a man who 'thinks he can do well enough without' the Eucharist 'must make up his mind to stay out of Heaven also' (Keble (1842e), 45; (1839b), 98).

If the Church's ministers and Sacraments are to be upheld, it follows that dissent from the Church must also be rejected. Keble offers such rejections in *Tracts nos. 4, 40* and *57*, and in two sermons in Volumes I and II. In 'The Unity of the Spirit', he exhorts his congregation to 'keep the Unity of the Spirit by means of [the] bond of peace' and asserts that 'one especial curse of the Antichristian power…is continual division and separation of what else was united' (Keble (1839l), 206, 208). He echoes this theme in 'The World's Conduct to the Man of Sorrows' when he speaks out against what he calls the 'very dangerous' notion that 'people may choose their own religion according to their own fancy of what will most edify themselves, and the consequent practice of running after strange teachers, without regard or reverence to the warnings of the Church' (Keble (1840e), 64).

Finally, Keble practices in his sermons the 'mystical' method of interpretation he defended in *Tract no.89*. In 'Christian Uprising', he writes that 'If Christians would but observe what they read or hear in the Bible, and what they experience in life…they would find that the whole world around them is…full of divine tokens; every thing almost would put them in mind, more or less directly, of JESUS CHRIST our SAVIOUR, and they would see that GOD meant it so to do' (Keble (1844d), 92). Many of his sermons, accordingly, contain typological readings of the Scriptures and the present day. When he looks into the Old Testament, he sees that Moses and David are forerunners of Christ; that the parting of the Red Sea and the lavers in the Tabernacle prefigure Christian baptism; and that 'Circumcision among GOD's ancient people' is a type of the cross of self-denial that all Christians are called to bear (Keble (1844f), 49; (1839a), 261; (1840c), 93; (1842c), 138; (1844e), 10). When he turns his attention to the New, he makes Paul out to be 'a Type, of the Church or Kingdom of CHRIST in *action* and *warfare*' and every mention of 'bread corn' in the Gospels and Epistles 'a token of something relating to the kingdom of heaven' (Keble (1839k), 249; (1844a), 28). Types can even be found in the world outside the Bible: in an interesting reversal of chronology, Keble places a type later in time than the thing it signifies, stating that the 'Bishops are living types of [Christ's] priestly and pastoral care' (Keble (1839d), 243).

This is not to suggest, however, that the *Plain Sermons* are simply tracts published under other names. Generally speaking, the tracts are addressed to the intellect; they answer the question 'What am I to believe?' The sermons, on the other hand, appeal to the will; they answer the question 'What am I to do?' When Keble addresses matters of doctrine, liturgy, or hermeneutics, his concern is therefore not with the reasons *why* something is true, but rather with how people are to behave *because* it is true. Because the Apostolic Succession is the foundation of the Church, Christians are to pray for and obey 'those whom the HOLY GHOST has set over [them], to be Bishops and

Priests among His people' (Keble (1842b), 295). Because the lessons in the Prayer Book have been arranged and preserved by God, they should listen to the Church when she uses the Book to speak 'a word of comfort or censure, of warning or encouragement' (Keble (1844a), 28). Because 'riches and good things here are but shadows, or tokens, or types of the true', Christians should leave lives of faithful stewardship, making 'up [their] minds to consider none of them as being properly [their] own' (Keble (1846e), 146).

The contrast between the tracts and the sermons is further enhanced by the fact that statements such as these are in the minority; most of the practical applications Keble suggests are not directly tied to a tenet of Anglo-Catholic doctrine. These applications address nearly every aspect of the Christian life: repentance when necessary, followed by obedience, self-denial, reverence, reflection and meditation, prayer and devotion, thankfulness, humility, patience, perseverance and preparation for the last days. They are often stated in rather general terms, which is probably fitting; specific instructions may not be equally relevant to every member of the congregation, so Keble leaves it up to each person to find a way to adapt his exhortations to his or her own life. Some are, however, quite specific. Keble doesn't merely suggest, for example, that people 'pray to God *regularly*' (Keble (1839f), 73); he suggests that they pray at least twice a day, morning and evening, in a place specifically suited to the purpose (Keble (1839e), 79).

Keble often makes his applications more concrete by holding up biblical characters as examples of behavior to be emulated or eschewed. Jesus is, of course, the ultimate positive rôle model, and His followers should strive to follow His example of engaging in 'active practical duties by day, and earnest devotion and meditation by night' (Keble (1846a), 52). Others include Mary, with her remarkable ability to bear tremendous pain; John, a model of 'amiable modesty' and an 'affectionate and teachable mind'; and Joseph, whose prompt action in fleeing to Egypt with the infant Christ teaches us *'Never to put by* GOD'S *warnings, but to act on them, in dutiful Faith, immediately'* (Keble (1844i), 81; (1840d), 289, 90; (1846c), 292). Christians should, Keble says, be like these men and women, and not like Ahab, who was guilty of 'rash impiety'; Pharaoh, who was 'apt to deal lightly with GOD's warnings'; or Judas, who embodies the disasters that can befall when hearts 'grow incurably hard' (Keble (1839c), 198; (1844f), 56; (1844g), 47).

Some of the characters Keble mentions are at least as instructive as examples as they were as types. It is interesting, and perhaps somewhat edifying, to see David as a type of Christ, but people are more likely to change for the better if they also learn, as he did, to truly repent and be restored (Keble (1842a), 153). Similarly, people may grow in contemplation by thinking about how Moses functions as 'a figure of the Law', but they will advance in holiness by emulating his 'loyal and devout spirit' (Keble (1840b), 119; (1846d), 175).

The typological character whom Keble invokes most often as a rôle model is the Apostle Paul. Not only is he an emblem 'of the Church or Kingdom of Christ in *action* and *warfare*', but he is also an exemplar of reverence, contentment, 'firmness, wisdom, courage, self-denial', and self-control (Keble (1844a), 23, 26, 28; (1844j), 210; (1846b), 27). Paul was unusual, to be sure, but he need not be unique. Keble notes that 'if there be any truth in the Bible, it is in the power of every one of us...to be like St Paul, if he will', and he echoes Paul's own words in I Corinthians 11. 1, exhorting his parishioners to 'be followers of St. Paul, as he was of Christ' (Keble (1844c), 279; (1844h), 71).

Keble's sermons, in short, are 'what his favourite Bishop Wilson said sermons should be, "pious instructions to lead men to heaven and save them from hell"' (Lock, 193). They are, moreover, instructions for *all* people, not just those of a particular faction or party. His denominational allegiances were explicit in the *Tracts*, but they tend to remain in the background of the *Sermons*; most of what he says is palatable not only to those affiliated with the Movement, but to believers of all persuasions. Keble's concern, in other words, is that those who hear or read his sermons become not better Tractarians, or even better Anglicans, but simply better Christians.

What is to be gained from a new consideration of Keble's prose such as the one I have suggested here? Additional study of the *Tracts for the Times* needs little justification. They are, after all, the flagship publications of the Anglo-Catholic revival, and our understanding of this revival cannot be complete without the fullest possible grasp of the texts that gave Tractarianism its name. More of a case may need to be made, however, for a study of Keble's sermons, which received little attention when they were first published and have remained largely unstudied for over one hundred and fifty years. I believe there is much to be gained from such a study. Work on the *Plain Sermons* and other addresses can enlarge our understanding of a range of subjects: Keble's hermeneutic and rhetorical strategies, his doctrinal and political views, his approach to parochial work and the cure of souls. They can profitably be studied in their own right, and fruitful comparisons can also be made to his *Tracts for the Times*, the *Letters of Spiritual Counsel and Guidance*, and *The Christian Year*.

Study of the sermons can also help to illuminate an important but too-often overlooked aspect of the Oxford Movement. In 1891, R.W.Church asserted that 'the Tracts were not the most powerful instruments in drawing sympathy to the movement... While men were reading and talking about the Tracts, they were hearing the sermons; and in the sermons they heard the living meaning, and reason, and bearing of the Tracts, their ethical affinities, their moral standard' (Church, 92–93). He was referring specifically to Newman's sermons at St Mary's, but his statement is equally applicable to

Keble's preaching. More recent scholars have echoed Church's views. F. L. Cross, for example, has stated that 'the story of [the sermons] is largely the story of the Revival', and Geoffrey Rowell has called Tractarianism not only 'a great revival of sacramental religion', but 'a great preaching movement' as well (Cross, 8; Rowell, 32). The preaching of the Oxford Movement has been briefly mentioned, but its significance has not been fully developed. There is an immense body of scholarship on the Movement, but only a handful of studies, such as Ronald McKinney's 'Preaching within the Oxford Movement' (*Homiletic and Pastoral Review*, 1985) and Cross' *Preaching in the Anglo-Catholic Revival* (SPCK, 1933), are specifically devoted to the Tractarians' pulpit work.

Much study, then, remains to be done. With nearly three hundred and fifty sermons by seven authors of the *Tracts for the Times*,[4] the *Plain Sermons* are an excellent place to begin a reconsideration not only of Keble's preaching, but of the homiletics of the Oxford Movement as a whole. The time has come to devote further scholarly attention to these important but nearly forgotten documents.

## Notes

[1] For the importance of the application in Victorian homiletics, see Ellison 18–19, 24. Keble's insistence upon it appears throughout his sermons, in statements such as 'the faith which is to justify and save us must run through our whole conduct' and 'Whether men will hear, or whether they will forbear, it is their Pastor's business to urge on them the truth, and their duties; it is their brethren's business, by practising the duties, to show that they believe the Truth' (Keble (1842f), 287; Keble (1844b), 62).

[2] Church-State matters are not entirely absent from the *Plain Sermons*. One takes the funeral of William IV as an occasion for reflecting upon the duties Churchmen 'owe to kings and princes' (Keble (1842d), 72). Another, entitled 'Kings to be Honoured for their Office' Sake', offers much the same argument as 'National Apostasy': Christians must try to advance the government's 'peace, prosperity, and welfare' even when it is guilty of 'encroachments' against the Church (Keble (1839d), 240). Statements like this, however, are relatively rare; a study of the rest of the *Sermons* shows that such issues are not Keble's primary concern.

[3] The first two 'Richard Nelson' *Tracts* (nos. 12 and 22) were written by Keble's brother Thomas. They record conversations that Nelson and the unnamed narrator have on key Tractarian themes such as apostolic succession and the dangers of making unwise alterations to the liturgy and Prayer Book.

[4] With 139 sermons, Keble was by far the most prolific contributor, followed by Isaac Williams (78), Thomas Keble (55), John Henry Newman (36) and E. B. Pusey (20). Robert Francis Wilson and Sir George Prevost had very limited involvement with both projects. Wilson wrote *Tract no. 51* and 7 *Plain Sermons*, Prevost the conclusion to *Tract no. 84* and 12 *Plain Sermons*.

## Works Cited

'Advertisement' to *Plain Sermons, by Contributors to the 'Tracts for the Times'*, I, 1–2.

Beek, W. J. A. M., *John Keble's Literary and Religious Contribution to the Oxford Movement*, Nijmegen: Centrale Drukkerij (1959).

Church, R. W., *The Oxford Movement. Twelve Years, 1833–1845*, ed. G. Best, Chicago: University of Chicago Press, 1970.

Coleridge, J., *A Memoir of the Rev. John Keble, M.A., Late Vicar of Hursley*, 2nd edn, Vol. 2, New York: Pott & Amery, 1869.

Cross, F. L., *Preaching in the Anglo-Catholic Revival*, London: SPCK, 1933.

Ellison, R. H., *The Victorian Pulpit: Spoken and Written Sermons in Nineteenth-Century Britain*, Selinsgrove, PA: Susquehanna University Press, 1998.

Keble, J., 'Adherence to the Apostolical Succession the Safest Course', *Tracts for the Times*, no. 4, new edn, London: Rivington, 1838a.

— 'Richard Nelson, No. III', *Tracts for the Times*, no. 40, new edn, London: Rivington, 1838b.

— 'Sunday Lessons, The Principle of Selection', *Tracts for the Times*, no. 13, new edn, London: Rivington, 1838c.

— 'Christ's Transfiguration', *Plain Sermons*, 1, 259–69, 1839a.

— 'Christian Fear of Relapse into Sin', *Plain Sermons*, 1, 88–98, 1839b.

— 'The Church an Unwelcome Prophet', *Plain Sermons*, 1, 196–205, 1839c.

— 'Kings to be Honoured for their Office' Sake', *Plain Sermons*, 1, 236–247, 1839d.

— 'Moral Benefits of Private Prayer', *Plain Sermons*, 1, 79–87, 1839e.

— 'Our Lord a Pattern of Private Prayer', *Plain Sermons*, 1, 71–78, 1839f.

— 'Sermons for Saints' Days and Holydays: No. 1, St. Matthias', *Tracts for the Times*, no. 52, new edn, London: Rivington, 1839g.

— 'Sermons for Saints' Days and Holydays: No. 2, The Annunciation of the Blessed Virgin Mary', *Tracts for the Times*, no. 54, new edn, London: Rivington, 1839h.

— 'Sermons for Saints' Days and Holydays: No. 4, St. Philip and St. James, *Tracts for the Times*, no. 60, new edn, London: Rivington, 1839i.

— 'Sermons for Saints' Days: No. 3, St. Mark's Day, *Tracts for the Times*, no. 57, new edn, London: Rivington, 1839j.

— 'The Sun of Righteousness', *Plain Sermons*, 1, 248–58.

— 'The Unity of the Spirit', *Plain Sermons* 1, 206–15, 1839l.

— 'Christian Ministers, Tokens of Christ's Presence', *Plain Sermons*, 2, 125–31, 1840a.

— 'Grace Well Used Attracts More Grace', *Plain Sermons*, 2, 118–24, 1840b.

— 'The Presence of God in Holy Places.' *Plain Sermons*, 2, 89–96, 1840c.

— 'Wishing for Christ's Coming', *Plain Sermons*, 2, 285–91, 1840d.

— 'The World's Conduct to the Man of Sorrows', *Plain Sermons*, 2, 58–65, 1840e.

— 'On the Mysticism Attributed to the Early Fathers of the Church', *Tracts for the Times*, no. 89, London: Rivington, 1841.

— 'Acknowledgment of Sin, the Only Comfortable Way', *Plain Sermons*, 4, 152–60, 1842a.

— 'Final Meeting of Pastors and People', *Plain Sermons*, 4, 294–301, 1842b.
— 'The Man after God's Own Heart', *Plain Sermons*, 4, 133–43, 1842c.
— 'On the Death of a King', *Plain Sermons*, 4, 71–80, 1842d.
— 'St. Peter's repentance', *Plain Sermons*, 4, 42–52, 1842e.
— 'Waiting for the Lord', *Plain Sermons*, 4, 285–93, 1842f.
— 'Apostolical Sympathy', *Plain Sermons*, 6, 22–31, 1844a.
— 'Christ and his Church in a Bad World', *Plain Sermons*, 6, 57–65, 1844b.
— 'Christian Energy', *Plain Sermons*, 6, 278–85, 1844c.
— 'Christian Uprising', *Plain Sermons*, 6, 92–100, 1844d.
— 'The Cure of Willfulness', *Plain Sermons*, 6, 9–14, 1844e.
— 'The Hardening of Pharaoh's Heart', *Plain Sermons*, 6, 49–56, 1844f.
— 'The Outcast's Place Filled', *Plain Sermons*, 6, 41–8, 1844g.
— 'Pressing Onward to the Cross', *Plain Sermons*, 6, 66–74, 1844h.
— 'Saint Mary Under the Cross', *Plain Sermons*, 6, 75–83, 1844i.
— 'St. Paul's Joy in Prison', *Plain Sermons*, 6, 204–11, 1844j.
— 'Christ's Own Preparation for His Passion', *Plain Sermons*, 8, 51–59, 1846a.
— 'How to Profit by Saintly Examples', *Plain Sermons*, 8, 25–33, 1846b.
— 'Our Lord's Nursing Father', *Plain Sermons*, 8, 285–92, 1846c.
— 'The Shining of Moses' Face', *Plain Sermons*, 8, 174–84, 1846d.
— 'The True Riches', *Plain Sermons*, 8, 145–50, 1846e.
— 'National Apostasy: Considered in a Sermon Preached in St. Mary's, Oxford Before His Majesty's Judges of Assize on Sunday, July 14th, 1833', London: A. R. Mowbray, 1931.

Lock, W., *John Keble: A Biography*, Boston: Houghton Mifflin, 1893.

*Plain Sermons, by Contributors to the Tracts for the Times*, 10 vols, London: Rivington, 1839–48.

Rowell, G., 'John Keble: A speaking life', *A Speaking Life: John Keble and the Anglican Tradition of Ministry & Art*, ed. C. R. Henery, Leominster, Herefordshire: Gracewing, 1995: 1–66.

# 7

# *LYRA INNOCENTIUM* (1846) AND ITS CONTEXTS

## J. R. Watson

When Keble said that 'if the Church of England were to fail altogether yet it would be found in my parish' (Battiscombe, 303), he was referring to a way of life that he had struggled to maintain since his appointment to Hursley in 1836. One of the principal features of that way of life was the attention given to children in church and in school. In church they were baptised, confirmed, and taught in the Sunday school. In the day school, the vicar himself taught for an hour in the morning and an hour in the afternoon. He is known to have taken a great interest in the bringing up of children, though childless himself, and to have expected from them respect, if not affection: 'I like them very much', he is reported as saying, 'if they would only like me; but they always do much better so long as they are under my wife' (Battiscombe, 178).

The teaching at Hursley, like everything else there, must be seen in a national context, even if it was often at odds with it. During the first half of the nineteenth century, the Church of England had become increasingly concerned with the education of children, both in terms of weekday education and of Sunday schools. Education was seen as necessary to guard against infidelity and social unrest, and to provide the nation with future church-going and respectable citizens, who would be taught to respect others, understand the needs of society, and know the Bible. The importance of religious and civil education was brought to the attention of the Church by discontent and unrest, particularly the Chartist riots of 1839 and 1840, and again in 1842. One answer to such uncomfortable manifestations of disaffection was perceived to be education; but there were widely-differing views about how this was to be implemented. The British and Foreign Schools Society, founded in 1814, existed to promote a general education, without specific religious ties; the National

Society for promoting the education of the poor, founded in 1811, was closely connected with the established Church. Owen Chadwick has described the ideal of the National Society as a village school intimately linked with the local church.

> In those schools all the children should be taught the liturgy and catechism of the Church of England. The parson was expected to hold his traditional place in the education of the people. The village school was 'his' school, the schoolmistress under his direction. (Chadwick, 338)

During the 1840s, when Keble was writing *Lyra Innocentium*, education was much in the minds of parish priests and their bishops, following the setting up by Lord John Russell of a Committee of Education and its system of School Inspectors, led by Sir James Kay-Shuttleworth. Kay-Shuttleworth's inspectors were independent of the Church. Their arrival on the scene was part of a perpetual struggle between Church and State, in which the State was attempting, very slowly and carefully, to gain more control over what went on in schools. Nonconformists, also, had their schools, and there were multiple skirmishes over education, between Church and Dissent, between Established Church and government, between the Protestant Churches and the Catholic Church, and between Churches and government. School management was one problem. The idea that churches might be places under a committee of management, on which the clergyman would have one vote, was seen by some as a threat to the authority of the parish priest. The failure of Sir James Graham's Factory Bill of 1843, with its provision for the education of working children between the ages of eight and thirteen in schools in which the schoolmaster must be a member of the Church of England, was a good example of the controversy which was aroused. The bill infuriated the Nonconformists, made the clergy anxious about State interference, and caused the government, which would have provided the money, to be concerned about the exclusion of good teachers and the spread of Puseyism.

In addition to these national concerns about education, which had repercussions at the parish level in the 1840s, there was also a thriving Sunday-school movement. The first Sunday schools had begun in about 1780, and the Sunday School Union itself was founded in 1803. The motive behind the first schools was educational and philanthropic in the widest sense, but they had begun to acquire a particularly religious purpose in the early years of the nineteenth century. A sermon preached at Belford in Northumberland in 1810, for example, was printed under the title of 'The Usefulness of Sunday schools for the prevention of vice, and the advancement of piety and religious knowledge'. In 1831 there was a Jubilee celebration of fifty years of successful endeavour, looking forward to the future as a golden age of religious instruction.

In Hursley, with Heathcote as the squire and Keble as the vicar, these questions would have been discussed; but it may be imagined that the question of education was stabilized at the parish level, both in the village school and the Sunday school. Controversy would have been excluded, or rather managed out of the way, by the simple expedient of keeping Dissenters out of the village: Heathcote would lease no land to them. It is probable that he was one of those Anglican squires who made it a condition of tenancy that the children of his tenants must be sent to Sunday school. In this 'autocratic kindness', as Barbara Dennis has charitably called it (Dennis, 36) church, school, and Sunday-school combined to promote the values and liturgy of the established Church. The prominent local families, the Moberlys and the Yonges, threw their weight behind Keble's efforts to reform and invigorate what he called in a letter to Newman 'a parish rather settled on its lees' (Dennis, 34). And although he was not always successful, to some outsiders he seemed to have created a little world that was an ideal English parish. Looking back in the 1880s, Thomas Mozley thought that 'When Sir William Heathcote invited Keble to Hursley, he created the most beautiful picture of English society that this century can show' (Mozley, I, 220).

The Yonges, Frances Mary and her daughter Charlotte, taught in the Sunday school, Charlotte teaching the littlest ones when she was only seven years old. She was an exceptional child, whom Keble liked and who loved him in return: her impeccably Anglican girlhood may even have led him into a false idea of what children were really like. So might Frances Mary's *The Child's Christian Year*, published in 1841. The title was an obvious gesture towards *The Christian Year*, which had reached its twenty-first edition in 1841. Yonge may have used her title for various reasons: as a tribute to Keble, or to catch the market, or simply as a descriptive title. Keble contributed a preface to it, in which he spoke of it as:

> One among many humble, but it is trusted not unavailing efforts, which are now being made in different quarters, to bring the whole body of our Church's teaching more into unison with the tone of her Prayer Book, and by consequence with that of the Ancient Universal Church.
> (Yonge, Preface, iii)

Yonge's book followed *The Christian Year* in its ordering, with hymns for every Sunday and for Saints' Days and other great Festivals. It used material from writers such as Joseph Addison, Reginald Heber, Newman, Keble himself, and Isaac Williams. Dissenters, and other such unsuitable persons, did not appear. Charles Wesley, though a loyal Anglican until his death and the author of 'Gentle Jesus, meek and mild', was excluded, perhaps because of his association with the Methodists; and Isaac Watts, whose *Divine and Moral Songs for Children* was the prototype for all such books, was a Dissenter. So he ruled himself out too. The book was indubitably a Heathcote-Keble-Hursley production, bearing on every page the stamp of a particular orthodoxy.

Keble's preface to it may have appeared modest, but it was signed with the most famous initials and parish in early Victorian religion, 'J. K., Hursley'. Its reticence was in keeping with the Oxford Movement emphasis on 'Reserve' in matters of religion, and it is dangerous to read into his tone something of an uneasiness with Frances Mary Yonge's work. Nevertheless, the awkwardness of his prose, and the lukewarm tone, suggest that there was in his mind a worry about the use of hymns in a book for children. He thought that 'the compositions preferred in it are such as may perhaps be found not ill-calculated gradually to raise and purify the standard by which the poor judge of religious poetry':

> The word Hymn, in their minds, has been too long associated with productions both in doctrine and manner very unworthy of that sacred name. It will be something, if in only one parish, we can preoccupy the minds and ears of the young with strains of a somewhat higher mood. (Yonge, Preface, iii–iv)

This reference to the popularity of hymns among the Nonconformists and the evangelical part of the Church of England suggests that Keble wanted to see *The Child's Christian Year* as a counter-influence to Wesley and Watts or to Newton and Cowper. If 'in only one parish', this kind of thing could be kept out, how much better things might be! His ideal went far beyond teaching Anglican hymnody, however. It was that 'young people' should conform to a certain pattern of churchmanship:

> The only Church Reform which can really deserve the name; – as things are at present to speak of such a thing sounds almost like talk in a dream: yet if the well-disposed of our young people were raised up in the tone of the Ancient Church, were taught to sympathize with her, and to look to her for sympathy, the spirit of discipline, it would seem, could not fail to revive, and what are now mere forms would again take to themselves power. (Yonge, Preface, iv–v)

This is not entirely preposterous, as the life of Charlotte Yonge demonstrates, but it presupposes enough well-disposed young people who would allow themselves to be raised up in the tone of the Ancient Church, which suggests a certain detachment from the day-to-day reality of village life. As Julian's *Dictionary of Hymnology* put it, the book was 'more fitted for the children of the educated classes than for the poor' (Julian, 222).

Certainly the hymns were not calculated to be popular. They were for the most part hymns that refer to the Prayer Book, its Collects, Epistles and Gospels, with no concessions to the child's mind. Unlike Ann and Jane Taylor's *Hymns for Infant Minds* of 1809, these hymns were designed for thoughtful and serious instruction Even Frances Mary Yonge seems to have perceived a problem, and felt constrained to defend her practice:

> The first impression on looking over this little book, will probably be that the hymns are too difficult, yet it is hoped they will not be thrown aside without a trial nor without being read in connection with the services of the day, which will often be found to clear up what otherwise appears obscure. (Yonge, Preface, vii)

The invitation to the Sunday-school teacher is plain. These hymns can be expounded in such a way as to make them useful and comprehensible to children. Although she would not have approved of its source, her preface echoes that of John Wesley in *Hymns for Children, and Others of Riper Years* (1790), in which Wesley said that 'There are two ways of writing or speaking to children: the one is, to let ourselves down to them; the other, to lift them up to us.' (Wesley, 1790, in Osborn, vi, 369) Yonge's book unhesitatingly takes the second of these courses.

Keble's book is different again. *Lyra Innocentium* of 1846 stands between *The Child's Christian Year* of 1841 and Cecil Frances Alexander's *Hymns for Little Children* of 1848 (containing 'All things bright and beautiful' and 'There is a green hill far away'), for which Keble also wrote a preface. *Lyra Innocentium*'s sub-title was 'Thoughts in verse on Christian children, their ways and their privileges.' These were to be 'thoughts on children' and not 'thoughts for children'. In the very brief 'Advertisement', Keble wrote:

> According to the first idea of this little work, it would have proved a sort of Christian Year for Teachers and Nurses, and others who are much employed about Children. By degrees it has taken a different shape...

The shape is a significant one, exploring the stages of a child's life, beginning with the newborn baby and ending with the Church. The poems are divided into sections. The first six deal with the child's experiences, beginning with 'Holy Baptism' and 'Cradle Songs', and continuing with 'Early Encouragements', 'Early Warnings', 'Children's Troubles' and 'Children's Sports'. Then follow 'Lessons of Nature', 'Lessons of Grace', and finally 'Holy Places and Things' followed by 'Holy Seasons and Days'. The speaker in the poems is normally in a position of authority – a priest, or a teacher, or an adult – but he or she learns from children too. That is why the epigraph was from Wordsworth, to whom Keble had dedicated his Oxford lectures as Professor of Poetry two years before:

> O dearest, dearest Boy! My heart
> For better lore would seldom yearn,
> Could I but teach the hundredth part
> Of what from thee I learn. ('Anecdote for Fathers')

Wordsworth was echoed in 'The First Smile', the poem which began the second section, 'Cradle Songs':

> But did the smile disclose a dream
> Of bliss that had been his before?
> Was it from heaven's deep sea a gleam
> Not faded quite on earth's dim shore?

This comes from the 'Ode: Intimations of Immortality from Recollections of Early Childhood', in which 'our Souls have sight of that immortal sea/ Which brought us hither'. To Keble, as to Wordsworth (and before him Vaughan) the 'angel-infancy' was perceptible, part of the innocence which he hoped to find in his parish children and which formed such a contrast to the warring factionalism of Victorian religion. It is salutary to remember that the years in which he was writing *Lyra Innocentium* were those of Newman's agonizing before and during his conversion to Rome: in Keble's poems the innocence of children was a sign of another world, the ideal world which he strove to create at Hursley. It was a world in which the children were baptised, grew into infancy, and had early encouragements and early warnings from their teachers (both lay and clerical). They have their troubles and their sports (Keble liked sports, and encouraged village cricket on a Sunday, until he fell foul of the sabbatarians); they have lessons of nature, and lessons of grace; and finally, they are led to 'Holy Places and Things' and 'Holy Seasons and Days'. Wordsworth's child has been thoroughly assimilated into the Anglican parish system. It was part of what Sheridan Gilley has called 'the Victorian Churching of Romanticism'. Keble's children in *Lyra Innocentium* may have begun with Wordsworth but they end up as innocents at the font or in Sunday school, and finally in the most important event of all, confirmation.

The first section, 'Holy Baptism', makes this very clear, for it is based on the Tractarian belief in Baptismal Regeneration, the doctrine which was to be so troublesome in the Gorham case a decade later (see Nockles 93–103). The newborn child is brought by the parents to 'Love's pure spring', and there 'Those wonders o'er again we see/ In saving mystery.' Until Baptism, the child's nature is unformed chaos, like the world before creation:

> All in the unregenerate child
> Is void and formless, dark and wild,
> Till the life-giving holy Dove
> Upon the waters gently move,

And power impart, soft brooding there,
Celestial fruit to bear. ('New Creation')

A newly-baptised child, on the other hand, is close to Jesus as never before and never again. This doctrine allows Keble to write tenderly about the death of a baby, which is, if baptised, 'Just touched with Jesus' light, then lost in joys above' ('Death of the Newly-Baptized').

Babes grow into infants, in the second section, 'Cradle Songs', still 'feeling Heaven so nigh' ('First Waking'), and still having 'recollection deep/ Of Eden bowers' ('Children with Dumb Creatures'). Yet they can go wrong in later life, however innocent they are in the cradle: 'Judas's Infancy' is a reminder that parents need to fear for the welfare of their children as well as dream for them:

O ye who wait with hearts too light
By Font or cradle, fear in time!
O let not all your dreams be bright,
Here in Earth's wayward clime!

From the foul dew, the blighting air,
Watch well your treasure newly won.
Heav'n's child and yours, unharmed by prayer,
May prove Perdition's son.

This protectiveness is continued in the next sections, 'Early Encouragements' and 'Early Warnings'. The first includes prayer, self-examination, confession and absolution; the second includes 'Danger of Praise', 'Fine Clothes', 'Disrespect to Elders' and, horror of horrors, 'Irreverence in Church':

O grief for Angels to behold
Within Christ's awful home!
A child regenerate here of old,
And here for lowliest adoration come,
Forgetting love and fear,
And with bold eye and tone bringing the rude world here!

Like Isaac Watts, Keble holds out the promise of eternal damnation for such. The saintly thrones are set and the doom is prepared

...that without hope or end
The Temple Roof will draw
Down on the irreverent head, there lingering without awe.

This is a reminder that Keble was a stickler for discipline, and that at least one of his parishioners described him as 'a very stern gentleman' (Battiscombe,

178). A few years later, Alexander was to tell children that 'the great God will not love them' if they misbehaved in church. Her directness is shocking, but it is better than Keble's artificial and confused verse (why 'without awe'?).

The ideal of the religious child is pervasive throughout the book, either in poems which criticise bad behaviour, or in those which celebrate a precocious Anglicanism. In 'Repeating the Creed', from the section 'Early Encouragements', Keble lovingly watches the praying child and imagines his imaginings:

> Down be his earnest forehead cast,
> His slender fingers joined for prayer,
> With half a frown his eye sealed fast
> Against the world's intruding glare.
>
> Who, while his lips so gently move,
> And all his look is purpose strong,
> Can say what wonders, wrought above,
> Upon his unstained fancy throng?
>
> The world new-framed, the Christ new-born,
> The Mother-Maid, the cross and grave,
> The rising sun on Easter morn,
> The fiery tongues sent down to save, –

From 'Early Encouragements' and 'Early Warnings', the growing child is shown with 'Children's Troubles' (including loneliness, shyness, bereavement, and orphanhood). In this section, the most unusual poem is 'Fire', in which the child who dies in a fire is invested with 'the Martyr's robe of flame' prepared for it by God ('O stern yet sweet decree!'). The idea of the child martyr may be consistent with a certain religious belief (compare Dylan Thomas's 'A Refusal to Mourn the Death, by Fire, of a Child in London') but it places that theology of suffering before natural human feeling. At the opposite extreme, full of sympathy and sensitivity, is the poem on stammering, in which the child is promised that one day

> ...the unchained voice
> Shall in free air rejoice:
> Thoughts with their words and tones shall meet,
> The unfaltering tongue harmonious greet
> The heart's eternal choice.

'Loneliness' in this section is one of the few places where the child's voice is heard. The child is alone, and afraid of the dark:

> Alone, apart from mother dear
> And father's gracious eye,

> From all the nursery's joyous cheer,
> Nor babe nor playmate by!

* * *

> Scarce dare I lay me down and sleep,
> Lest in half-waking dream
> Dimly all ways to dance and creep
> The forms around me seem.

But the voice of the adult breaks in: 'I bid thee at no shadows start:/ The Upholder is at hand.'

The section on 'Children's Sports' continues this adult's idea of childhood. The sports are 'Gardening', 'May Garlands', 'Sunday Nosegays', 'Dressing Up', 'Pebbles on the Shore', 'Bathing', and (extraordinarily) 'Enacting Holy Rites'. 'May Garlands' will give a flavour of the whole. It begins:

> Come, ye little revellers gay,
> Learners in the school of May,
> Bring me here the richest crown
> Wreathed this morn on breezy down.

But the reader is urged to remember that yesterday's garlands have now withered:

> They are gone – and ye must go,
> Go where all that ever bloomed,
> In its hour must lie entombed.

The lessons of spring are also that

> None of all the wreaths ye prize
> But was nursed by weeping skies.
> Keen March winds, soft April showers,
> Braced the roots, embalmed the flowers.

Therefore, says the moral

> Stern self-mastery, tearful prayer,
> Must the way of bliss prepare.
> How should else Earth's flowerets prove
> Meet for those pure crowns above?

In order to prepare for such a heavenly crown, the growing child needs to take heed of the next two sections, 'Lessons of Nature' and 'Lessons of Grace'. The first of these shows Keble's delight in the natural world, but inexorably draws obvious lessons from it; the second shows him as a teacher. Hursley was a place where 'the emphasis was on teaching, not preaching' (Battiscombe, 176), and poems such as 'David's Childhood' and 'The Boy with the Five Loaves' are versifications of Sunday-school homilies. All of these lead inexorably to the centre of Keble's parochial existence, 'Holy Places and Things', and 'Holy Seasons and Days', in which he celebrates the church and its services, and specific events of the church's year.

Lyra Innocentium is therefore not a book for children. Nor is it 'a sort of Christian Year for Teachers and Nurses'. As the Advertisement says, 'by degrees it has taken a different shape'. That shape is one which sees a child's life as a childless clergyman might see it (one of the poems, 'Looking Westward', begins 'Had I an infant, Lord, to rear/ And mould in Jesus' Law'). Through baptism the child is regenerate: he or she then grows up, through infancy and later childhood, to learn the lessons from the natural world and from the biblical stories. At the centre of the village in which the child lives, the church is a sacred space, into which are – or should be – subsumed all the aspirations and longings for a higher life, one which is more than the day-to-day business of survival.

To this end, Keble stayed at Hursley while the religious controversies of the 1840s raged around him. Lyra Innocentium is a revelation of his reasons for staying. It shuts out the world of controversy; it cares for the parish children, with a limited understanding of a child's needs and a rigorous application of Church teaching; it finds lessons in the beauty of the natural world in such a place – as David L. Edwards has written, 'The whole countryside was an extended church, where nature preached' (Edwards, 80). At the centre of it all was the church itself, where Keble was constant in prayer and in his concern for the rightness of worship, and where 'the children of the parish were his special concern' (Battiscombe, 178). He was assiduous in teaching them, but knew that they did better under his wife. It is not difficult to see why: the insistent concern with the religion of children and their position vis-à-vis the Church ignored much of what makes children children: the necessary element of play which Blake understood so well and which Winnicott has emphasised so productively is represented here only by the rather decorous 'Children's Sports'. In the same way, Hursley managed to avoid much of what was going on in England in the nineteenth century. But there was something valuable and idealistic in its attempt, and Lyra Innocentium, awkward, authoritarian, tender, bigoted, churchy, well-meaning, aspiring, clumsy, obvious, fussy, didactic, shows something of the attractions and the drawbacks of country Anglicanism in the nineteenth century.

## Works Cited

Alexander, H. C. F., *Hymns for Little Children*, London, 1848.

Battiscombe, Georgina, *John Keble, A Study in Limitations*, London: Constable, 1963.

Chadwick, Owen, *The Victorian Church*, Part 1, 3rd edn, London: A & C Black, 1971.

Dennis, Barbara, *Charlotte Yonge (1823–1901), Novelist of the Oxford Movement*, Lewiston, Queenston, Lampeter: Edwin Mellen, 1992.

Edwards, David L., *Leaders of the Church of England, 1828–1944*, London: Oxford University Press, 1971.

Gilley, Sheridan, 'John Keble and the Victorian Churching of Romanticism', *An Infinite Complexity: Essays in Romanticism*, ed., J. R. Watson, Edinburgh: Edinburgh University Press, 1983.

Keble, John, *Lyra Innocentium*, Oxford: Parker, 1846.

Julian, John, *A Dictionary of Hymnology*, London: John Murray, 1892.

Mozley, Thomas, *Reminiscences, Chiefly of Oriel College and the Oxford Movement*, London, 1882.

Nockles, Peter Benedict, *The Oxford Movement in Context*, Cambridge: Cambridge University Press, 1994.

Wesley, John, 'Preface to Hymns for Children' (1790), in Osborn, G., *The Poetical Works of John and Charles Wesley*, London: Wesleyan–Methodist Conference Office, 1868–72).

Wesley, John and Charles, *Hymns for Children*, Bristol: Farley, 1763 (reprinted with Preface, 1790).

Winnicott, D. W., *Playing and Reality*, London: Tavistock, 1971.

Yonge, Frances Mary, *The Child's Christian Year* (1841), 4th edn, Oxford: Parker, 1846.

# PART III

Influence and Resistance: Literary Heirs and Successors

# 8

# 'HEALING RELIEF...WITHOUT DETRIMENT TO MODEST RESERVE...' KEBLE, WOMEN'S POETRY AND VICTORIAN CULTURAL THEORY

## Emma Francis

In 1993, contained within her landmark study *Victorian Poetry: Poetry, Poetics and Politics*, Isobel Armstrong published the essay which marked the commencement proper (after several valiant false starts) of the project which, perhaps more than any other, has energised, revolutionized and problematised Victorian studies over the past decade – the rediscovery and revaluation of the full range of poetry written by British and Irish women in the nineteenth century. Much as the personnel Armstrong discusses – Letitia Landon and Felicia Hemans, Dora Greenwell and Jean Ingelow, Christina Rossetti, Adelaide Anne Procter, Amy Levy, Mathilde Blind, Augusta Webster and others – have been extensively pursued in the intervening decade, perhaps the full implications of one of the most important theoretical and methodological questions her essay raises have yet to be explored. Armstrong argues that if the huge diversity of nineteenth-century women's poetry can be seen as a 'tradition', it is in the respect that it is an 'expressive' tradition.

Pointing to the way in which in different ways across the period, women's poetry is concerned with the themes of 'movement beyond the boundary, with escape, with ex-patriotism and return [and is] deeply preoccupied with displacement' (Armstrong, 336), Armstrong traces the work which metaphors of breathing and breath, air and musical vibration do 'as the representation of the imprisoned life of emotion seeking to escape or to take form' (Armstrong,

337). She demonstrates that women poets essentially 'invent' the dramatic monologue form, a decade or more before Robert Browning. Women poets, in the main, use the form not to gain access to masculine subjectivity and its supposed cultural authority, but to represent the subjectivities of other women. These are often marginal, dangerous, 'sinful' subjectivities, of the prostitute, the child-killer, the raped or abused woman, experiences which demand exposure, yet which challenge and confound Victorian epistemology. The mask becomes one of the quintessential expressivist strategies of women's poetry throughout the nineteenth century, used to reveal and conceal, to encounter and to distance female subjectivity. Armstrong argues that the Victorian woman's poem represents an overdetermination of a general tendency within Victorian poetics. It is, profoundly, the 'double poem', in which a limpid, disciplined lyricism often conceals highly charged, disturbing meaning underneath (Armstrong, 326).

Armstrong is committed to developing an aesthetic account of women's poetry, as a corrective to the tendency she identifies within much late twentieth-century feminist criticism of this work, of attempting to mine the poetry for explicit feminist polemic which is recognisable within modern-day terms. Modern-day critics, she argues, 'retrieve the protest, but not the poem' (Armstrong, 319). Ten years after Armstrong's essay, even in the wake of a great deal of fine work over this period on nineteenth-century women poets, feminist criticism has found it curiously difficult to shake this tendency, of focusing largely on political – that is feminist polemical – content. It is still paying less attention than it should to the way in which the poetry is in dialogue with and determination of the cultural politics and poetic theory of its period.

Of course, the two issues, aesthetics and politics, feminism (or the lack of it) and form are intimately bound together, and this is why it is so vital to re-open Armstrong's question of the relationship of the expressive theory of poetry, and Keble as a central proponent of that theory, with nineteenth-century women's poetry. As Emma Mason argues elsewhere in this volume, following Armstrong's insights critics of both Romantic and Victorian women's poetry now consider a discussion of feeling and sentiment and the metaphors which carry them essential. Affect, in short, has become politically and intellectually significant. However, as Mason points out at the start of her essay, 'how such feeling was rendered and also what such feeling constituted, remain unresolved.' Equally, the contours in the map of nineteenth-century cultural theory have yet to be fully redrawn to take account of the significance and prominence of Keble and expressive theory.

This volume is testimony to the increasing recognition of Keble's importance to nineteenth-century cultural theory. As part of this, the role his account of poetry played in the legitimation and development of a distinct mission for women's poetry is at last receiving sustained attention. The work of G. B. Tennyson, in his seminal *Victorian Devotional Poetry* some quarter-century ago, established the role of Keble's legacy for Christina Rossetti. Tennyson positions Rossetti as a late Tractarian poet, whose adoption of Keble's aesthetic is intelligible in terms of her profound commitment to the doctrinal basis of High Anglicanism. This line of enquiry is growing in the study of Rossetti and Adelaide Anne Procter, for example. Gill Gregory's recent monograph study of Procter places considerable emphasis on her religious affiliations and her own understanding of her aesthetic as doctrinally and denominationally driven and accountable. Equally, recent work on Rossetti, including that emanating from feminist critics, has been characterised by greater emphasis upon her later, devotional writings, which were largely ignored or glossed over as an embarrassment in the initial recuperation of her poetry in the 1980s. Mason's study of Dora Greenwell, to be published later this year, also establishes the importance of Keble's aesthetic for a poet who was working at the same time and in some respects in the same aesthetic space yet was some way distant from High Anglican orthodoxy, a line of enquiry she extends in her essay in this collection.

However, I want to approach Keble's relationship with the poetry in a slightly different way, not primarily via individual poets and poems, but by looking at the permeation of the terms of his arguments, of the claims he makes about the nature and power of poetry, into the critical discourse, into some of the literary theory and literary history, produced in the middle two quarters of the nineteenth century, which explored the role and permission of women's poetry within Victorian society, its 'proper sphere and powers of usefulness', as one critic whom I will discuss puts it in her 1842 study (Stodart). This nineteenth-century criticism, often contained in extensive and lengthy volumes of commentary or heavily annotated anthologies, has thus far not been systematically explored. I think it is important to look at this material and to take it seriously, as it is the site for the development of a gendered cultural theory and of a legitimation of women's poetry, which is unique in the modern period.[1] Reading this contemporaneous criticism allows us to construct an account of Victorian women's poetry and its relationship with Victorian culture which is very different from the story generated by the first wave of Anglo-American feminist criticism in the late 1970s and 1980s, that women's poetry was discouraged or even prohibited by nineteenth-century patriarchy (see Gilbert and Gubar). Even the vast work of recovery of women poets of the period, undertaken over the past decade, which has made clear the enormous amount of poetry written by women in the nineteenth century, has not fully dismantled this repressive hypothesis. Refocusing on Keble's poetic theory, understanding the arguments he made about the role of the poet and the relationship of poetry with society and examining the use made of these arguments by the theorists of women's poetry is key to this dismantling. Sometimes these writers are in violent opposition to his theological affiliation. The things which Keble said about poetry, the role he imagined for the poet in society had a resonance for women's poetry and its critics far beyond strict doctrinal or even predominantly religious concerns. Therefore this essay has much less to say about God than perhaps any other in this volume. The obscuring of Keble's central role in nineteenth-century cultural politics has hindered more than just the study of women's poetry, of course. But in spite of his almost complete silence on women's poetry – the only woman poet mentioned in *Praelectiones Academicae* is Sappho and she is discussed only briefly – I believe that without a proper appreciation of Keble we will continue to misunderstand several aspects of the role and the extent of the legitimation of the Victorian woman poet.

\*\*\*

Keble, as G. B. Tennyson wryly pointed out, did himself few favours in relation to posterity. *Praelectiones Academicae*, the series of forty lectures he gave during his tenure as Oxford Professor of Poetry (1832–1841) which constitute the fullest and most systematic explication of his poetic theory, were delivered and published initially in Latin, and did not become generally available in the vernacular until the early twentieth century in the translation of E. K. Francis (Keble, 1912). Of course, Keble did allow access to his theory in English. Mason argues here that Keble's 1838 review of J. G. Lockhart's *Life of Sir Walter Scott* was Christina Rossetti's introduction to his theory. This publication, within the *British Critic*, was culturally prominent enough to be regarded as a more general point of access for women and for other readers who might not have heard, or been able to read, *Praelectiones Academicae*. However, it would be correct to say that Keble's choice to cloak the most substantial and prominent statement of his thesis with the modest veil of a dead language has created a barrier to the appreciation of its centrality to nineteenth-century cultural theory. It has been less available in the process of the reconstruction of the cultural politics of women's poetry than it should have been.

Keble's poetic theory, as many have pointed out, is fundamentally indebted to and revisionary of Romanticism. Keble is committed to a Wordsworthian account of the crucial role of emotion and its overflow within poetry. Yet Keble moralizes, privatizes, psychologizes, we might almost say Victorianizes, Wordsworth. Rather than celebrating, as the Preface to *Lyrical Ballads* does, the moment of spontaneous overflow, Keble valorizes the disciplines and restrictions which poetic language places upon emotion. Expressivism is a dialectical theory in which emotion is dependent upon the stylistic and formulaic constraints of poetic language to bring it into representation.

> Poetry is the indirect expression in words, most appropriately in metrical words, of some overpowering emotion, or ruling taste, or feeling, the direct indulgence of which is somehow repressed...the conventional rules of metre and rhythm may evidently have the effect of determining in some one direction, the overflow of sentiment and expression, wherewith the mind might otherwise be oppressed...the rules may be no less useful, in throwing a kind of veil over those strong and deep emotions, which need relief, but cannot endure publicity. (Keble (1838), 6, 17)

For Keble, as for Wordsworth, emotion is 'natural', but, departing from his Romantic precursor, Keble argues that a tendency to rein in, to reserve, to conceal this emotion, in short to be 'shamed' by emotion, is an equally strong impulse.

> We may note too that men so wrought upon...by human emotions...very often exhibit excessive shamefacedness, being overquick and sensitive in their sense of shame as in everything else. (Keble (1912), 20)

Poetry, for Keble, is the solution to these conflicting impulses: it 'gives healing relief to secret mental emotion, yet without detriment to modest reserve, and while giving scope to enthusiasm, yet rules it with order and due control' (Keble (1912), 22).

It is important to emphasize that for Keble these aspects of modesty, indirection and 'shame' are not indicative of political or aesthetic inferiority. Rather it is precisely these characteristics which Keble spends the majority of *Praelectiones Academicae* tracing at length, and celebrating, in the work of those whom he identifies as 'primary poets' – Homer, Pindar and Aeschylus, Dante, Spenser and Shakespeare. Moreover, he explicitly declares that this response of 'shame', the impulse to control and conceal emotion, is the mark of a fully developed civilization. Whereas the 'savage' will cry out unimpeded, the civilized and 'those of a more delicate sensibility' will be amenable to the disciplinary control of 'shame' and release their emotion under strictly controlled circumstances, 'especially such as "live the lives of freeborn citizens in a happy country", conditions which, as Cicero justly notes of the citizens of Rome, "give men's minds a more delicate sensibility"' (Keble (1912), 20).

This linkage of the modesty and indirection of expressive poetics with Classical Republicanism is indicative of the politically and aesthetically central role Keble envisages for this poetics. That this perspective on the politics and poetics of modesty has largely eluded feminist criticism until now goes a long way to explaining the problems which it had and continues to have with some of the strategies of Victorian women's poetry. Sandra Gilbert and Susan Gubar in their seminal *Madwoman in the Attic*, identified what they term an 'aesthetics of renunciation' in the work of Christina Rossetti (539–80). They point, largely accurately, to Rossetti's refusal explicitly to repudiate patriarchy, her emotional reserve and control, her disciplining of challenging insights inside tight, sparse, lyric structures. However, working from a twentieth-century politics and cultural theory, they go on to paint a picture of this as a sign of Rossetti's disablement, repression and fractured poetic identity. Quite simply, the restoration of Keble to our account of mainstream nineteenth-century cultural theory collapses this repressive account.

In her recent study, *Women's Poetry and Religion in Victorian England* Cynthia Scheinberg has argued that Keble's shifting of the account of the relationship between religion and poetry was crucially enabling for women poets in the nineteenth century. Scheinberg argues that Keble repudiates an account of 'the poet as prophet' in favour of one of the poet as 'handmaid of poetry', which she claims enabled women to insert themselves into poetic identity more easily (Scheinberg, 18–19). Egocentric didacticism was replaced by an account of poetry as subservient to a higher authority within devotional lyric. I think that this observation is correct, but I would go further and argue that the permission which Keble's notions of modesty, indirection, concealment and 'shame' as the currency and essence of poetry granted to women poets has implications far wider than the field of explicitly religious poetry. Expressive theory dovetailed with the work of explicit articulation of the cultural 'mission' of the woman poet, and with the discourses of what came to be organized under the heading of 'woman's mission', which is the basic work of this theoretical and critical material. As Joseph Bristow and other have pointed out, great anxiety assailed the poetic identities and mission of the early Victorian male poet (Bristow, 1987). By contrast, women poets and their critics maintained a strong conviction of the moral and social importance of women's poetry, which increased rather than decreased after 1830. The legitimation of this mission was made on the basis, precisely, of gender. It was argued that women poets offered a different vision and, specifically, that their poetry spoke from an indirect relationship with the political. This criticism does not maintain, as has sometimes been assumed and claimed within contemporary feminist criticism, that women poets were entirely excluded from the public sphere. Rather the argument is that women's poetry enacts a socially enobling performance of the virtues of the private sphere inside the public sphere. So-called 'private' emotions and virtues, emanating from and superintended by femininity are, in a sense, crucial elements of the 'public' sphere. The theorists working within this dialectic make arguments directly analogous to Keble's understanding of the power of modesty, indirection and concealment in their arguments for the power and importance of women's poetry.

Mary Ann Stodart, who wrote one of the most extensive works within this genre, *Female Writers, Thoughts on Their Proper Sphere and Powers of Usefulness* (1842), uses expressivist terms to secure her case for poetry as the 'proper sphere' of the woman writer. From Virginia Woolf onwards, feminist critics have assumed that that since the later eighteenth century the novel has been the literary form granted to women by patriarchal culture, assumed both by themselves and by men to be more amenable and appropriate to female talents and concerns because its mainstay is matters in which women are supposed to be expert – the mechanics of 'private', emotional and domestic life. Poetry, by contrast, twentieth-century critics have argued, deals with the universal and 'public', and is thus unfitting, or at least uncomfortable, for women to attempt. Stodart produces a precise reversal of the terms of this argument, stating that for women it is, in fact, the novel which is the improprietous form, fraught with a peril of self-revelation that she figures as something like symbolic soliciting:

> [O]ne stronghold of women, in fictitious narrative is her knowledge of the human heart. Her sphere of observation is limited, and it is from herself that she learns to know others. Now in this laying bare of the workings of the inward heart there is a peculiar inconvenience for the delicate and sensitive woman. It is like proclaiming to the public that which passes within her own breast. It is more – it is placing a glass window in her bosom that every passerby may look in and see the workings of her heart. It is needless to point out the obvious inconveniences, every woman of ordinary delicacy of feelings instinctively perceives them, and like the mimosa plant, shrinks away from danger. (134)

In this extraordinary metaphor of visual anxiety, Stodart secures the claims of women to poetry on the grounds of propriety as well as ability. She argues that because of its preoccupation with the more elevated and universal category of 'truth', poetry bypasses the difficulties for women of immodest personal display which fiction, with its dependence on more debased details of 'fact', gives rise to. Stodart does not cite Keble by name, possibly because as a fiercely anti-Catholic, Low-Church Protestant she would have regarded his doctrinal affiliations with suspicion. J. H. Newman was, after all, during the 1840s arguing for the compatibility of Anglican doctrine with the Church of Rome. Indeed, Stodart believed that it was vital to educate women in theology in order that they would be alert to the wiles of popery in all its forms. Her text celebrates the work of several women writers who were instrumental in advancing the cause of Low-Church Protestantism (80–1). But it is clear that Stodart's study, published the year Keble stepped down from his post at Oxford, is committed to the notions of modesty, concealment and indirection central to expressive poetics. Stodart's insistence that it is poetry, rather than the novel which is the 'proper sphere' of the woman writer becomes more intelligible when we realize that she was not revolting against patriarchal hegemony, as Gilbert and Gubar might suggest, but was simply affiliating her thesis with a dominant poetic theory of her period, giving Keble's account of poetry as a concealing 'veil' of representation a specifically gendered inflection.

Jane Ysgafell Williams, another important critic, who produced what is probably still the most chronologically extensive account of British women's literature up to the mid-nineteenth century, also makes use of Keble's account of the economy of restraint and discipline of emotion in the production of poetry. Her mammoth text, *The Literary Women of England* (1861) in some 560 pages traces a history of women's writing from antiquity to 1860, culminating in an extended study of the career of Felicia Hemans, whom Williams regards as the epitome of what women's poetry could achieve. Williams works with an account of the generation of poetry which is at once deeply indebted to Keble's terms and explicitly feminized. She locates the emotional centre of Hemans' life and the dynamic inspiration of her poetry in her relationship with her mother. The death of her mother was, according to Williams, the crucial transition point in her poetic career, precisely because it generated a critical mass of emotion which could be disciplined to produce her finest work.

> Her mother's death, casting back upon herself many feelings which would otherwise have ebbed away secretly and safely, probably led afterwards to that fervid utterance of her very soul in poetry, which tended for a time to transform an innocuous and pleasing occupation into an exhausting and health-destroying process. (Williams (1861), 440)

In this account, a dangerous build-up of the affective state necessary for the production in the poetry, a stoppage in the channels by which emotion would, under normal circumstances, have leaked 'safely' and unpoetically away, propels Hemans into a new phase of creative intensity. It is caused by a profound psychic and emotional investment in another woman and it is modeled directly on the dialectic of restraint and overflow, concealment and expression which Keble outlines. It is worlds away from the 'anxiety of authorship' which the Anglo-American feminist account of Gilbert and Gubar envisages and it is worth dwelling on the very different places in which the two accounts locate the points of stoppage, of release and of the danger inherent in the emotional economics of poetic creation. The tortures which Hemans suffers in Williams' version are the result of her loss of her mother, they have nothing to do with men. They work to facilitate rather than suppress her poetry, they provide the crucial dialectic of enabling restraint – Keble's point of 'shame' – which allows emotion to build up to the point when it can be expressed in more and more intense poetry.

By contrast, Gilbert and Gubar explore an equation of women, poetry, emotion and restraint which is quite different. In their story, emotion is the pain inflicted by the oppression and abuse Judith Shakespeare and her literary daughters suffer at the hands of men. The stoppage occurs at the point of creativity. Judith dies because she is prevented from releasing the poetry within her by a patriarchal demand for modesty and restraint, which prevents and completely blocks, rather than creating poetry:

> locking women into 'the common sitting room' that denies them individuality, it is a murderous phantom that if it didn't actually kill 'Judith Shakespeare', has helped to keep her dead for hundreds of years, over and over again, separating her creative spirit from 'the body which she has so often laid down' (Gilbert and Gubar, 188).

This brief sketch of the way in which some nineteenth-century critics of women's poetry engage with Keble's terms obviously serves merely to open the question of his importance for the history of women's poetry. But his importance to this history is fundamental. Indeed, there were those outside of the discussion of the role and status of women's poetry within the nineteenth century who spotted that Keble's work explored a vindication of the relationship between the feminine and poetry. John Shairp made this point in his essay on Keble, published in 1866:

> True, [in Keble's poetry] the woman's heart everywhere shows itself. But as it has been said that in the countenance of most men of genius there is something of a womanly expression not seen in the faces of other men, so it is distinctive of true poetic temper that it ever carries the woman's heart within the man's. (96)

His account of the way in which restraint, modesty, shame and indirection, terms which during the Victorian period became increasingly inflected with femininity, might be understood as poetically enabling, as indicative of a central rather than a marginal civic and aesthetic position, as the key to rather than the death of creativity, is an important corrective to the repressive hypothesis which still has large influence on the reading of women's poetry.

Keble, in short, gives us a more sophisticated account of power within poetic language. Our understanding of nineteenth-century cultural theory, in all its permutations, is dominated by Matthew Arnold. Arnold's account of the aggressive clash of Hellenism and Hebraism, perhaps, has overshadowed Keble's more dialectical, expressive model. We must investigate in much greater depth the extent to which nineteenth-century women poets and their critics availed themselves of Keble's theory. This investigation will be part of the reconstruction of Keble's importance, and substantiate his claim to a place beside Arnold as a point of reference in Victorian cultural theory and politics.

## Note

[1] My study, *Women's Poetry and Woman's Mission: British Women's Poetry and the Sexual Division of Culture, 1824–1894*, will discuss this body of criticism in more detail.

## Works Cited

Armstrong, Isobel, *Victorian Poetry: Poetry, Poetics and Politics*, London: Routledge, 1993.

Bristow, Joseph, *The Victorian Poet: Poetics and Persona*, New York, London, Sydney: Croom Helm, 1987.

Gilbert, Sandra and Gubar, Susan, *The Madwoman in the Attic: The Woman Writer and the Nineteenth-Century Literary Imagination*, New Haven and London: Yale University Press, 1979.

Gregory, Gill, *Adelaide Anne Procter*, Aldershot: Ashgate, 1999.

Keble, John, 'Memoirs of the Life of Sir Walter Scott by J.G.Lockhart', *British Critic* (October 1838).

— *Occasional Papers and Reviews*, ed. E. B. Pusey, Oxford and London: James Parker and Co., 1877.

— *Keble's Lectures on Poetry 1832–1841*, trans. Edward Kershaw Francis, 2 Vols, Oxford: Clarendon Press, 1912.

Mason, Emma, *Nineteenth-Century Women Poets*, Writers and Their Work, London: Northcote, 2004, forthcoming.

Scheinberg, Cynthia, *Women's Poetry and Religion in Victorian England*, Cambridge: Cambridge University Press, 2002.

Shairp, John, *John Keble: An Essay on the Author of the 'Christian Year'*, Edinburgh: Edmonston and Douglas, 1866.

Stodart, M. A., *Female Writers: Thoughts on Their Proper Sphere and Their Powers of Usefulness*, London: R.B. Seeley and W. Burnside, 1842.

Tennyson, G. B., *Victorian Devotional Poetry: The Tractarian Mode*, Cambridge, Mass.: Harvard University Press, 1980.

Williams, Jane Ysgafell, *The Literary Women of England*, London: Saunders and Otley, 1861.

# 9

# 'HER SILENCE SPEAKS': KEBLE'S FEMALE HEIRS

## Emma Mason

That nineteenth-century women's poetry forged, and is founded on, an expressive tradition is a claim that, since Isobel Armstrong's celebrated *Victorian Poetry*, might be made almost without question. Allusions to fountains, streams, sentiment, gush and feeling are rarely missed within criticism of both Romantic and Victorian women's poetry written both then and in our own period of scholarship. Both the ways in which such feeling was rendered and also what such feeling constituted, however, remain unresolved. The hymnal strains of Isaac Watts and the Wesleys, the associationist theories of David Hartley, the benevolent philosophies of Shaftesbury and David Hume, and the profound exploration of feeling Wordsworth enacted in his poetry and critical prose all impact on the way many eighteenth and nineteenth-century women poets exhibited emotion in their work. Yet, as Emma Francis also notes in this volume, the influence of John Keble on those women writing verse later in the century remains largely unexplored, his relationship with Charlotte Yonge commanding those fascinated by the preacher's relationship to women's writing. His shaping of an at once restrained and intensely emotional poetics is nevertheless fundamentally central to the poetry of several nineteenth-century women poets – Dora Greenwell, Cecil Frances Alexander, Caroline Leakey, Bessie Parkes, Adelaide Anne Procter – wary of their assumed proclivity to extreme sentimentalism. Writing in the shadow, not simply of Wordsworth or Tennyson, but the emotive Charlotte Smith, Letitia Landon and above all, the phenomenally popular Felicia Hemans, later nineteenth-century women poets struggled to work free of the identity their predecessors had forged: that of the 'poetess'. The ardent Hemans, for example, was regarded as a poetess because she wrote from what was perceived as a feminine space, sensitive to feeling and designed to encourage her readers into a gentle and consolatory state of weeping. As one of Adelaide Anne Procter's few twentieth-century commentators declares of her subject:

> She appears to have taken over where Felicia Hemans left off, as the sweetly feminine and refined purveyor of pretty sentiments in verse, the graceful, tender poetess, the mainstay of bijou almanacs, birthday books and musical evenings. (Maison, 636)

While Hemans undoubtedly wrote what was considered some of the best poetry of the nineteenth century, as attested to by Wordsworth, William Gladstone and Tennyson, her many imitators failed to hit the pitch her demonstrative poetics reached. The Countess of Blessington even felt moved to write a scathing account of such deriders in the form of her own poem, 'Stock in Trade of Modern Poetesses' (1833), accusing the poetess of issuing nothing more than 'Bursting tear and endless sigh – / *Query* – can she tell us why?' (ll.25–26). No wonder Cecil Frances Alexander, famed for her hymns, 'All Things Bright and Beautiful' and 'There is a Green Hill Far Away,' and commented on also in this volume by J. R. Watson, found excessive displays of feeling in poetry vulgar and inappropriate. As her husband and editor, William Alexander declared:

> Sentimentality is either an ostentatious display of ill-regulated emotion or a theatrically made claim to a feeling which we really do not possess. To be treated as a poetess on the pose, and honoured by a scented *douche* of 'gush,' was abhorrent from [Cecil's] love of perfect sincerity. (W.Alexander, xviii)

So too did Procter's distinguished editor, Charles Dickens, distance her from such sentimentality, insisting that 'she would far rather have died without seeing a line of her composition in print, than that I should have maundered about her as "the Poet," or "the Poetess"' (Dickens, xxvii). For Dickens, writing in the 1870s, the roles of poet or poetess are problematic, each owing what he perceives as an awkward debt to a 'feminine' form of expression. This, argued William Michael Rossetti, was what had made Hemans the poet she was, claiming as he did for her an almost pure sensibility evoked in her poetry through 'sentiment without passion, and suffering without abjection' (Rossetti, xi). Yet he also admitted that Hemans had successfully regulated her representation of feeling by implementing a 'deep religious sense.' This is the sense that Keble was to inherit from Hemans and Wordsworth, his *Lectures on Poetry* (1832–41) dedicated to the latter and founded on both the possession of a 'full heart' and its correct religious management through what he called the 'stay of passion' (Keble, I, 19).

This essay will explore the attraction Keble's regulated poetics held for nineteenth-century women poets, already assumed to be inherently of full heart and designated the guardians of right and religious feeling throughout the period. While John Ruskin notoriously warned women to refrain from theological inquiry, Keble perhaps unwittingly forged a path on which women could explore this priestly and often esoteric realm, albeit in disguise as lady hymn-writers assumed to be meek and clichéd. Indeed the refusal by women poets to stray into any obvious originality in their verse adhered strictly to a Tractarian dislike for it, and does not reveal a group of writers curbed by religious language. The latter point was a criticism once flung at Christina Rossetti, the most well-known of Keble's heirs – who is not dealt with here simply because much recent work has already established her as an exceptionally intricate and aesthetically well-tuned theological thinker and versifier.[1] A great reader of the *British Critic*, the back issues of which were kept at her church library, Rossetti would certainly have encountered Keble's 1838 review of J. G. Lockhart's *Life of Sir Walter Scott*, wherein the central tenets of the Latin *Lectures* were outlined in English.[2] It is here, for example, that Keble straightforwardly declared: 'Poetry is the indirect expression in words, most appropriately in metrical words, of some overpowering emotion, or ruling taste, or feeling, the direct indulgence whereof is somehow repressed' (Keble (1838), 6). Standing as the foundational argument for the *Lectures*, this statement, echoed in John Henry Newman's essay 'Poetry' (1829) and Isaac Williams' *Tracts* addressing reserve (1838–40), held an alluring appeal for the woman poet, already assumed to be an individual constituted of bound emotion. The consequences of such an appeal for Greenwell, Alexander, Leakey, Parkes and Procter are outlined below in Part II; in Part I, we will attend to Keble's *Lectures* themselves, observing specifically those aspects of his poetics by which these women poets were so captivated.

I

It is often noted that for the Oxford Movement, poetry was synonymous with religious truth and offered believers the best, and most appropriate, way of communicating and understanding their faith. Romantic poetic theory had already established the abstract and supernatural, even sacramental, element within poetry and Keble in particular extended this work by delineating the spontaneous overflow of feeling as a spiritual process (Keble, I, 54). Poetic feeling did not simply explode for Keble, being rather the product of a build-up of pressure or tension that contained such force within a religious frame. To explore the manner by which such feeling might be cautiously expressed, Keble set out to write a series of lectures on the subject, so fulfilling his role as Oxford Professor of Poetry which he occupied from 1831 to 1841. His *Lectures on Poetry* were delivered to the University between 1832 and 1841, and aimed, he wrote to John Taylor Coleridge, nephew of the poet, 'to consider poetry as a vent for overcharged feelings, or a full imagination' (Prickett, 281). This Wordsworthian notion of poetry as overflow had indeed been introduced to Keble by John Taylor, who had brought with him to Corpus Christi, where they had been undergraduates together, copies of both the *Lyrical Ballads* and Wordsworth's *Poems in Two Volumes* (Martin, 73). Wordsworth's impact on Keble deserves a separate discussion, but it is notable that many of the women most influenced by the preacher were also drawn to the laureate. Greenwell, for example, was the intellectual confidant of William Knight, the most prominent and respected of Wordsworth's Victorian editors; and Procter was introduced to the poet via her father, Barry Cornwall. While there is much that differs in the poetic theories of Keble and Wordsworth, both focus on poetic feeling as a restorative and healing faculty available to those able to access or develop their own emotions. As Keble argues:

> Poetry properly and truly so called can only be comprehended with a mind full to overflowing, and, consequently, by men whose feelings are so strong that they cannot suppress them and yet shrink from wholly revealing them. (Keble, I, 57–8)

Within the *Lectures*, Keble is preoccupied with the expression and suppression of emotion as a way of addressing three issues: first, he wanted to assert, prefiguring Arnold, that poetry and religion were united by the emotive effect they could produce within individuals; second, he sought to illustrate how this effect was ultimately consolatory and soothing, producing those whom it affected as model religious citizens; and third, he wanted to consider ways by which such an effect could be schooled so as not to produce too much feeling, which might send the individual into derangement or mental illness. For Keble, these three points are bound together by the subject of feeling, flagged up by continual references to the importance of a 'full heart,' a metaphor indicating the capacity of the individual to experience, control and shape emotion into a conductor through which 'Divine wisdom' may enter (Keble, I, 62). All of this can best be done, Keble suggests, through poetry itself, that which fills up the heart with tender feelings as it guides and composes the mind to worship and prayer (Keble, II, 482–3). The Prayer Book and Gospels are also essentially poetic in this sense, full of balmy truth and highlighting the potentially sacramental nature of human experience. How, then, does poetry infuse the reader with such feeling? For Keble, the answer lies in poetry's rhythm and measured sound; its ability to renew memories; and its role in fuelling the imagination. In these processes, he argues in the first *Lecture*, poetry:

exhibits, assuredly, wonderful efficacy in soothing men's emotions and steadying the balance of their mind. For while we linger over language and rhythm, it occupies our minds and diverts them from cares and troubles: when, further, it gives play to Imagination, summons before us the past, forecasts the future, in brief, paints all things in the hues which the mind itself desires, we feel that it is sparing and merciful to the emotions that seethe within us, and that, for a while, we enjoy at least that solace which Dido once fruitlessly craved, to her woe: 'a transient grace / To give this madness breathing-space.' (Keble, I, 21–22)

Poetry does not simply offer relief here, but is defined *as* relief, calming and regenerating the harried and heartbroken, 'a kind of medicine divinely bestowed upon man: which gives healing relief to secret mental emotion, yet without detriment to modest reserve' (I, 22). The last clause of this statement concludes Keble's first lecture in order to highlight the importance of humility, restraint, control and temperance in the expression and experience of emotion. For poetry might produce and linguistically figure feeling, but it does so without spilling it forth, attentive to the 'stay of passion' as a rhythmical, melodious and deliberate genre able to marshal feelings as it releases them. To simply announce one's private, inner feelings in a public and open sense is, for Keble, crude and immodest, undermining that which is expressed. Like biblical parables, which indirectly and metaphorically communicate specific messages, poetry obliquely hints at its subject matter, so implicitly coaching readers to proclaim their own feelings in an encoded manner.

In this sense, poetry accords with Tractarian reserve, that doctrine which insisted believers hold back, or disguise, the tenets of their faith-system for fear it would be misunderstood, distorted or derided by unbelievers (see Gilley). Indicating, then, that God's scriptural laws were to remain hidden to all but the faithful, devotional writing and biblical exegesis alike were meant to render religious truth through metaphor, figure and allegory in a way only the initiated believer could understand. Reserve also prevented an increasingly literate secular audience from accessing scriptural law, while underlining the fact that some of God's tenets were simply beyond human comprehension, revealed at last to the faithful in heaven. Significant to this discussion is how Keble uses reserve in his *Lectures* to highlight the importance of controlling one's emotional expression through poetry, that genre which allows the individual to be wary and slow to give his or her confidence. For even as Keble promotes the benefits of experiencing feeling through poetry, he recognises that 'only one among a thousand' will 'not cool before' the 'warm feelings of another':

And truly, when men's minds are keenly alive to all that affects that which they have most at heart, no wonder that those who would otherwise be eloquent in glowing words and phrases often withhold and restrain themselves from some fear of ridicule. For what is more liable to be ridiculed than deep emotion and mental struggle exhibited in the absence of any sympathy, when there is no response of affection? (Keble, I, 76)

Affection and sympathy, popularly debated in the eighteenth century, seem outmoded and insincere by the nineteenth, Keble suggests, undermined by the fervour and romance promoted by Hemans, Byron and Shelley, not to mention that Wordsworthian feeling even Keble feared was too 'radical.'[3] What was needed, he argued in the sixth *Lecture*, was an investment in a certain type of emotion that Quintilian had identified as, Keble translates, 'character,' that which calms, persuades and gives expression to moral emotion. For Quintilian, this moral emotion was of a very different order to that other kind of emotion translated by Keble as 'feeling,' that which excites, overpowers and benefits the individual caught up in the 'very whirl and rush of passion' (Keble, I, 88).

The ideal poet, of course, can harness both, each giving rein to various aspects of the imagination. Sappho, for example, the only woman poet Keble discusses in any detail, is applauded for developing a metre in which her muse is 'sometimes sad and sobbing, sometimes laughing and jesting ... partly broken up in spasmodic bursts, partly borne onward swiftly and evenly as though with a favouring breeze' (Keble, I, 325). Yet it is principally 'feeling' rather than 'character' with which Keble associates Sappho, her verses platforms on which 'she seeks remedy for present passion' (Keble, I, 89). Such an association has much to do with Keble's sense of Sappho's lyrical style, which for him is somewhat lawless and enthusiastic. As he argues in the twenty-fourth *Lecture*, lyric poetry, with its emphasis upon metre and rhythm, tends to carry both the poet and reader away: it being 'far more easy to pretend to feel a strong emotion in a short poem'; and lyric feeling being 'quick and impulsive' as opposed to those more enduring emotions expressed within elegies, epics or odes (Keble, II, 96–7). Further still, lyric threatens to topple the definition of poetry Keble has hitherto outlined, pouring forth, rather than holding back the poet's feelings. For while poetry is heralded within the *Lectures* for its capacity to place feeling 'behind a veil,' lyric demands that 'everything is uttered in the poet's own person,' his or her subjectivity 'exposed to the full blaze of daylight' and forthrightly breaking the rules of reserve (Keble, II, 97, 99). Far safer, Keble argues, is for poets to play a different part to that of themselves in their verses, adopting a role or 'choosing subjects somewhat remote from those which in truth hold their affection' (Keble, II, 99). Yet even as such a view is forwarded, the *Lectures* never refuse the importance of expressing emotion, it seemingly being better to licence the 'outspoken freedom' of lyric than to silence 'hol[y] feeling and thought' (Keble, II, 198). 'The central point of our theory,' Keble reminds his reader in the twenty-eighth *Lecture*, 'is that the essence of all poetry is to be found, not in high-wrought subtlety of thought, nor in pointed cleverness of phrase, but in the depths of the heart and the most sacred feelings of the men who write' (Keble, II, 201).

## II

While Keble very much had in mind 'the men who write' in his *Lectures*, the poetic theory outlined there was profoundly enabling for the woman poet, assumed to have a greater capacity for sensibility and sentiment but also prone to severe criticism if considered too candid regarding her personal feelings. The feminised aesthetic Keble promoted also justified poetical careers for religious women, able to adopt reticently the role of theological observer or even cleric while freed from accusations of vainly flaunting religious learning suitable only for men. This was certainly the case for Dora Greenwell, a respected theologian and essay writer, whose various publications addressed the social, as well as spiritual, implications of worship and faith. While her most quoted work in recent criticism is the radical pamphlet, 'On Single Women' (1862), Greenwell was primarily committed to establishing herself as a religious poet. She did so not only by drawing on Tractarian poetics, but also by embracing Quaker, Methodist and Evangelical traditions of hymn-writing. In her collection of essays, *Liber Humanitatis* (1875), for example, Greenwell argued that she considered poetry the 'natural ally of Christianity,' both giving 'wings to the fettered soul' and speaking 'to man of something that is far beyond' (Greenwell (1875), 119). Yet she also worried that poetry had the capacity to lead one 'upon dangerous, forbidden paths,' intoxicating those poets of 'ardent feeling' whose verses 'let in heaven upon the soul, and flood it' with a 'warmth and radiance' that is so intense it is doomed to fade into a cool indifference (123, 126). Such poets, Greenwell asserts, 'pass through vehement, overstrained emotion into an apathy, a weariness of men and things,' that Christianity avoids by living 'to order and to law,' regulating fierce feeling in the manner Keble suggests (126–7). The preacher's reserved poetics, then, doubtless introduced to Greenwell by her Tractarian brother, Alan, arrested Greenwell whose sonnet, 'Reserve,' stresses the imperative of encoding emotion within verse, especially when addressing God:

> Now would I learn thee like some noble task
> That payeth well for labour; I would find
> Thy soul's true Dominant, and thus unwind
> Its deeper, rarer harmonies, that ask
> Interpreting; for like a gracious mask
> Is thy calm, quiet bearing; far behind

> Thy spirit sits and smiles in sunshine kind,
> And fain within that fulness mine would bask.
> Set if thou wilt this bar betwixt thy tide
> Of feeling and the world that might misknow
> Its strength; use ever with the crowd this pride,
> 'Thus fare, and yet no farther shall ye go;'
> But not *with me*, dear friend, whose heart stands wide
> To drink in all thy Being's overflow.

The 'rarer harmonies' that constitute emotion within the believer here are gently unravelled rather than oozed forth, the object of her worship lying hidden behind a veil of benevolence, a 'gracious mask.' If we assume that on at least one level this poem addresses God, the narrator even entreats him to aid the believer in holding back strong emotion, asking him to set a 'bar' between the 'tide / Of feeling' that pushes to flow forth so that the true overflow might be of God into the believer. This regulating power is essential in allowing the believer to experience emotion: the uneasy narrator of Greenwell's 'A Thought at Midnight', for instance, is unable to 'feel' at all in her state of 'flutter'd ... unrest' (ll. 8–9).

Serenity, calm and tranquillity are almost requirements to enable worship within such logic, as Edward Pusey reiterated in his sermons, encouraging the believer to 'commune' with God 'in stillness'. 'He will fence thee round,' wrote Pusey of God, 'that nothing outward break in upon the sacred stillness of thy soul, which seeketh to be hushed in Him' (Pusey, 200–1). This hushed state for Greenwell and Keble, however, could only be truly induced by poetry. Greenwell literally enacted such a proposition in 'Silence,' a poem wherein the narrator describes her experience at a poetry reading she encounters deep in the countryside as part of an afternoon walking group. Already embraced within a natural scene parallel to that spiritually heightened one Wordsworth painted in 'Nutting,' the group attentively listen to a poet modelled on Keble's ideal versifier:

> suddenly the reader's voice let fall
> Its flow of music; sweet as was the song
> He paused in, conquered by a spell more strong
> We asked him not its cadence to recall.
> It seemed as if a Thought of God did fill
> His World, that drawn unto the Father's breast,
> Lay hushed with all its children. This was Rest,
> And this the soul's true Sabbath, deep and still. (ll.25–32)

Consoling and tender, the poet renders the narrator entirely comforted and released from earthly pressures: again, emotion is imperative here, the narrator wishing to move beyond the linguistic representation of feeling to that which only the heart might discern. Language is inadequate to feeling, it seems, useful only to let loose that which flows through us when caught by poetry, but which itself is clamped down by God:

> Speech is but a part
> Of Life's deep poverty, whereof the heart
> Is conscious, striving in its vague unrest
> To fill its void; but when the measure pressed
> And running over, to its clasp is given,
> It seeketh nothing more, and Earth is blest
> With Silence – even such as in Heaven! (ll.37–43)

Packed with biblical references – the deep poverty of life (II Corinthians 8), the need to fill a void (Proverbs 11), the image of a cup running over (Psalm 23), the charge that believers refrain from seeking too much (Deuteronomy 7) – the poem highlights the impossibility of vocalising one's desire for God by relying heavily on scripture. As Dolores Rosenblum suggests, lyric prayers and devotional utterances 'are inexhaustible in that the suppliant cannot say the same thing often enough, nor can she say too much': reserve forges a barrier to dangerous expression while the recital of prayer is an act with no bounds (Rosenblum, 152).

The repetition of scriptural phraseology in poetry accords with Keble's poetic theory because it cuts off the reader from the poet's subjectivity, at the same time as hinting that it lies beyond the words within feeling. As Keble stated in his final *Lecture*, poetry and religion alike own a 'tender and keen feeling for what is past or out of sight or yet to come,' even as they possess 'the power of guiding and composing the mind to worship and prayer' (Keble, II, 482–3). Lulling the reader into a state of expectant meditation, Keble's religious poet is ideally suited to address the transcendent and intangible, encouraging believers to anticipate Christ's renewal and second coming without passionately desiring it like those too fervent mystic writers. Here is Cecil Frances Alexander precisely fulfilling the requisite of reserve in her translation of the Irish hymn, 'St Patrick's Breastplate,' the reiteration of her experience of Christ underlining his ubiquitous presence in the world without pre-empting what is 'yet to come':

> Christ be with me, Christ within me,
> Christ behind me, Christ before me,
> Christ beside me, Christ to win me,
> Christ to comfort and restore me,
> Christ beneath me, Christ above me,
> Christ in quiet, Christ in danger,

Christ in hearts of all that love me,
Christ in mouth of friend and stranger. (ll.53–60)

There is no unlocking of religious mystery here, nor any strong betrayal of the poet's emotion. Instead, readers glean such emotion by themselves being caught up in the rhythmic flow of the verse, relying as it does on a pulsating beat that owns a sensory quality tantamount to feeling.

Alexander was intimately familiar with Keble's work, dedicating her *Verses for the Holy Seasons* (1846) to him as he would edit her *Hymns for Little Children* (1852); and, with Harriet Howard, writing a series of Tractarian pamphlets for Keble and Newman (Leighton and Reynolds 217–18). William Alexander alleged that his wife had been attracted to the Oxford Movement because of 'its profound psychology of the passive emotions and insight into the danger of playing upon them – with its severe self-analysis, its rigid reserve, its dislike of self-exhibition' (W. Alexander, xviii). Even Alexander's juvenilia verses are suspicious of what she called 'o'erwrought feeling' in her poem, 'King Edward's Dream,' and she insisted, according to William, that 'a good hymn must be *poetry*: but poetry in essence and by suggestion, poetry with a timid air and tremulous voice, recognised by a look of bashful beauty, half hiding herself' - a statement that directly recalls Keble's manifesto of Reserve (W. Alexander, xxv). William even claimed that Alexander avoided the expression of religious emotion in poetry, letters and general conversation alike (W. Alexander, xix). Yet her hymns break faith with this assertion by focusing in on pouring 'streams of grace' ('At Jacob's Well'), the value, as well as danger, of passion ('The Pilgrim') and the agonising sufferings endured by Christ ('There is a green hill far away'). Like Greenwell, however, Alexander intimates that true religious emotion might only be captured in a space beyond words, such as music, which for her at once controls and expounds feeling. In 'Church Bells,' for example, an emotive chime is struck to 'trace,' rather than declare, hidden feeling:

They tell of high and holy thought,
Pure feelings hallowed long . . .

Back to my soul that music brings
Dreams of mine early innocence,
Which ever loved in outward things
To trace a hidden sense. (ll.9–12; 17–20)

The aery but resounding peal of church bells emits the same conciliatory power as Keble's 'true' poetry, producing an untouchable feeling that seems almost to marry moral emotion with a more weighty sense of passion. Evoking that which is held within the believer, the bells recall both the dream world and external reality to privilege the experiential element of each as they are filtered through the religiosity of church music.

Certainly Keble associated gentle, salvific poetics with music, writing in the thirty-second *Lecture* of the potential of a 'single chord' to 'call out an echo in our inner spirit.' To the 'judgement of trained ears,' he claimed, 'even isolated notes are said to give sufficient suggestion of a complete harmony,' music purging feeling from us as 'moisture rise[s] from the surface of the sea' or 'as if some one were unravelling a web and drawing out the threads one by one' (Keble, II, 309). This sentiment is recorded not only by Alexander, but also by Caroline Leakey, in her poem, 'Cathedral Bells':

> Then one full thrilling bell
> On the calm'd air doth swell;
> One solitary note,
> On stillness sent afloat,
> Like an ancient memory,
> Enthralled by spirit power,
> To wander through the belfry
> At each lone curfew hour (ll.50–58).

Elsewhere, Leakey becomes almost obsessed with the 'silence' by which she feels pursued in the aftermath of sound, welling up within to vitalise her listening powers ('The Music of the Rills'); or in need of re-tuning to render God the sole focus of the feelings produced ('O harp of God!').[4] In 'Cathedral Bells,' however, it is precisely Keble's notion of the 'single chord' or 'solitary note' that impresses itself upon the reader, that which is cast out into the world to become what Leakey calls a kind of 'spirit power,' parallel to that numinous essence Hazlitt so famously argued poetry becomes (see Hazlitt). The tone summoned here is indeed ghostly, exciting a feeling that stalks through the church after dark to fan the flame of those willing to embrace it, a handmaiden to poetry in the same way as poetry lends religion expression.[5]

If Alexander and Leakey were both compelled by the intonation of a musical note, Adelaide Anne Procter engaged herself in the task of reserving the audible or phonetic in her much anthologised poem, 'A Lost Chord.' Favourite poet of Queen Victoria and, in the mid-nineteenth century, second only to Tennyson in popularity, Procter explored the potency of restrained and silenced narration in verse and prose, but it is her religious lyrics that wrangle most effectively with the difficulty of emotive articulation. Like the spring on a pinball machine, Procter's expression is pulled back so tightly that it always promises to shoot forth with an overflow of feeling, but instead becomes radically intensified because unreleased. The troubled mix of reserve and expressivity in 'A Lost Chord' leaves feeling arrested between a state of withdrawal and overflow, moulding it as does a nebulous and uncertain quality that seems to come from nowhere:

> I do not know what I was playing,
> Or what I was dreaming then;
> But I struck one chord of music,
> Like the sound of a great Amen.
>
> It flooded the crimson twilight
> Like the close of an Angel's Psalm,
> And it lay on my fevered spirit
> With a touch of infinite calm. (ll.5–12)

Procter fulfils Keble's philosophy almost exactly, poetic form and rhythm used to evoke a sense of tranquillity while the very subject matter underlines poetry's medicinal effects. The struck chord is gently suspended on the narrator's spirit to calm and comfort her, like the 'sound of a great Amen,' but then disappears to dissolve individual feeling into an appreciation of God:

> I have sought, but I seek it vainly,
> That one lost chord divine,
> Which came from the soul of the Organ,
> And entered into mine. (ll.21–4)

The description of feeling slipping away or becoming unobtainable even while it resides somewhere inside of us here might be read almost as a textbook explication of reserve. Refraining from any kind of blunt definition, the poem allusively communicates both the importance and inevitability of using feeling as a curative while controlling its impact by cloaking it with what Keble calls modesty or 'religious reverence' (see, for example, Keble, II, 79). Nowhere does feeling flood or spill here, but is instead dispatched from one unfathomed location – the 'soul of the Organ' – to another, the narrator herself. As Procter claimed in her other celebrated poem addressing music, 'A Tomb in Ghent,' melody will forever unite and restore feeling to all those who are prepared to engage with it on an experiential level. The poem's gentle portrayal of the romance between an organist and his lover is thus haunted throughout by the strains of 'Some strange old chant, or solemn Latin hymn,' directing the lovers, and the reader, to raise their eyes 'up to Heaven' in order that music might overflow from the heart (ll.196–7, 288).

Able to evince, through poetry, the holding taut of violent and furious emotion within the self, Procter continually satisfied Keble's aesthetic mandate in a manner recognisable to her fellow poets. Bessie Parkes, for example, who followed Procter into Tractarianism and then Roman Catholicism, prosodised her friend's unusual capacity to 'weave mysterious rhymes' framed by 'kind human melody,' offering 'relief in song' to her readers ('For Adelaide,' ll.6–7, 13). Parkes herself struggled with the reserved aspects of Keble's poetics, worrying in her poem to Procter that they were elitist and 'abstruse' (l.2). Even more unnerving to Parkes, however, was the emotional exhaustion she associated with feeling, that which she considered had to be wrung from the heart only to 'show / What coarse and sensual meanings lurk below' ('The World of Art,' ll.59–60). Yet Parkes also recognised how enabling feeling might be for penetrating religious questions, writing in 'Stoneleigh' of what she perceived as a dynamic 'interior radiance' that illuminates the individual and so too 'the shadowy places round us' (ll.46–7). Her fear, in line with Keble, was that too much emotion might mentally break believers so that while God might be hidden from them, they would nevertheless encounter occasional glimpses of his power or spirit that could prove fatal. As she declared in her disarming poem, 'Mysteries':

> Sometimes from that most glorious shore
> Where Christ the Lord sits evermore
> Comes a faint wind; aside one moment rolls
> The awful curtain; on our trembling souls
> A vision of the Eternity which is,
> Hath been, and ever shall be, very nigh
> To the dear dreaming earth sweeps gloriously.
> A moment hear we symphonies of Heaven,
> A moment see blue depths thro' vapours riven, -
> Then darkness steals upon us, and we seem
> As though our hearts had fir'd at some unstable dream. (ll.9–19)

Discerning the pitfalls of spending one's life committed to a riddle that may not be solved, Parkes intuitively brings out those moments when heaven seems near or, as Keble writes, the moisture, here the 'vapours,' seem to rise from the sea and promise revelation. The ensuing darkness is crippling for the narrator, perhaps because she relies too much upon emotion in the poem, confessing, in Wordsworthian mode, that she lives only for those 'glorious days when we seem knit / To some great Heart' (ll.30–1). Looking for Christ to 'perfect everything,' however, she falls short of reaching the 'great truth,' fancying that it might be half seized but acknowledging that it always escapes behind her (ll.41, 54–7).

Procter may have suffered from the same unease, but the momentum of her poetry comes in its ability to bear down and reserve such strain in order to seek different ways of communicating faith. 'Murmurs,' for example, characterises the prospect of annunciation as a whispered undertone unable to become fully vocalised, the speaker urging the reader to 'Listen, and I will tell thee / The song Creation sings' (ll.13–14). Softly intimating the poem's religious nature by deeming it a 'holy song,' the narrator cloaks her meanings in shadowy metaphors: they echo, ripple and glitter in an attempt to be amplified through the 'little voice' of the believer, but such a voice turns down its own volume in accordance with reserve. 'Unexpressed' too bares the silent soul the believer owns until seated in heaven, the poem a catalogue of varying attempts, all failed, to express what 'Dwells within the soul of every Artist' (l.1). As in Blake's *Laocoön* (c.1818), Procter's 'Artist' embraces all who profess faith, the very act of doing so an aesthetic creation. The poem insists, however, that for every artist, 'the best remains unuttered,' the 'deepest beauty' always veiled 'to mortal eyes' (ll.3, 7–8). Only God has access to the full resonance of what the artist endeavours to fix in form:

> No real Poet ever wove in numbers
> All his dreams; but the diviner part,
> Hidden from all the world, spake to him only
> In the voiceless silence of his heart. (ll.21–4)

The poet's most divine harmonies are thus too bright for the mortal world, murmuring within a still human heart that contains and restricts powerful feeling until it is ready to burst forth in more sacred realms. The poet's 'numbers' here – the stanzaic units that contain and regulate the feeling put forth – cannot entirely effuse his or her dreams or feelings but their diviner part – their poetical nature – is so obviously prayer-like that God hears the poet's faith even when he or she is silent. As Keble wrote in his *Lectures*, 'the variety of the poet's numbers are of great import in guiding us to his personal feeling and disposition: just as a man's walk is an index to the movements of his mind' (Keble, II, 106). Meaning can be communicated within poetry, then, but the religious feeling behind it is always held back and reserved until heaven is achieved.

### III

The impact of Keble's *Lectures* on nineteenth-century poetics is still largely elided by literary critics, and yet its diffuse message seems to have touched many poets with religious, if not explicitly Tractarian, concerns.[6] Such an impact was compounded for religious women poets who found themselves in a position of being ministered to by male priests as Keble argued Christianity ministered to poetry. The 'handmaid' of religion, and one figured, as this discussion has outlined, through submission, piety, modesty and reserve, poetry forged a feminised aesthetic that was profoundly hospitable to women. The lyric expression of Greenwell, Alexander, Leakey, Parkes and Procter might seem supine or passive, but it is powerfully and radically so, aligning itself with a strong poetic tradition for which Keble, like Newman and Williams, effectively argued. These women refused, rather than were prevented from, gushing forth lyrical religious feeling, and were consequently granted an enduring, if serene, voice that marks hymns and verses still current today. Occupying a religious realm to which Victorian cultural and political debate remained yoked throughout the century, such women subtly defied the warning of Ruskin not to dabble in matters theological and embraced the Tractarian mode. It is in this sense that they accord with what Keble's Tractarian friend, Isaac Williams, summed up in his own appraisal of women's lyrical expression, found within his poem, 'The Song of the Blessed Virgin':

> She has no voice; but in that Virgin's song
> Divinely meditates her holier praise, [ . . . ]
>
> We seize her mantle, ere she heavenward springs,
> And wait her voice, - from her no accent breaks,
> Her voice is with her God, her silence speaks. (ll.15–16, 75–7)

## Notes

1. Stuart Curran's dismissive analysis of Rossetti's poetry was at one time commonplace (see Curran); recent criticism of the poet tends to be more attentive, however, particularly regarding religion, see, for example, Arseneau, D'Amico and Mason.
2. The review text was John Gibson Lockhart, *Memoirs of the Life of Sir Walter Scott, Bart*, 7 vols (London: Murray and Whittaker, 1838).
3. Keble wrote to his brother on January 23, 1844, 'You see the Praelectiones are now all in print and they are waiting only for the Index, Title and Preface. Now I have always intended to write a few lines of dedication to old Mr Wordsworth: but Mrs JK has started a doubt on account of his having begun life as a Radical'; in Martin, 81.
4. Both of these poems are from Leakey's longer sequence, *Shadows of Death*, parts IV and XXIX.
5. Keble claims: 'In short, Poetry lends Religion her wealth of symbols and similes: Religion restores these again to Poetry, clothed with so splendid a radiance that they appear to be no longer merely symbols, but to partake (I might almost say) of the nature of sacraments,' II, xl, 418.
6. A recent notable exception is Scheinberg.

## Works Cited

Alexander, Cecil, Frances *Poems*, London: Macmillan and Co., 1896.

Alexander, William, 'Preface,' Cecil Frances Alexander *Poems*, London: Macmillan, 1896.

Armstrong, Isobel, *Victorian Poetry: Poetry, Poetics and Politics*, London: Routledge, 1993.

Arseneau, Mary, 'Incarnation and Interpretation: Christina Rossetti, the Oxford

Movement, and "Goblin Market"', *Victorian Poetry* 31:1 (1993), 79–93.

Blessington, Countess of, 'Stock in Trade of Modern Poetesses', *The Keepsake*, ed. Frederic Mansel Reynolds, London: Longman, Rees, Orme, Brown, Green and Longman, 1833, 208–9.

Curran, Stuart, 'The Lyric Voice of Christina Rossetti', *Victorian Poetry* 9 (1971): 287–99.

D'Amico, Diane, *Christina Rossetti: Faith, Gender and Time*, Louisiana: Louisiana University Press, 1999.

Dickens, Charles, 'Introduction' (1866), *Legends and Lyrics Together with a Chaplet of Verses*, London: George Bell and Sons, 1877, xi–xxxi.

Gilley, Sheridan, 'John Keble and the Victorian Churching of Romanticism', *An Infinite Complexity: Essays in Romanticism*, ed., J. R. Watson, Edinburgh: Edinburgh University Press for the University of Durham, 1983, 226–39.

Greenwell, Dora, *Poems*, London: William Pickering, 1848.

— 'An Inquiry: As to how far the spirit of poetry is alien, and how far friendly, to that of Christianity', *Liber Humanitatis: A Series of Essays on Various Aspects of Spiritual and Social Life*, London: Daldy, Isbister and Co., 1875, 118–44.

— 'Our Single Women', *Essays*, London and New York: Alexander Strahan, 1866, 1–68.

Hazlitt, William, 'On Poetry in General', *Lectures on English Poets and The Spirit of the Age* (1818), London: J. M. Dent, 1910, 3–18.

Keble, John, 'Memoirs of the Life of Sir Walter Scott by J.G.Lockhart', *British Critic* (1838), John Keble, *Occasional Papers and Reviews*, Oxford and London: James Parker and Co, 1877.

— *Keble's Lectures on Poetry 1832–1841*, trans. Edward Kershaw Francis, 2 vols, Oxford: Clarendon Press, 1912. Reprinted in Gavin Budge, ed. *Aesthetics and Religion in Nineteenth-Century Britain*, 6 vols, Bristol: Thoemmes, 2003.

Leakey, Caroline W., *Lyra Australis; or Attempts to Sing in a Strange Land*, London: Bickers and Bush, 1854.

Leighton, Angela and Margaret Reynolds, eds, *Victorian Women Poets: An Anthology*, Oxford: Blackwell, 1995.

Maison, Margaret, 'Queen Victoria's Favourite Poet', *The Listener and BBC Television Review* April 29, 1965.

Martin, Brian W., *John Keble: Priest, Professor and Poet*, London: Croom Helm, 1976.

Mason, Emma, 'Christina Rossetti and the Doctrine of Reserve', *The Journal of Victorian Culture* 7:2 (2002): 196–219.

Newman, John Henry, 'Poetry: With Reference to Aristotle's Poetics', *The London Review* 1:1 (1829): 153–71.

Parkes, Bessie Rayner *Poems*, London: John Chapman, 1852.

— *Poems*, 2nd edn, London: John Chapman, 1855.

Prickett, Stephen, 'Tractarian Poetry', *A Companion to Victorian Poetry*, Richard Cronin, Alison Chapman and Antony H. Harrison, eds, Oxford: Blackwell, 2002, 279–90.

Procter, Adelaide Anne, *Legends and Lyrics Together with a Chaplet of Verses*. London: George Bell and Sons, 1866.

Pusey, Edward Bouverie, *Sermons During the Season from Advent to Whitsuntide*. Oxford, 1848.

Rosenblum, Dolores, 'Christina Rossetti and Poetic Sequence', *The Achievement of Christina Rossetti*, ed., David A. Kent, Ithaca: Cornell University Press, 1987, 132–56.

Rossetti, William Michael, 'Prefatory Notice', *The Poetical Works of Mrs Felicia Hemans*, ed., William Michael Rossetti, London: E. Moxon, Son, & Company, 1873, xi–xxviii.

Ruskin, John, 'Of Queen's Gardens', *Sesame and Lilies, Unto This Last* (1865/71). London: Cassell and Company, 1907.

Scheinberg, Cynthia, *Women's Poetry and Religion in Victorian England: Jewish Identity and Christian Culture*, Cambridge: Cambridge University Press, 2002.

Williams, Isaac, *Tract no. 80*, 'On Reserve in Communicating Religious Knowledge (Parts I–III)', *Tract no. 87*: 'On Reserve in Communicating Religious Knowledge (Conclusion: Parts IV–VI)', *Tracts for the Times by members of the University of Oxford: Volume IV for 1836–7*, 6 vols, London: J. G. & F. Rivington, St Paul's Church Yard and Waterloo Place, Pall Mall; & J. H. Parker, Oxford, 1833–41.

# 10

# 'FOR RIGOROUS TEACHERS SEIZED MY YOUTH': THOMAS ARNOLD, JOHN KEBLE AND THE JUVENILIA OF ARTHUR HUGH CLOUGH AND MATTHEW ARNOLD

## Daniel Kline

I do not know whether you have ever seen John Keble's Hymns. He has written a great number for most of the holidays and several of the Sundays in the year, and I believe he intends to complete the series. I live in hopes that he will be induced to publish them; and it is my firm opinion that nothing equal to them exists in our language.

> Thomas Arnold, letter to J. T. Coleridge, 3 March 1823,
> *Life and Correspondence of Thomas Arnold*

'The Doctor' was no poet.
Mary Ward

The juvenilia of Arthur Hugh Clough and Matthew Arnold is characteristic of most initial essays in poetry in that it is filled with both the acknowledged and unacknowledged voices of others.[1] Two Victorian assessments of Clough and Arnold make this point explicitly and suggest the presence of two very different influences in their earliest poetry. The first comes from Samuel

Waddington's 1883 monograph on Clough, in which he draws a parallel between Clough's poetry and the sermons of A.P. Stanley and suggests that the similarity between the two writers has an obvious explanation:

> And, indeed, are not these in a measure but different pipes of the same organ stop, – are they not two fragrant flowers gathered from the same holy garden,– the work and wisdom of two scholars that had been nurtured and trained under the fostering care of one and the same master, that great and good man the late Dr. Arnold? (Waddington, 17)

The second comes from Matthew Arnold's younger brother Tom who wrote to his granddaughter Dorothy on her birthday in 1896[2]:

> I send the new volume of your uncle Matt's poems, containing the prize poems, as a little birthday present; I hope you have not got it. The prize poems are quite worth reprinting, particularly the Rugby one; of which the 'Anklänge' with Byron are obvious, but people will not so readily notice how great the influence of Keble's 'Christian Year,' its phrases, its turns, its cadences,– must have been on my brother at that time. (Brotherton MS)

At first glance, the acrimonious personal history and strongly opposed political and ecclesiastical positions of Thomas Arnold and John Keble would seem to augur against their simultaneous co-existence as influences on the poetry produced at Rugby between 1836 and 1841. This essay confronts this problem by exploring the extent, nature and implications of John Keble's thought and work on the earliest poetry written by Thomas Arnold's star pupil and eldest son.

David Riede has asserted that the presence of other voices, particularly the voices of previous poets, in juvenilia constitutes 'a kind of poetic lalling' (32) that can be detrimental to a poet's efforts to establish a distinctive and authoritative voice and persona. In what follows, I wish to explore one aspect of this 'lalling' in the very earliest poems of Clough and Arnold, and the specific and largely unacknowledged voice of John Keble as it emerged at Rugby in the mid-1830s as a counter-spirit to the dominance of Thomas Arnold. In what ways does Keble contribute to or, conversely, help alleviate the poetic lalling in Clough and Arnold? More particularly, I will argue that Keble's influence on the juvenilia of Clough and Arnold differs, intriguingly, in both scope and degree. Clough's first poems are characterized by a broad but ultimately passing interest in Keble, one clearly subordinated to the ideas of Thomas Arnold. Matthew Arnold's early poetry, meanwhile, reveals a more sustained, detailed and focused engagement with Keble's work, particularly his ideas on Reserve.

In his magisterial study of Matthew Arnold, Lionel Trilling points out the two poles that Keble and Thomas Arnold represented: 'Matthew Arnold, then, had his baptism between the ideals of ecclesiastical dogmatism and ecclesiastical democracy' (Trilling, 39). In this examination of Clough's and Arnold's juvenilia, I want to broaden and modify Trilling's observation and restate it in order to suggest that Matthew Arnold *and* Arthur Hugh Clough had their aesthetic and linguistic baptism between the two positions embodied in the thinking of Thomas Arnold and John Keble.

In certain respects, the influence of Keble's writing at Rugby in the 1830s is not unimaginable given the personal history that he shared with Thomas Arnold. From their days at Corpus Christi and then Oriel, up to the time of his own doubts surrounding ordination, Thomas Arnold viewed Keble as a close friend whom he trusted for guidance and later asked to be the godfather to his eldest son in January 1823. His regard for Keble as a poet is evident from the encomium that serves as one of the epigraphs to this essay, although his enthusiasm for *The Christian Year* waned, not surprisingly, throughout the 1830s. As it did for so many nineteenth-century families, *The Christian Year* occupied an honored place among the Arnolds and their circle.[3] It was a common companion in their weekly devotional exercises, which, as Stanley reports, generally included

> The common reading of a chapter in the Bible every Sunday evening, with repetition of hymns or parts of Scripture, by every member of the family – he [Thomas Arnold] would himself repeat his favourite poems from the Christian Year, or his favourite passages from the Gospels. (Stanley, I, 236)

Thomas Arnold also admired Keble's prose, including his 1825 essay 'Sacred Poetry': 'How pure and beautiful was J. Keble's article on Sacred Poetry in the Quarterly, and how glad am I that he was prevailed on to write it. It seems to me to sanctify in a manner the whole number' (Stanley, I, 80). Even taking into account the deterioration of their friendship, which began with Thomas Arnold's support for Roman Catholic Emancipation and reached its nadir with his 'Oxford Malignants' essay[4], which was written for the *Edinburgh Review* in the midst of the Hampden Affair, an awareness of *The Christian Year* and its author continued to entangle itself in the texture of daily life at Rugby and in the Arnold family. Critics have identified paraphrases and echoes from Keble's poems in Thomas Arnold's letters and journals that postdate the estrangement (see Noonkester), and Park Honan notes that:

> [D]espite her husband's feelings, Mrs. Mary Arnold never blotted a vivid Keble lyric ['Second Sunday After Advent'] from her journal. 'If

ever your lives are passing away in careless peace,' she told her children, 'I would entreat you to think of the injunction contained in these lines. God grant that your mother herself may bear it in mind–

> Think not of rest; though dreams be sweet
> Start up & ply your heavenward feet.
> Is not God's oath upon your head
> Ne'er to sink back in slothful bed,
> Never again your loins untie
> Nor let your torches waste and die...?' (Honan 6)

Keble, then, remained a constant if somewhat muffled voice at Rugby during the period when Clough and Arnold were students there.

Given the popularity of *The Christian Year* and its persistent presence at Rugby, it is not surprising that it came to influence the poetry written by Clough and Arnold during their respective tenures at the school. In the final stanza of his Rugby prize poem, 'The Close of the Eighteenth Century,' Clough compares the human race guided providentially through history to a 'bark' invisibly piloted by God through 'Time – that ocean vast and wide' (*Poems*, 180). Although the image is reminiscent of Shelley's 'To Wordsworth,' Keble's 'Sixth Sunday After Epiphany' from *The Christian Year* is more likely the source.[5] In an immediate sense, then, Keble's poems provided an ample resource of images, tropes, and lines that, given the symbolic capital accruing to the collection with each successive edition and glowing testimonial, young poets such as Clough and Arnold echoed and reechoed. This is certainly the case in much of Clough's other juvenilia, particularly in his sustained burst of poetic composition in the first six months of 1836. For example, in one poem from this period, 'An Apology,' Clough attempts to explain and defend his procrastination and the neglect of his editorial responsibilities for the *Rugby Magazine*. He writes:

> Yea, thou hast come, and in the morn
> I quickly leave my slothful bed,
> Ere scattered are the mists of dawn
> Or the hot sun is overhead.
> The dew is bright, and in the trees
> The leaves are singing to the breeze
> And oh! my heart is in me stirred. (ll.41–47)

These lines, which are among the more serious in what is essentially a light-hearted piece, echo, both thematically and linguistically, the first, and much more solemn, poem in *The Christian Year*, 'Morning':

Thou rustling breeze so fresh and gay,
That dancest forth at opening day,
And brushing by with joyous wing,
Wakenest each little leaf to sing; – (ll.4–8)

Elsewhere, in the contemporaneous (Spring 1836) poem 'Lines,' the speaker's inability to respond sympathetically or imaginatively to the natural world issues in the conviction:

For I am sure as I can be,
That they who have been wont to look
On all in Nature's face they see,
Even as in the Holy Book;
They who with pure and humble eyes
Have gazed, and read her lessons high,
And taught their spirits to be wise
In love and human sympathy,
That they can soon and surely tell
When aught has gone amiss within,
When the mind is not sound and well,
Nor the soul free from taint and sin. (ll.17–28)

Here Clough echoes the famous opening lines of Keble's poem 'Septuagesima Sunday':

There is a book, who runs may read,
Which heavenly truth imparts,
And all the lore its scholars need,
Pure eyes and Christian hearts.
The works of God above, below,
Within us and around,
Are pages in that book, to shew
How God himself is found. (ll.1–8)

Besides these and other examples of 'Anklänge,' to use Tom Arnold's phrase, from *The Christian Year*, Clough's interest in Keble at this early stage in his career is more extensive. Many of Clough's poems from this period apparently restate or parallel some central tenets of Keble's poetics, which he elucidated and circulated during the 1830s. The fullest expression of Keble's theory of poetry occurs in the first six of the forty lectures he delivered as Oxford Professor of Poetry between 1832 and 1841. Keble argues that poetry is 'a kind of medicine, divinely bestowed on man, which gives healing relief to secret mental emotion or overpowering sorrow, yet without detriment to modest reserve, and while giving scope to enthusiasm yet rules it with order and due control' (*Lectures on Poetry*, I, 22). As this striking metaphor and the subtitle to the published lectures (*De Poeticae vi Medica*) suggests, the foundation of Keble's poetics is his conviction of poetry's therapeutic function as it provides healing relief to the inner turmoil of the poet and (by extension) the reader. In this way, it functions in a manner akin, but not equal, to religion. The specifics of the transmission of these ideas from Oxford to Rugby remains conjectural, but given the extensive network of communication between Rugby and the Oxford colleges, it seems more than likely that many of Thomas Arnold's students would have been generally familiar with the content of the course that Keble was delivering during these years. Besides, Keble's *Lectures on Poetry*, although the most elaborate and detailed exposition, was only one of several places in which Keble's poetics were aired. Thomas Arnold and the students of Rugby would have encountered versions of the central tenets of his theory in the aforementioned essay 'Sacred Poetry' (1825), the 'Advertisement' to *The Christian Year* (1827), or Keble's review of Lockhart's *Life of Scott* (1838). William Beek adds to this list in his succinct overview of the development and circulation of Keble's aesthetics:

> Keble's ideas about poetry, its functions and place in the whole of God's ordinance, were first sketched in outline in his review of Copleston's *Praelectiones Academicae* in the *British Critic* in 1814, and in his article on *Sacred Poetry* written for the *Quarterly Review* of 1825. Their fullest statement, however, is found in his *Lectures on Poetry*, which he delivered in the University of Oxford as Professor of Poetry during the years 1832–1841, and in his review of Lockhart's *Memoirs of the Life of Sir Walter Scott, Bard* published in the *British Critic* in 1838. The same ideas also form part of the foundation of his *Tract no. 89* on *The Mysticism attributed to the Early Fathers of the Church*, printed in 1841. (86)

It is perhaps not surprising then that Keble's ideas on poetry find expression in several of Clough's early poems. Once again, in 'An Apology,' which he wrote for *The Rugby Magazine*, Clough gestures to Keble's notion of poetry as a divine gift:

> Least, least of all forget I thee
> Thou gentle power of poesy,
>
> ...
>
> I have not lost, (oh first come death!)
> The gentle thoughts that spring at even,
> The love and hope and humble faith,
> The 'angel's food' that falls from heaven;

Deep feelings yet my bosom fill
And airy forms are with me still,
Yet safely it may be averred,
I cannot write a single word. (ll.4–16)

Poesy is understood here in its Kebleian sense as a quality or a process rather than a well-wrought finished artifact, and Keble's 'divinely bestowed' medicine is imaged as manna that acts upon a bosom that is filled to overflowing with deep feelings. Another and more sustained example of the undercurrent of a Kebleian aesthetic is found in 'The Exordium of a Very Long Poem.' This poem, also written in the spring of 1836, falls into two sections. The first half of the poem describes a rural autumn nightscape, where a persistent breeze and a shining moon monopolize the speaker's attention. The solitary moon shines and adds beauty and grandeur to everything else in the scene. The second half of the poem reveals that the preceding description has been the vehicle in a sustained metaphor and that the tenor of this metaphor is poetry itself. The poem draws an extended analogy between the nature and effects of the moon and the nature and effects of poetry. As Clough describes the power of poetry, the Kebleian overtones are pronounced:

Yet, blessed Spirit, yet vouchsafe to take
Our thoughts and words to dwell thine or beside;
Yet let our earthly souls in that bright wake
Still, still with fond and springing rapture ride;
This burning thirst, those high desires still slake
And joy as in these hues; albeit denied
The excellence of thy one light, unmeet
For weaker souls, yet these be very sweet.
('Exordium', *Poems* 33–40)

The poem thus potentially embraces two aspects of Keble's thinking on poetry: it represents it as a divine source for the alleviation of feeling and also makes use of analogy, which as Keble and later Tractarian writers would argue, is a central technique of the other cornerstone of Keble's theory of poetry – the idea of Reserve.

In the end, however, these aspects of Keble's poetics are subordinated, as Samuel Waddington notes above, to the moral, intellectual, and aesthetic-linguistic principles of Thomas Arnold. 'The Close of the Eighteenth Century' in spite of its many echoes from *The Christian Year* is a *Rugby* prize poem and thus, among other things, an articulation of Thomas Arnold's theory of history and his moral teachings (see Biswas, McCrum and Williamson). The range of Clough's diction, syntax, figurative language and linguistic self-reflexivity in this poem and others such as 'The Poacher of Dead Man's Corner,' 'The

Effusions of a School Patriarch,' and 'Rosabel's Dream', as well as prose essays for *The Rugby Magazine* such as 'Macaulay's "Battle of Ivry"', situate Clough's juvenilia firmly under the aegis of Dr. Arnold's more moderate, latitudinarian and Broad Church-rooted aesthetic and linguistic ideas, ideas scattered throughout his diverse body of writing. Clough was too much the Doctor's disciple, the Galahad of the Rugby set (Williams, 24), to commit himself fully or for a sustained period to the ideas of one of Thomas Arnold's great Tractarian adversaries. Yet in the poems that I have been considering, there is the suggestion of a surge in interest in Keble, on Clough's part, during the winter and spring of 1836. This interest intensifies in the midst of a confluence of important events in his Rugby career. These events included his contradictory sense of an elevated responsibility at Rugby (editor of the *Rugby Magazine* and head of the School House) mixed with the initial steps toward a post-Rugby education (preparation for the Balliol Scholarship), and his condemnation of Thomas Arnold's ill-advised involvement in the Hampden Affair and its aftermath as he confided to J. N. Simpkinson (*Correspondence*, I, 47). The spring of 1836 was a productive period of poetic composition for Clough. It was also a period that brought many of his anxieties about Thomas Arnold, the Rugby community and his place in it into focus, and his passing interest in Keble's theories at this same time appears to have been, at least partially, enmeshed with these anxieties. Even if it was an interlude in Clough's juvenilia, the presence of Keble's ideas on poetry at the borders of Clough's work does suggest that as a renowned poet with a fully articulated aesthetic theory, Keble was a figure of considerable importance and attraction to apprentice poets such as Clough and Matthew Arnold. The Kebleian counter-spirit at Rugby would become more pronounced and sustained in the juvenilia of Matthew Arnold who succeeded Clough as Rugby's resident poet in the autumn of 1837.

As Clough was establishing himself in his rooms at Balliol in October, Matthew Arnold was commencing his Rugby career. In one of his earliest pieces of schoolwork, his entry for the Latin essay prize that autumn, he provides an indication of his own interest in Keble. Arnold's entry was ultimately unsuccessful but among the English epigraphs and quotations that he sprinkled liberally throughout the text, which included selections from Byron, Pope and Southey, there is also one from Keble's poem for 'St. Andrew's Day' in *The Christian Year*:

> E'en round the Death bed of the good
> Such dear Remembrances will hover
> And haunt us with no vexing mood
> When all the Cares of Life are over. (Balliol MS)

The inclusion of Keble's poetry in such a context indicates, for Arnold as well as for Clough, the symbolic capital that his work embodied even in a supposedly antagonistic institution. The boldness of Arnold's inclusion of Keble also points to the more prominent and specific place that Keble occupies in his juvenilia. The relationship to Kebleian thought expressed in his juvenilia is qualitatively different to that seen in Clough's early poems.

One evident explanation for this difference is that Arnold's exposure to the work of Keble was much more systematic and personal than it ever was for Clough. Keble and his work occupied a familiar place in the rhythms of daily life as Arnold grew up in Laleham and then Rugby, and in one anecdote from early in Arnold's life, Park Honan notes that as a young boy he 'learned to repeat Keble's lyrics in exchange for his mother's ardent attention' (12). A further layer of exposure to Keble and his ideas occurred in 1836 when Thomas Arnold decided to send Matthew and Tom to his own alma mater, the Winchester Grammar School. Matthew Arnold had already produced a series of poems characterized in Riede's words by a 'self-conscious echoing of an earlier poetic tradition' (32); poems which showed that he had read his copy of *The Christian Year* with care and attention. This was particularly true, for example, when he composed 'Lines written on first leaving home for a Public School' which he wrote upon his arrival at the Winchester Grammar School. Nicholas Murray points out:

> One of the first things that Matthew did on arrival at Winchester was to write another poem, *Lines written on first leaving home for a Public School*. It bears the mark of his enforced rote learning of his godfather John Keble's *The Christian Year* (1827). (25)

The echoing of both content and formal aspects of *The Christian Year* is reminiscent of the many echoes of the poems found in Clough's juvenilia, some of which have been discussed above. But, this was simply an initial step in Arnold's engagement with Kebleian thought, and his Winchester experience would be crucial in moving him beyond a repetition of Clough's involvement with Keble's poetry and poetics. Biographers have tended to elide the significance of Matthew Arnold's year at Winchester. Yet Thomas Arnold's decision to send his sons to Winchester is curious, given that it was a High-Church bastion with Tractarian sympathies and its Headmaster, George Moberley, was sympathetic to the Tractarians and was a close friend of John Keble, who lived near the school at Hursley. Keble's proximity to the school allowed Matthew and Tom to make at least one visit to his vicarage.[6] The Arnold sons may also have heard Keble's famous Visitation Sermon, 'On Primitive Tradition Recognized in Holy Scripture,' which was delivered in Winchester Cathedral shortly after their arrival in September 1836. Thomas Arnold's concerns about Tractarian influence on his sons may have been heightened when Moberley approached Matthew about a Heathcote Scholarship in November 1836. The required subscription to the Thirty-Nine Articles ran counter to Thomas Arnold's advocacy of a more comprehensive National Church and he advised his son to decline the scholarship offer. At the end of the school year, Thomas Arnold, perhaps fearing that his sons were being proselytized at Winchester, abruptly removed Matthew and Tom from the school. In a certain sense, however, Matthew Arnold was already partially converted, in literary terms, to some of Keble's aesthetic positions and his interest in the work and thought of his godfather was strengthened. While Clough's poetry reveals a general interest in Keble's poetics or echoes lines from *The Christian Year*, Matthew Arnold's juvenilia focuses more specifically on a particular aspect of that theory, namely the idea of Reserve and the kinds of expressive possibilities and limitations it imposed on a young poet.

The divinely bestowed expression of overpowering emotion offers the first and most important component of Keble's theory of poetry. It was this aspect of Keble's theory – its divine origin and expressive orientation – that Clough appears to have developed in some of his early poems. But according to Tractarian thought, the *way* in which this emotion and feeling is expressed is of equal importance. In a restatement of the concurrent argument he was making in the *Lectures on Poetry*, Keble argued in his review of Lockhart's *Life of Scott* (1838) that 'poetry is the indirect expression in words, most appropriately in metrical words of some overpowering emotion or ruling taste or feeling, the direct indulgence whereof is somehow repressed' (6). It is here and elsewhere that the concept of Reserve and its role in regulating expression emerges as an important aspect of Keble's theory. The idea of Reserve is most closely tied to the work of Keble's Tractarian associate and fellow poet Isaac Williams. In *Tracts* 80 (1838) and 87 (1840), combined under the title 'On Reserve in Communicating Religious Knowledge,' Williams exhaustively outlined the concept of Reserve. As the title of the combined tracts indicates, Reserve is considered as a mode of disclosure and is tied to communication, specifically the interaction between the divine and the human. For a variety of reasons ranging from the finite comprehension of human beings, self-protection and selective dispensation, the divine spirit communicates in ways that are indirect, partial, and veiled. Williams traces the history of the concept from the life of Christ (most dramatically in the very fact of incarnation), his teaching by parables and miracles, to the adoption of reserve in Scriptural typology, and to the Church's embrace of the concept in the sacraments and liturgy. Williams' treatment of Reserve circles frequently around the importance of language. The use of tropes, linguistic ambiguity, and the flexibility and depth of Scriptural language are all aspects of language that are tied to Reserve. Williams' connection of Reserve with certain linguistic qualities is indebted to

Keble who first explored the idea of Reserve in a specifically linguistic and aesthetic context in his Oxford prize essay 'On Translation from Dead Languages'.[7] He also raised the subject in his essay 'Sacred Poetry' where, among other things, he rated Spenser's indirect, veiled allegorical mode as superior to Milton's admittedly powerful but overly bald, direct, and iconoclastic style. Keble's poetic practice, specifically his choices of diction, metrical patterns, syntactic construction and figurative language in *The Christian Year* have also been viewed as examples of his own commitment to Reserve in his poetry. It would have been in this specific aesthetic context and not the more theologically charged context of the *Tracts for the Times* that Clough and Arnold initially encountered Reserve. Although he did not pursue it in his juvenilia, one of Clough's essays for *The Rugby Magazine*, 'Sonnets in the Abstract', points to an awareness of Reserve, in the way that Keble initially elucidated it, and its place in relation to the expressive impulses of the poet. In this essay Clough wrote that the constraints of genre and metre in restraining the emotions and feelings of the poet made the sonnet: 'a profitable exercise in that first spring of poetry, and is a useful curb on, and corrective of its flightiness' (*Prose*, 49). It is the post-Winchester juvenilia of Matthew Arnold, however, that more fully explores Reserve as it was understood as a crucial aspect of Keble's poetics.

As one of the two pillars of Keble's poetics, it is striking that upon his return to Rugby after the year at Winchester, Reserve, or at least Arnold's understanding of it, occupies an increasingly prominent place in Arnold's early poetry in terms of both form and content. Indeed, Arnold seems to have gleaned that Reserve was also a mode of personal behavior and could be located in the quotidian events and details of life. One of Arnold's classmates at Rugby described his behavior upon his return from Rugby as 'reserved' (Wymer, 168) and when Arnold took a Continental tour just prior to enrolling at Rugby he was struck by the reserved simplicity of the language of the epitaphs in French cemeteries (*Letters* I, 22–32). What is more tangible, however, is that from this point on a form of Kebleian Reserve emerges with greater prominence and variety in Arnold's juvenilia. While the post-Winchester juvenilia may continue the 'poetic lalling' that Riede speaks of in terms of its dependence on predecessor poets (most notably Byron), it is a lalling that is complicated by Arnold's sense of the uses of Kebleian Reserve.

Reserve is connected to one of the most notable features of Matthew Arnold's post-Winchester juvenilia. These poems range across a wide spectrum of topics, but they are linked by a pervasive sense of silence. This silence becomes more noticeable when the poems are compared to the decidedly more effusive selections from Arnold's pre-Winchester work, including 'Mary Queen of Scots, on her departure from France,' 'The First Sight of Italy,' and 'Reply to a declaration, that he would not live by the Sea, made in verse by H.H.'. By contrast, a silence settles over the poems that Arnold composed after his return from Winchester. In 'Inspired by Julia Pardoe's *The City of the Sultan*' the Greek woman who is the subject of the poem braves the plague to nurse her afflicted lover and dies herself with a Stoic fortitude characterized by her near silence: 'But not one word, or look, or sigh,/ Might tell the storm that raged within' (ll. 27–8). In 'Land of the East,' the divine spirit is associated with a single voice, the pillar of a cloud, and the rushing wind in contradistinction to the modern condition of apostasy, which is linked to the arrival of the 'unrestrained' 'busy hum/Of many voices' (ll. 33–4). Finally, in 'Alaric at Rome,' the Visigoth king does not utter a word in the poem that bears his name. These poems are dominated by a quietness that is in many ways an radical interpretation of Keble's theory of Reserve. Arnold creates characters, such as Alaric or the Greek heroine in 'Inspired by Julia Pardoe's *The City of the Sultan*', who embody restraint. This reserve, in spite of the Byronic 'Anklänge' of the poems, differentiates them from a Childe Harold or from Byron himself – whom Arnold would later point out in 'Stanzas from the Grande Chartreuse,' in an assessment which Keble would have undoubtedly endorsed, as bearing 'Through Europe to the Ætolian shore/ The pageant of his bleeding heart' (ll. 135–6).

Arnold also attempts to practice the Reserve he dramatizes in many of the distinct linguistic features of these poems. For example, the silence of the Greek woman in 'Inspired by Julia Pardoe's *The City of the Sultan*' is broken only once in the poem when she compares her lover's suffering with her own impending death:

> Mid death and corruption thy tomb shall be–
> But mine where the breeze is fresh and free;
> In a lazar vault thy ashes lie–
> But mine beneath the glorious sky.
> And when the Chains of Death are riven
> My spirit shall mount unrestrained to heaven–
> Before th' awakening voice shall come
> To burst the cerements of thy tomb. (ll. 43–50)

The emotional climax of the poem is peculiarly restrained by some archaic diction choices by Arnold, notably 'lazar' and 'cerements,' particularly since they are the only places in the poem where the diction draws attention to itself in this way. Moreover, the couplets have a distancing effect, which is heightened by the fact that this is the only stanza in the poem where Arnold employs a rhyming couplet scheme. Thus, at the moment in the poem where the reader most expects a powerful expression of feelings and emotion, the language becomes restrained, reserved, and artificial.

Arnold's last Rugby poem was 'Alaric at Rome'. The first third of the poem is a meditation on Rome's ambivalent historical legacy occasioned by the sight of the ruins of the city. The remainder of the poem treats Alaric's final and successful siege of Rome and speculates on his thoughts as he surveys his conquest the following morning. As he does with 'Inspired by Julia Pardoe's *The City of the Sultan*,' Arnold demonstrates an interest in investing the language and structure of the poem with the idea of Reserve. Although, as noted above, the poem opens with a meditation on Roman ruins, Arnold withholds the proper name of the city for as long as possible by utilizing a series of apostrophes that identify Rome as 'imperial city' (l.19), 'wondrous chaos' (l. 43), and 'solemn grave' (l. 49). Of course, given the title of the poem, the city's identity is an open secret, but it is not named explicitly until the thirteenth stanza. This periphrastic opening is a strategy of Reserve, particularly when the entire meditation is compared with the passage from Byron's *Childe Harold* on which it is based. Byron's direct address 'Oh Rome, my Country! City of the Soul' is revised here in ways that orient Arnold more fully with Kebleian Reserve. Further, in the pre-Winchester poem, 'The First Sight of Italy,' Arnold unreservedly apostrophizes Italy in a manner that eschews the circumlocutions of the opening of 'Alaric at Rome.'

There are other ways in which Arnold's language in 'Alaric at Rome' experiments with a Kebleian sense of Reserve, but the poem is also interesting in the opposition it establishes between classical, cultured Roman reserve and the loud, rude, barbaric Visigoths. This reserve is revealed in the poem's repeated association of Rome with 'whispers' (l. 66), 'mute memorial' (l. 58) and above all 'eloquent silence' (l. 67). These traits emerge more forcefully when compared with the characterization of the barbarian Visigoths who are repeatedly linked to the 'hoarse onset' (l. 110), the 'wild shout' (l. 112), and the jarring 'bursting shout' (l. 132). Intriguingly, Alaric, as the representative of the Visigoths, has more in common in his brooding, reserved silence with the city he has just conquered than with his own warriors. The central image of the poem is the silent, reserved Alaric looking down upon what is in many ways a mirror image in the silent, quiet city. It is tempting, in many respects, to read 'Alaric at Rome' as an allegory about two different kinds of language – opposing Roman silence to barbarian noise – and to see in it an early embrace on Arnold's part of the classical purity that he would struggle towards throughout the 1840s and advocate in the famous 1853 Preface. In any event, Arnold's juvenilia concludes, with 'Alaric at Rome', in the strange transformation of a Germanic Visigoth barbarian into something that very much resembles a Stoic Roman philosopher. That he associated the former with his father and the latter with Keble (and later his associates at Oxford) is apparent in the first poem that he wrote at Balliol in December 1841. In a humorous, private and unpublished fragment entitled 'The Incursion,' Arnold records a conversation between two Oxford citizens, Jenkins and Tomkins, who meet in dread anticipation of an invasion from the north (Warwickshire presumably) of a barbarian horde (likely a joking reference to Dr. Arnold's journey to deliver his first lecture as Regius Professor of Modern History). The values of the Oxford citizens are the values of Keble and his Tractarian allies. 'Decorum, seemliness, propriety' ('Incursion', l. 56) are threatened by the 'barbarian hordes' (allied with Dr. Arnold and his Rugby disciples) who 'brawl and riot in the heart of Oxford' (l. 10).

In 'Stanzas from the Grande Chartreuse' Matthew Arnold speaks of an unnamed group of rigorous teachers who seized his youth. Thomas Arnold has always been included in this group by critics. However, if we are considering the poetic education of Arthur Hugh Clough and Matthew Arnold with Mary Ward's candid assessment of her grandfather in mind – 'The Doctor was no poet' – the teaching of John Keble becomes vitally important in our considerations of the juvenilia of these two poets.

In the end, this assessment of the place of Kebleian aesthetics in the juvenilia of Arthur Hugh Clough and Matthew Arnold leads to three significant conclusions. First, by stressing Clough's passing interest in Keble at this point in his career and suggesting a more detailed engagement on Matthew Arnold's part, I am reasserting the familiar judgment of contemporaries and subsequent critics who see Clough as the scion of Thomas Arnold's Rugby experiment and Matthew Arnold as a lesson in filial insouciance. I have, in many ways, rehearsed this argument, but I have also attempted to represent it in a slightly different key by exploring the difference between Clough and Arnold through the varying influence of John Keble and his work. Second, the debates on poetry and poetics that mark high points in the Clough and Arnold correspondence at Oxford and beyond, are in many ways anticipated and, perhaps, partially precipitated by an aesthetic-linguistic rift that emerged from their varying responses to Rugby and Keble. Finally, many critics, including others in this volume, have stressed the lasting and far-reaching influence of Keble's poetry and ideas on subsequent Victorian poets including Tennyson, Hopkins and Christina Rossetti. As I demonstrate here, this influence also had a more immediate impact in the largely unexpected location of Rugby under Dr. Arnold, and on two poets at the very outset of their poetic careers.

## Notes

[1] For previous discussions of Clough's and Arnold's juvenilia see Biswas 45–58 and Riede 32–5.

[2] For the sake of clarity when discussing multiple members of the Arnold family at once, I will observe the following conventions: I will refer to Dr. Thomas

Arnold as Thomas Arnold; his second son and namesake will be referred to as Tom Arnold; his eldest son, the poet, will be referred to as Arnold or Matthew Arnold.

3 The immense popularity of *The Christian Year* has been documented extensively both in terms of its circulation and the ecumenical character of its readership. See Cruse 47–8, Martin, and Tennyson 227–30.

4 'The Oxford Malignants' essay was written in the wake of Renn Dickson Hampden's censure by Convocation in 1836. As a liberal theologian, Hampden's appointment as Regius Professor of Divinity had angered much of Oxford. The Tractarians helped to lead a well-orchestrated campaign to question his orthodoxy, and Arnold was a leader in the small but vocal minority that defended Hampden. Meriol Trevor summarizes the significance of Arnold's essay in the *Edinburgh Review*: 'In his hardest hitting style he let fly against the moral wickedness of the revivers of priestcraft in Oxford. By using the Puritans' term 'malignants' he identified the Apostolicals with the High Church tradition stemming from Laud and the Caroline Divines...Keble, who really was a spiritual descendent of this school, was so pained...that he could never feel the same towards him afterwards' (Trevor, 36). It seems to have been the vehemence of Arnold's attack that was so damaging to the friendship. The Tractarian J. B. Mozley commented that Arnold 'wielded a pen as if it were a ferule' (Fitch, 139).

5 The relevant lines from 'Sixth Sunday After Epiphany' are:

> That on thy guiding hand unseen
> Our divided hearts may lean
> And this our frail and foundering bark
> Glide in the narrow wake of thy beloved ark. (*Christian Year* 13–16)

If Clough was reading *The Christian Year* week by week in the winter of 1836, he would have come to this poem at the same approximate time he was at work composing his Rugby prize poem. We might observe the same parallel in Arnold's use of a quotation from 'St. Andrew's Day' in his entry for the Latin prize in the autumn of 1837 (discussed later in this essay).

6 For accounts of this visit see Honan 30 and Hamilton 36; Tom Arnold also recounts a visit in his autobiography *Passages of a Wandering Life*, 15.

7 See Shaw's discussion of this essay and the concept of Reserve and its uses in Victorian poetry (66–74).

## Works Cited

Arnold, Tom, *Letter*, Brotherton MS, Brotherton Library, Leeds University.
— *Passages of a Wandering Life*, London: Edwin Arnold, 1900. Arnold, Matthew *Notebook*, Balliol ms., Balliol College, Oxford.
— *The Poems of Matthew Arnold*, ed., Kenneth Allott and Miriam Allott, London: Longman, 1979.
Beek, W. J. M., *John Keble's Literary and Religious Contribution to the Oxford Movement*, Nijmegen: Centrale Drukkerij N.V., 1959.

Biswas, Robindra Kumar, *Arthur Hugh Clough: Towards a Reconsideration*, Oxford: Clarendon Press, 1972.

Clough, Arthur Hugh, *The Correspondence of Arthur Hugh Clough*, 2 vols, ed. F. L. Mulhauser, Oxford: Clarendon Press, 1957.

— *The Poems of Arthur Hugh Clough*, ed. F. L. Mulhauser, 2nd ed., Oxford: Clarendon Press, 1974.

— *Selected Prose Works of Arthur Hugh Clough*, ed. Buckner B. Trawick, University of Alabama Press, 1964.

Cruse, Amy, *The Victorians and Their Reading*, Boston: Houghton-Mifflin, 1936.

Fitch, Joshua, *Thomas and Matthew Arnold and Their Influence on English Education*, New York, 1898.

Hamilton, Ian, *A Gift Imprisoned: The Poetic Life of Matthew Arnold*, New York: Basic Books, 1999.

Honan, Park, *Matthew Arnold: A Life*, Cambridge MA: Harvard University Press, 1983.

Keble, John, *The Christian Year*, Oxford, 1868.

— *Keble's Lectures on Poetry, 1832–1841*, trans. Edward Kershaw Francis, 2 vols, Oxford: Clarendon Press, 1912.

— 'Review of Lockhart's Life of Sir Walter Scott', *Occasional Papers and Reviews*, Oxford, 1877, 1–80.

Martin, Brian, *John Keble: Priest, Professor and Poet*, London: Croom Helm, 1976.

McCrum, Michael, *Thomas Arnold, Head Master: A Reassessment*, Oxford: Oxford University Press, 1989.

Murray, Nicholas, *A Life of Matthew Arnold*, London: Spectre, 1996.

Noonkester, Myron C., 'Thomas Arnold and Keble's *Christian Year*', *Notes and Queries*, 239 (1994), 384.

Riede, David G., *Matthew Arnold and the Betrayal of Language*, Charlottesville: UP of Virginia, 1988.

Shaw, W. David, *The Lucid Veil: Poetic Truth in the Victorian Age*, London: Athlone, 1987.

Stanley, A. P., *The Life and Correspondence of Thomas Arnold* (1845), 2 vols, New York: AMS Press, 1978.

Tennyson, G. B., *Victorian Devotional Poetry: The Tractarian Mode*, Cambridge MA: Harvard University Press, 1981.

Trevor, Meriol, *The Arnolds: Thomas Arnold and His Family*, London: The Bodley Head, 1973.

Trilling, Lionel, *Matthew Arnold*, New York: Norton, 1939.

Waddington, Samuel, *Arthur Hugh Clough: A Monograph* (1883), New York: AMS Press, 1975.

Ward, Mary, *A Writer's Recollections*, London: W. Collins, 1918.

Williams, David, *Too Quick Despairer: A Life of Arthur Hugh Clough*, London: Rupert Hart-Davis, 1969.

Williamson, Eugene L., Jr, *The Liberalism of Thomas Arnold: A Study of His Religious and Political Writings*, University of Alabama Press, 1964.

Wymer, Norman, *Dr Arnold of Rugby*, London: Robert Hale, 1953.

# 11

# *IN MEMORIAM* AND *THE CHRISTIAN YEAR*

## Marion Shaw

There is a copy of *The Christian Year* in the collection of books from Tennyson's library in the Tennyson Research Centre in Lincoln. There is also a copy of Keble's two-volume *Praelectiones*, with some pages uncut and the rest cut somewhat jaggedly. *The Christian Year* is a small (approximately 7cm by 11cm), rather frail volume which has been rebound. Its date is 1831 and its place of publication Oxford. Pasted inside the front cover is a label bearing the names of 'Alfred and Emily Tennyson', almost certainly in Tennyson's hand. The title page has 'J. W. Brook' and below it 'Friskney'. Friskney is a village near to Lincoln. It seems that Tennyson obtained this volume second hand, some time after his marriage to Emily in 1850. The handwriting on the inside cover is not that of the young Tennyson but of the older, even elderly, Tennyson. The contents page has been marked in pen and in pencil with between one and seven small lines against almost all of the titles of poems. Inside, there are a few pencil marks, only one of which, against the last line of the poem for the Third Sunday in Lent, seems to be a definite line indicating significance to the reader. The other marks look to be no more than someone pausing with a pencil on the page as they make their way through the book. Nothing about these unobtrusive marks looks in the least as if they have been done by Tennyson, who always scored quite firmly. The evidence suggests that it is Emily's reading we are seeing traces of, and indeed, *The Christian Year* would have been very much to her heart.

As far as physical evidence is concerned, there is, then, none to suggest a direct influence or link between *The Christian Year* and *In Memoriam*. There is no mention of Keble in any of the documents relating to Tennyson's youth in

Lincolnshire when he was preparing his first volume of poems, *Poems by Two Brothers* (1827), or at Cambridge where he began there, also in 1827, the year that Keble's book was published. There is, in fact, no mention of Keble in any of Tennyson's surviving letters. But this is not to say very much. Tennyson was a reluctant letter-writer and what letters he did write rarely spoke about poetry. He was the least theoretical of poets: no prefaces, essays, *apologias* or manifestos outlining his views on poetry or on his own practice as a poet. There are only a few remarks, apparently off the cuff, prompted usually by exasperation at the obtuseness of reviewers and readers.

When Tennyson joined, briefly, the Apostles at Cambridge he came into contact with a circle of young men who were intensely theoretical, one of whom was only too ready to act as Tennyson's literary adviser and promoter. Arthur Hallam's views on the nature and purpose of poetry were very different from Keble's. Hallam's approach was aesthetic, rather than dogmatic or philosophical. In his review of Tennyson's *Poems, Chiefly Lyrical*, Hallam claimed that in his worship of beauty, Tennyson was a true poet, a 'Poet of Sensation', aligned with Shelley and Keats, not Wordsworth. Wordsworth's 'error' was that he piled up 'his thoughts in a rhetorical battery...instead of letting them glow in the natural course of contemplation, that they may enrapture. [Much of his poetry] is good as philosophy, powerful as rhetoric, but false as poetry' (Jump, 36). For Keble, on the other hand, the beauty of poetry, like that of nature, was only a means to an end, to demonstrate the glory of God. The due training of the Christian soul is not to be beguiled by 'Nature's beauteous book' but to read through and beyond it as a way to 'see the King's full glory.'[1] The beauty of poetry exists to reveal religious truth, which reciprocates by endowing poetry with radiance and significance. Wordsworth for Keble is the 'true philosopher and inspired poet', who 'by the special gift or calling of Almighty God...failed not to lift up men's hearts to holy things' (Keble (1912)). As the advertisement to *The Christian Year* makes clear, poetry's purpose is to cultivate 'a sober standard of feeling in matters of practical religion' and to act as a kind of intermediary between the anxious, excited seeker after truth and the '*soothing* tendency of the Prayer Book'. Poetry is a vehicle for God's message, and the poet God's instrument, as Keble makes clear in 'Palm Sunday':

> Ye whose hearts are beating high
>     With the pulse of Poesy...
> Know ye, who hath set your parts?
> He who gave you breath to sing,
> By whose strength ye sweep the string,
> He hath chosen you, to lead
> His Hosannas here below. (CY, 77)

Hallam did not mention *The Christian Year* but it is inconceivable that he did not know it. He begins his review of Tennyson's poems with a contemptuous comment on Robert Montgomery's poetry, particularly his long religious poem, *The Omnipresence of the Deity* (1828), describing the great popularity of this 'poetaster' as a 'curious phenomenon...partial and transient though it be, of himself and others of his calibre.' *The Omnipresence of the Deity* is, like Keble's poem, a celebration of the influence of God 'not only [on] creation, but human life, in all its diversified forms of happiness and woe'. It traces the changing moods of nature, the progress of the seasons, the presence of God in all human affairs and in the 'heavenly rites of His Church' (Montgomery, 'Introductory Analysis'). And like *In Memoriam*, it uses many of the rituals and images of mourning: yew trees, bells, the burial of the dead, the anniversaries of the year, time as a healer and destroyer; and it makes an anecdotal progression through a loosely constructed narrative. Like both Keble's and Tennyson's poems it is in sections of varying lengths, but it differs in its use of the heroic couplet and in its ornate and tired eighteenth-century poetic diction. It is, however, even now, easy to see why it was so popular, and it testifies to a taste in religious poetry, of Paleyan persuasion, which Keble and Tennyson refined and challenged.

Hallam's influence on Tennyson remained but it was moderated by other demands and opinions, and doubtless would have been had Hallam lived beyond 1833. Two related issues bore on Tennyson: popularity and social relevance. Hallam thought popularity no sign of greatness, rather the reverse. Relevance, like popularity, had once co-existed with beauty, in the days of Homer, Shakespeare and Milton, but in this current 'period of degradation' they are dissociated: 'In the old times the poetic impulse went along with the general impulse of the nation...modern poetry, in proportion to its depth and truth, is likely to have little immediate authority over public opinion' (Jump, 40–1). But other voices said differently: not just the advice of his religious-minded friend R. C. Trench, 'Tennyson, we cannot live in Art' (Martin, 147) but reviews of his poems by serious thinkers like John Stuart Mill and John Sterling. Mill's review of *Poems, Chiefly Lyrical* and *Poems* (1833) implicitly takes issue with Hallam, agreeing that the true poet is endowed by nature with 'fine senses' but also 'has been a great thinker; – has had a philosophy...has had his mind full of thoughts, derived not merely from passive sensibility, but from trains of reflection, from observation, analysis, and generalisation' (Jump, 92). In other words, the poet is a teacher, and should seek to have authority over public opinion.

Section 9 of *In Memoriam*, the first Tennyson wrote, composing it within days of learning of Hallam's death, is a graceful description of the voyage of the ship bearing Hallam's body. It is followed in an early manuscript by sections

17 and 16, and the three are numbered in such a way as to comprise a small sequence in which the voyage, the safe arrival and the burial of the body form a narrative of departure and return, modelled on the classical forms of the propemptikon and the prosphonetikon (Shatto and Shaw, 172). They are, in fact, very much in the Hallam mode, being fanciful, unphilosophical, aesthetic. As the composition of *In Memoriam* unfolded such sections did not disappear but became interspersed amongst sections 'full of thoughts', as J. S. Mill put it, and 'reflection...observation, analysis, and generalisation.' Through the seventeen years to its publication in 1850, the poem was taken hold of by the age in which it was being written, and from its Apostolic roots in Hallam's cult of beauty, it grew into the dogged, troubled, relevant and argumentative long poem of 1850. Tennyson maintained that such a sequence of poems had not been his original intention: 'I did not write them with any view of weaving them into a whole, or for publication, until I found that I had written so many' (Hallam Tennyson, I, 304–5). Even as late as 1848, he told his publisher, perhaps disingenuously, that he had been writing 'for his own relief & private satisfaction some things that the public would have no interest in, and would not care to see' (Shatto and Shaw, 18).

The cumulative nature of *In Memoriam's* composition, and the hesitancy and reticence of its author, echoes the way in which *The Christian Year* came into being. Keble wrote the first of its poems, the one for the Third Sunday after Epiphany, more than ten years before the publication of the whole poem, whilst he was working as a curate in two small parishes near his birthplace of Fairford. In 1825 he wrote to a friend,

> I have got a few attempts at hymns by me, which I have from time to time written, principally for my own relief. My plan was to have one, if I could, for every Sunday and Holy Day in the year, taking a hint for the subject of each from something or other in the proper Psalms or lessons for the day, and in that way I thought to go on, revising and making as perfect as I could, till the day of my death, and then, if it were thought worth while, they might be published (Battiscombe, 83).

*The Christian Year* might well not have appeared in Keble's lifetime had it not been for mounting awareness of its existence and the advice of friends that it should be published before it could be pirated. Keble was not confident of its success: 'It will be still-born, I know it very well' (Battiscombe, 104). In the event, it was immediately and lastingly successful. By 1837 there were sixteen editions, and ninety-five by the time of Keble's death in 1866. The estimate is that by 1873 nearly 400,000 copies had been sold (G. B. Tennyson 227–8). It was indeed a poetry bestseller. Its influence permeated the thought and literature of the age, even to so distant a point as *Jude the Obscure* (1895), and it is an important point of reference in that summary of Victorian religious doubts, Mrs Humphry Ward's *Robert Elsmere* (1881).

One of the causes of Keble's reluctance to publish was a fear that he 'should do something or other to disgrace the truths he endeavoured to recommend.' This is an anxiety announced but also resolved in the first of the hymns he wrote:

> Worthless and lost our offerings seem,
> Drops in the ocean of his praise;
> But Mercy with her genial beam
> Is ripening them to pearly blaze,
> To sparkle in His crown above,
> Who welcomes here a child's as there an angel's love.
> ('Third Sunday after Epiphany', CY, 45)

Self-doubt and a sense of an almost sacrilegious imprudence on the poet's part are recurrent notes in *In Memoriam*: 'I am not worthy ev'n to speak / Of thy prevailing mysteries,' (Section 37, ll. 11–12); 'My words are only words, and moved / Upon the topmost froth of thought.' (Section 52, ll. 3–4). In *The Christian Year*, however, the belief in God's redemption, and in His translation of human efforts into divine harmony, is a constant source of comfort and purpose: 'When souls... / Waste their impassion'd might on dreams of earth, / He opens Nature's book, / And on his glorious Gospel bids them look, / Till by such chords... / Their lawless cries are tun'd to hymns of perfect love' ('Fourth Sunday after Epiphany', CY, 47). There is no such reassurance in *In Memoriam*. To a modern age, one of its most attractive features is a search, occurring in more that twenty of its sections, for poetic legitimacy. Unlike Keble, Tennyson has no reliable field of reference for his poetry; what assurances he has are secular, and therefore fallible. His 'mortal lullabies of pain' may lie neglected on a market stall, or be made into curl papers or a lining for a box, and even if they are read a thousand moons later, they will be little more than a curiosity, 'sung by a long-forgotten mind' (section 77). The fact that this hardly matters to the poet – 'To breathe my loss is more than fame' – is no guarantee of ultimate significance. Even section 103, in which the barrier between life and death is breached by the muses, 'all that made life beautiful here,' as Tennyson described them, and 'which we hope will pass with us beyond the grave' (Shatto and Shaw, 262), are no more than a dream.

So poetic embarrassment about touching on 'mysteries' arises from different attitudes to the function of poetry in *The Christian Year* and *In Memoriam*. In Keble's case, the humility and simplicity of his writing was also an expression of his poetical creed. In his essay 'Sacred Poetry,' published in the *Quarterly Review* in 1825, and therefore written during the composition of *The Christian*

*Year*, Keble takes as his ideal model the Psalms, which, he says, are free from ostentation and striving after effect. It is their subject matter which is important, not the art with which it is disclosed. Those who write sacred poetry 'should seem to write with a view of unburthening their minds, and not for the sake of writing; for love of the subject, not of the employment.' Such poetry should be 'fervent, yet sober; awful, but engaging, neither wild and passionate, nor light and airy' (Keble (1877), 81–91). Keble would later develop these views into what M. H. Abrams has called 'the most sensationally radical criticism of their time' (Abrams, 145). This sensational contribution to the Wordsworthian notion of poetry as an expression of emotion was the idea of repression, or, as G. B. Tennyson describes it (G. B. Tennyson, 34), a 'veiling and speaking of sacred things by indirection.' By analogy with nature, which expresses yet also veils the glory of God, so poetry should act with a delicacy, tact and reserve in relation to the poet's emotions. In the case of sacred poetry especially, there may and should be rapture and inspiration but in 'speaking to or of the true God [the poet] is all dignity and calmness.' Such 'deceiving poetry,' as Isobel Armstrong calls it (Armstrong, 72), which works in disguise, has the advantage of attracting a wider audience, which is, as it were, beguiled into devotional thought.

This approach is very far from the extravagances of *The Omnipresence of the Deity*, and also from most of Tennyson's poetry before *In Memoriam*. There are examples of a plain style – what Keble might have called 'a kind of plain chant' – in Tennyson's work in the years to 1850 but what the public most thought of as Tennysonian was a much more luxuriantly expressive kind of writing than *In Memoriam* would offer. It is tempting to speculate that Tennyson may have been influenced by the example of *The Christian Year*, its 'dignity and calmness,' but it is perhaps more fruitful to see both *In Memoriam* and *The Christian Year* as a response to and part of the great phase of hymn writing beginning in the early years of the nineteenth century and continuing to flourish throughout the rest of the century. As J. R. Watson points out, writers like James Montgomery, Reginald Heber and Henry Hart Milman (and one may include Tennyson's College contemporary, Henry Alford, later Dean of Canterbury, who published a book of hymns in 1844) had

> turned hymn-writing from an art form for an Evangelical and Dissenting minority into an art which had something in common with the hopes and aspirations of other Romantic period poets...Their poetry included sacred poems as well as hymns, and they brought the two genres together: the process was completed by Keble (Watson, 326–7)

It made available poetry that was popular and accessible to an increasingly literate yet not classically educated audience, and that made Scripture familiar and memorable to that audience and catered for their Romantic and devotional aspirations. Hymns took on the guise of spiritual autobiography for the common man and woman, particularly where a personal voice or narrative was used, as in James Montgomery's diurnal route through stages of worship in 'For the Morning of the Sabbath:'

> From Thy house when I return,
> May my heart within me burn;
> And at evening let me say,
> 'I have walked with God today.'

Of course, *The Christian Year* was published as collection of poems, not of hymns, which assumes a musical accompaniment. Some of its poems, such as 'First Sunday in Lent' (CY, 64–5) or 'Twentieth Sunday after Trinity' (CY, 185–6), are probably too complicated, metrically or as narratives, to be suitable for congregational singing. But when *Hymns Ancient and Modern* was compiled and published in 1860, with a music edition in 1861, to become the authoritative hymnbook of the Church of England, several of Keble's poems were included, and an extract from the first poem of *The Christian Year*, 'Morning', took second place in the new hymnbook, to become the well-loved hymn beginning:

> New every morning is the love,
> Our wakening and uprising prove;
> Through sleep and darkness safely brought,
> Restored to life, and power, and thought.

Keble could now be sung, as well as read, by all classes, from the wealthiest to the poorest, and throughout England's widening empire:

> Where truth embodied in a tale
> Shall enter in at lowly doors…

> Which he may read that binds the sheaf,
>   Or builds the house, or digs the grave,
>   And those wild eyes that watch the wave
> In roarings round the coral reef. (IM, 36, 7–16)

The model of *The Christian Year*, in which the poems follow the Church calendar, may very well have influenced the design of *Hymns Ancient and Modern*, in its progress of the Christian soul through the year.

At its finest, Keble's hymn-poetry demonstrates the harnessing of Romantic feeling and imagery to Christian humility and restraint. His poem 'Wednesday before Easter', a first-person narrative, opens passionately with a rocking, pulsating rhythm:

> O Lord my God, do thou thy holy will
>     I will lie still—
> I will not stir, lest I forsake thine arm,
>     And break the charm,
> Which lulls me, clinging to my Father's breast,
>     In perfect rest.
>
> Wild Fancy, peace! Thou must not me beguile
>     With thy false smile:
> I know thy flatteries and thy cheating ways;
>     Be silent, Praise,
> Blind guide with siren voice, and blinding all
>     That hear thy call. (CY, 84)

But this is followed by four ten-line stanzas of self-denial, in a quietened and chastened rhythm:

> Come, Resignation, spirit meek,
> And let me kiss thy placid cheek,
> And read in thy pale eye serene
> Their blessing, who by faith can wean
> Their hearts from sense, and learn to love
> God only, and the joys above.

The final stanzas return to the earlier rhythm but the alternating dimeter lines, with a greater use of enjambment, now reflect a calm and purposeful resignation and the relinquishing of earthly pleasures:

> Mortal! If life smile on thee, and thou find
>     All to thy mind,
> Think, who did once from Heaven to Hell descend
>     Thee to befriend:
> So shalt thou dare forego, at His dear call,
>     Thy best, thine all. (CY, 86)

The text for this poem is Luke 22.42, describing Christ's moment of 'weakness' followed by His immediate submission to the will of God: 'saying, Father, if thou be willing, remove this cup from me: nevertheless not my will, but thine, be done.' Keble takes this sublime moment from the Christian story and transposes it into the life of the individual in which sensuous and imaginative pleasures take the place of Christ's temptation, and commonplace suffering and desolation become the way to God's presence:

> Meek souls there are, who little dream
> Their daily strife an Angel's theme,
> Or that the rod they take so calm
> Shall prove in Heaven a martyr's palm.

Though never conceived as a collection of hymns, *In Memoriam* has a number of features in common with hymns that created a familiar resonance for its readership. It uses long measure (8.8.8.8), one of the commonest hymn metres, and the majority of its sections are between four and eight stanzas in length, the commonest length for a hymn. It makes use of biblical incidents, as in sections 30–2, the Lazarus sequence, or the more glancing reference to Exodus in 96. 18–22: 'And Power was with him in the night...But in the darkness and the cloud, / As over Sinai's peaks of old.' This kind of oblique reference to the Bible, which momentarily evokes a scriptural image rather than developing it fully, is very frequent in *In Memoriam*: section 43 provides a good example of this unobtrusive yet pervasive allusive force. Line 4 uses the image of 'claspt in clay,' and this is reminiscent of Job 10. 9: 'Remember, I beseech thee, that thou hast made me as the clay.' There is a continuing allusion to Job in the following lines: 'No visual shade of some one lost, / But he, the Spirit himself, may come' which recall the spirit in Job 4. 15, 16 that 'passed before my face...It stood still, but I could not discern the form thereof.' And John 1. 23 – 'I saw the Spirit descending from heaven like a dove, and it abode upon him' – becomes 'Descend, and touch, and enter...That in this blindness of the frame / My ghost may feel that thine is near.'

In relation to Charles Wesley's hymns, Donald Davie has described this evocation of a wealth of biblical authority and association as a 'field of force,' in which the often plain and simple diction of the hymnist is given a profound dimension. Davie's example is Wesley's use of the word 'disorder'd' of our fallen natures:

> Expand Thy wings, celestial Dove
> Brood o'er our nature's night,
> On our disorder'd spirits move,
> And let there now be light.

Here 'the activity of the Holy Spirit in the human soul is described in terms which recall the Creative Spirit of *Genesis* [so that] the word 'disorder'd' is set against the vast image of primeval chaos' (Davie 73–4). In this way, ordinary hymn-singing worshippers felt themselves moved by a sense of grandeur in their own lives, which was nevertheless legitimate: a romanticism which was both permitted and within their comprehension. It is also important to remember that hymns are sung, that music is the most emotive of the arts, and that singing in church is a communal activity in which the individual is absorbed into the group, part of something greater than the self.

*In Memoriam's* 'way of the soul' [2] charts its progression through the anniversaries of Hallam's birth and death, through seasonal change, from the autumn of his death to the spring two and a half years later, and through paired sections that mark the lightening of grief, such as the yew tree sections, 7 and 109. Only the sections describing three Christmases (28–31, 78, and 104–6) relate in any way to the Christian year, 'in conscious subversion of the fixed significance of the Christian seasons,' as Patrick Scott suggests (146). This is one of the major differences between the two collections of poems; although *In Memoriam* could give rise to profound religious feeling and spiritual exaltation, it did not do so by orthodox means. Not only in its structure is this unorthodoxy evident; there is a persistent turning away from the consolations of scripture and of religious belief. Although there are many occasions when *In Memoriam* and *The Christian Year* begin with the same impulse towards consolation, they do not arrive at the same conclusion. A stanza in Keble's poem 'Evening', for example, draws on 24. 29 of St Luke's gospel, in which some of the disciples on the road to Emmaus ask Jesus, whom they do not yet recognise, to stay with them: 'Abide with us: for it is toward evening, and the day is far spent.' In *The Christian Year* this becomes:

> Abide with me from morn till eve,
> For without Thee I cannot live:
> Abide with me when night is nigh,
> For without Thee I cannot die. (CY, 5)

As in the poem for the Wednesday before Easter, Keble personalises the scripture, making it into an individual and also a more intensely felt plea. He familiarises the Gospel incident but stays within the parameters of Christian faith. With Tennyson is quite different: the gospel image, even more intensely realised, is behind section 50 of *In Memoriam* in the repeated 'Be near me' of the opening line of each stanza. Here physical terror – 'When the blood creeps, and the nerves prick' – and anger at the impersonal forces of Time and Life and the viciousness of mankind, are far removed from Keble's 'howling wintry sea' which need not be feared since 'We are in port if we have Thee.' The presumed 'Thee' (there is no addressee) of section 50 of *In Memoriam* is not the Jesus of the road to Emmaus, who can steer through the tempest, but the shadowy, uncertain figure of the dead Hallam, whose ghost would not be believed even if it did appear, as Tennyson tells us in section 92: 'If any vision should reveal / Thy likeness, I might count it vain / As but the canker of the brain.' The ending of Keble's poem comes to rest in loss of self in God's love after death:

Come near and bless us when we wake,
Ere through the world our way we take:
Till in the ocean of our love
We lose ourselves in heaven above.

This is an idea that *In Memoriam* toys with but rejects:

That each, who seems a separate whole,
  Should move his rounds, and fusing all
  The skirt of self again, should fall
Remerging in the general Soul,

Is faith as vague as all unsweet:... (*IM*, 47, ll.1–8)

Instead of the Christian belief in a single resurrection, Tennyson posits the ancient, heretical notion of many afterlives of the individual soul before immersion into the Universal soul. Even then, it would be after 'at least one last parting! and would always want it again of course,' as Tennyson told his friend Knowles (Shatto and Shaw, 211–13).

The Bible is also subtly turned away from its purpose in section 54, in the allusion to Jeremiah 1. 6: 'Then said I, Ah, Lord God! Behold I cannot speak: for I am a child' which becomes the final stanza of 54 in *In Memoriam*:

So runs my dream: but what am I?
  An infant crying in the night:
  An infant crying for the light:
And with no language but a cry.

Those who knew their scripture would recognise that the helplessness of this final stanza runs contrary to the robust rejoinder God gives to Jeremiah: 'But the Lord said unto me, Say not, I am a child...Then the Lord put forth his hand, and touched my mouth. And the Lord said unto me, Behold, I have put words into thy mouth.' A similar deflation occurs in section 7 in the allusion to Luke 24. 6, in which the women at the empty tomb of Jesus are told by angels that 'He is not here, but is risen.' In section 7, the quotation breaks off, and its triumphant second part is transformed into the banality of daily life: 'He is not here; but far away / The noise of life begins again.'

Even more daring is the subversion in section 18 of the incident from II Kings, 4. 34, in which Elisha restores life to an apparently dead child: 'And he went up and lay upon the child, and put his mouth upon his mouth, and his eyes upon his eyes, and his hands upon his hands: and he stretched himself upon the child; and the child waxed warm.' In section 18, in an almost blasphemous transposition, the narrator imagines performing Elisha's role; but this is a secular fantasy not a biblical miracle, and in any case it does not succeed:

> Ah yet, e'vn yet, if this might be,
>   I falling on his faithful heart,
>   Would breathing thro' his lips impart
> The life that almost dies in me;
>
> That dies not, but endures with pain...
>   Treasuring the look it cannot find,
> The words that are not heard again.

Such examples can be replicated throughout the poem; an allusion is made, its 'field of force' exploited, but, in Patrick Scott's words, 'the perspective is radically subjectivised' (Scott, 148). A sceptical imperative undermines a surface piety; indeed, one could say that in this respect Tennyson's surfaces are *not* intimate with his depths.[3] The relation between them is full of cross-currents and turbulence.

With *The Christian Year* it would seem to be quite otherwise. The structure of the collection and the textual impulse for each poem are clearly part of Christian belief and worship. But if it had been as straightforwardly simple as this suggests, would it have caught the imagination of its nineteenth-century readers so forcefully? R. S. Edgecombe, for all his devotedly respectful attention to the poem, has to conclude that the poetry, in spite of its 'gentle, unstrenuous verse,' is 'full of quiet surprises':

> Biblical events are given quirkish turns and integrated into the experience of nineteenth-century Christians, daring elisions of item with item all but hide behind the even tread of the verse, and allusions develop new resolutions in the poetic acoustic into which they have been transposed. (Edgecombe, 167).

Over a third of the biblical epigrams for each poem are taken from the Old Testament, with Keble showing a particular predilection for Genesis and Isaiah. This allows him more narrative scope and a greater emotional range than if he had used only the New Testament. It also seems to relate to the indirectness of Keble's aesthetic. It allows for subtle cross-referencing between the two Testaments and also enables a tangential approach to some of the issues he wished to address. For example, the poem for the Monday before Easter takes as its text Isaiah 63. 16: 'Doubtless thou art our father, though Abraham be ignorant of us, and Israel acknowledge us not.' Surprisingly, Keble begins his poem with a reference to Andromache's farewell to Hector in the *Iliad*. This is the kind of love, Keble suggests, that 'by Faith's undying glow, / We own the Crucified in weal or woe.' From this, the poem moves into a domestic landscape that *In Memoriam* would come to use so evocatively (in sections 100–2, for example):

> Strange to our ears the church-bells of our home,
> The fragrance of our old paternal fields
> May be forgotten; and the time may come
> When the babe's kiss no sense of pleasure yields
> Even to the doting mother; but thine own
> Thou never canst forget, nor leave alone.

This leads to a rebuke to the 'vain and selfish' individuals who believe they are unloved: 'Thou art thy Saviour's darling – seek no more.' A desire to trace 'Christ's musings' during the unaccounted days of Passion week, where scripture is silent, to be able to read the stones where Christ knelt, or mingle our tears with His blood – all such contact would frame ' a guardian spell / To chase repining fancies, as they rise, / Like birds of evil wing, to mar our sacrifice.' But the final stanza rejects this idea:

> So dreams the heart self-flattering, fondly dreams; –
> Else wherefore, when the bitter waves o'erflow,
> Miss we the light, Gethsemene, that streams
> From thy dear name, where in His page of woe
> It shines, a pale kind star in winter's sky?
> Who vainly reads it there, in vain had seen Him die. (CY, 80–1)

The poem has come a long way from its origins in a chapter of Isaiah that describes the anger of God against the Israelites, and ends with a plea that He will return to protect them. It also significantly omits the reassuring conclusion of Isaiah 63. 16: 'thou, O Lord, art our father, our redeemer; thy name is from everlasting.' In a typical Keble movement, this difficult poem for the Monday before Easter denies the directness of the scriptural text and instead insists on the veiled and delicate presence of Christ's light: 'a pale kind star in winter's sky.' Is this the star of the Nativity, and is Keble establishing a link between the everlasting God of the Old Testament and the renewal of that presence in the birth of Christ? If the modern Christian soul cannot comprehend these complex relations and subtle hints, then actual attendance at the death of Christ, which the poem has imagined, would also be meaningless. For the nineteenth-century believer, particularly the nineteenth-century Protestant believer, this, then, will be the way forward. Revelation no longer has credence; instead the signs of God's presence must be interpreted, must be registered in the delicate and veiled manifestations of what is seen and endured in the everyday world. God works in a mysterious way, through 'duplicity, subterfuge and subliminal manipulation' (Armstrong, 72).

For Tennyson, revelation was also not to be taken in any surface sense, whether of the Paleyan kind – 'I found Him not in world or sun, / Or eagle's wing, or insect's eye,' (*IM*, 124. 5–6) – or the scriptural:

> There lives no record of reply,
> Which telling what it is to die
> Had surely added praise to praise…
>
> The rest remaineth unreveal'd;
> He told it not; or something seal'd
> The lips of that Evangelist. (*IM*, 31, 6–16)

To Tennyson, the sealed lips of the Evangelist are not the discretion or indirectness of the poet but the failure of divine mystery either to exist at all or to be explained in other than human terms:

> What find I in the highest place,
>     But mine own phantom chanting hymns?
>     And on the depths of death there swims
> The reflex of a human face. (*IM*, 108, 9–12)

If faith is to be found anywhere, it is in a subjective state of feeling, owing little to external authority: 'like a man in wrath the heart / Stood up and answer'd "I have felt."' (*IM*, 124, ll.15–16).

To Keble such incipient humanism would have been untenable. His manipulation of scripture is to interpret and explicate its message for the times in which he lived and for times to come. The poem for the Tuesday of Easter Week, 'To the Snowdrop,' seems at first glance a simple expression of God's purpose manifested in nature. Its text is Matthew 28.8, describing the discovery by the two Marys of the risen Christ and their departure from the sepulchre in 'fear and great joy [to] bring his disciples word.' This is one of the supreme moments of Christianity, yet Keble's poem is troubled and pessimistic. Joy in the beauty and promise of snowdrops soon turns to dismay at the discrepancy between human acceptance of what the snowdrop signifies and the scepticism of those who 'smile in scorn' at the Bible's message. It is as though fear that too great a Wordsworthian dependency on nature, a kind of secular or materialist pride, will distract the would-be believer. In his poem, 'To a Snowdrop', published in 1819, Wordsworth's snowdrop, like Keble's, is praised for its fortitude, valued as a 'venturous harbinger of Spring', and it too gives rise to thoughts – it is a 'pensive monitor of fleeting years' – but these are time-bound and mortal. For Keble this was not sufficient; Wordsworth's book of nature had to be rewritten as the book of God, and the snowdrop's 'shy averted smiles,' like Keble's own poetry, read as a warning that such beauty exists not in itself or as a measure of mortality but as a means to God. Even in this there is a lesson: only the meek and lowly, those who have, like the snowdrop, been buffeted by the harsh winds of fortune, those who are credulous and those in 'want and pain,' 'have seen the angels near, / And kiss'd the Saviour's feet.' The poem ends with a call to first principles – 'And of our scholars let us learn / Our own forgotten lore.' (CY, 100–2). In this poem, as in so many of the poems in *The Christian Year,* a circuitous journey has been taken; to follow it from the originating text, through the introductory stanzas on the snowdrop, and the concluding lesson on humility and trust, makes challenging and disconcerting reading.

Patrick Scott rightly suggests that in spite of his orthodoxy Keble 'certainly fostered no illusions about easy interpretative agreement among readers' and he quotes Keble's words from *Tract no. 89*:

> ...if our words seem often full of a deeper meaning than we intended, if the same words produce on us quite a different effect at different times, it is natural that we should be constantly able to find new meanings in Divine language, and that it should speak a different language to those whose hearts are prepared to receive it. (Scott, 152)

Such interpretative uncertainty exposes a dilemma for the Christian Romantic poet between beauty as the object of poetry and poetry as the expression of God's teaching in a strife-torn and restless age. This will be a conflict rehearsed with greater rhetorical violence by G. M. Hopkins later in the century. *The Christian Year* is in many respects a tortured poem, struggling within the confines of Christian orthodoxy to make literal scripture more accessible, more relevant and more open to metaphoric interpretation, than hitherto. The connection between the snowdrop and the resurrection is no facile undertaking for Keble; in unstrenuous verse, as Edgecombe puts it, the most strenuous and far-reaching argument is made. *In Memoriam*'s arguments are not so constrained: its doubts are larger, it does not have to force answers upon its own questions. It has broken free of the Christian apologia that *The Christian Year* cannot, by its very nature, abandon.

## Notes

[1] John Keble. *The Christian Year: Thoughts in Verse for the Sundays and Holydays Throughout the Year.* New York: D Appleton and Co., 1975. 'Fourth Sunday in Advent,' 14. This edition uses the third edition of *The Christian Year*, 1828, the earliest complete edition. The first and second editions ended with the poem on the Commination Service, that is, without the last six poems of the third edition. Henceforth *The Christian Year* will be noted in the text as CY.

[2] Tennyson sometimes referred to his long poem during its composition as 'The Way of a Soul.' See Shatto and Shaw 22–3.

[3] T. S. Eliot uses this expression in 'Tennyson's *In Memoriam*,' (in *Selected Prose*, ed. John Hayward, Harmondsworth: Penguin, 1953, 184). Eliot's essay, published in 1936, stated that 'Tennyson's surface, his technical accomplishment, is intimate with his depths: what we most quickly see about Tennyson is that which moves between the surface and the depths, that which is of slight importance.' I am arguing against this position (always assuming I know what it means) in that it seems to me that what moves between surface and depth is most fascinatingly subversive and, in Keble sense, veiled.

## Works Cited

Abrams, M. H., *The Mirror and the Lamp; Romantic Theory and the Critical Tradition*, New York: Norton, 1958.

Armstrong, Isobel, *Victorian Poetry: Poetry, Poetics and Politics*, London and New York: Routledge, 1993.

Battiscombe, Georgina, *John Keble: A Study in Limitations*, London: Constable, 1963.

Davie, Donald, 'The Classicism of Charles Wesley', *Purity of Diction in Engllish Verse*, Oxford: Oxford University Press, 1967.

Edgecombe, R. S., *Two Poets of the Oxford Movement: John Keble and John Henry Newman*, New Jersey: Associated University Presses, 1996.

Eliot, T. S., 'Tennyson's *In Memoriam*', *Selected Prose*, ed. John Hayward, Harmondsworth: Penguin, 1953.

Jump, John D., ed., *Tennyson: The Critical Heritage*, London: Routledge & Kegan Paul, 1967.

Keble, John, *The Christian Year: Thoughts in Verse for the Sundays and Holydays Throughout the Year*, New York: D. Appleton, 1975.

— *Lectures on Poetry, 1832–1841*, trans. Edward Kershaw Francis, Oxford: Oxford University Press, 1912.

— *Occasional Papers and Reviews*, Oxford: 1877.

Martin, R. B., *Tennyson: The Unquiet Heart*, Oxford: Oxford University Press, 1980.

Scott, Patrick, 'Rewriting the Book of Nature: Tennyson, Keble and *The Christian Year*', *Victorians Institute Journal*, 17, (1989).

Shatto, Susan and Marion Shaw, eds, *Tennyson: In Memoriam*, Oxford: Oxford University Press, 1982.

Tennyson, G. B., *Victorian Devotional Poetry: The Tractarian Mode*, Cambridge, Massachusetts: Harvard University Press, 1981.

Watson, J. R., *The English Hymn: A Critical and Historical Study*, Oxford: Clarendon Press, 1997.

# 12

# 'A HANDMAID TO THE CHURCH': HOW JOHN KEBLE SHAPED THE LIFE AND WORK OF CHARLOTTE YONGE, THE 'NOVELIST OF THE OXFORD MOVEMENT'

## Ellen Jordan, Charlotte Mitchell and Helen Schinske

In the late 1880s Charlotte Yonge (1823–1901), one of the most popular women novelists of the second half of the nineteenth century who had been editing a magazine for girls, the *Monthly Packet*, since 1850, wrote to the magazine's publisher: 'My object always was to make the Packet a handmaid to the Church' (GC: Yonge, IV, 5: CMY to A. D. Innes). We shall be arguing in this chapter that this aim was not restricted to this publication, but applied to all Yonge's writings, and that it was a direct result of her coming under the influence of John Keble at an early age.

Yonge's novels were admired by Tennyson, Kingsley, Rossetti and William Morris (Hayter, 1–3; Thompson), she became the first woman vice-president of the Society of Authors (Keating, 28), and she had a dedicated High Anglican following that relied on her not just for fiction but for appropriate reading for young people, and for school textbooks promoting what they called 'Church principles'. Several biographies of her have been written, but this chapter is based on the further insights into her life and career that have come out of the project on which the authors are working of transcribing and annotating all her known letters.

Charlotte Yonge was born in 1823 in Otterbourne, a village lying on the main road between Winchester and Southampton. Her father had been an officer in the 52$^{nd}$ Regiment and had fought at Waterloo, but had retired to marry and had then settled with his wife as manager of the small estate bought three years earlier by his mother-in-law (Dennis, 7). For seven years she was the only child until her only sibling, her brother Julian, was born. Her parents had plenty of time on their hands and so put considerable effort into her education. She was obviously a bright little girl who responded readily to the rigorous demands made of her. When she was five years old, for example, her mother noted that in the last 6 months: 'C. has done...1016 lessons; 537 very well; 442, well; 37, badly.' (Coleridge, 62)

She remembered her girlhood at Otterbourne as solitary, though Barbara Dennis has pointed out that she had lots of relations nearby, but she contrasted this life with the summer visit her family made to her father's family in Devonshire, where she stayed with two large families of cousins and enjoyed the interaction enormously. She also later described herself as 'a great chatterbox', getting excited by games, screaming with laughter, and making outrageous jokes. A good deal of teasing went on among the cousins, all of which she seems to have taken in good part, and there are several approving examples in her early fiction of teasing, joking adolescent boys. When she was thirty-three she described herself to the illustrator Jemima Blackburn: 'I am personally a great coward and not at all enterprising, I was as a girl rather wild and scrambling, but it went off, I fancy from leading a quiet life.' (UIUC: CMY to JB, 7, 24 January 1856) The 'quiet life' does not seem to have bored her. She was a great reader and her mother appears to have shared all her interests, while to earn her father's approval she tried hard to become regular and thorough.

Her parents were conventionally religious and took very seriously the obligations that were increasingly seen as going with landed property, possibly influenced in this by being in the same parish as Sir William Heathcote, who became celebrated for his paternalist management of his estate. It seems likely that they gave the land for the allotments that still exist at Otterbourne, and they certainly set up the Sunday and then National schools in the village, which became one of Yonge's life-long interests. She began taking a Sunday School class very young, and was still going every day to the National School when she was in her seventies.

The arrival of John Keble at Hursley in 1836 was probably the most significant event in Charlotte Yonge's life. He prepared her for confirmation, and she took on board his principles and religious orientation wholeheartedly and held to them unquestioningly for the rest of her life. Furthermore, friendship with Keble incorporated the whole Yonge family into an intellectual and clerical social network they would not have encountered otherwise, though they were obviously capable of taking their place in it. George Moberly (1803–1885), then headmaster of Winchester College and later Bishop of Salisbury, used to rent a farm nearby each summer (Moberly, 4–6) and provided Yonge with another large family to observe. Various other clergy later of great significance were drawn into the district by Keble and a local clerical family also provided Yonge with her greatest friend and mentor Marianne Dyson (1809–1878), the sister of the clergyman in the neighbouring parish of Dogmersfield. Another great acquisition for Yonge was the family of Keble's lifelong friend John Taylor Coleridge, who were also distant relatives of her own. The whole family visited the Kebles and included her in their activities, building up connections that lasted all her life.

This was the world into which Charlotte Yonge 'came out'. We tend to think of young women coming-out in Jane Austenish terms; balls, dinner parties, flirtations etc., and Charlotte Yonge must have had many opportunities for going to parties and balls in Winchester, and also in London, and in the houses where she and her mother were guests. Such gaieties, however, figure very little in her fiction and not at all in her reminiscences. She suffered always from paralysing shyness, which manifested itself either as, as one acquaintance put it, 'a very cold and unapproachable manner' (Coleridge, 288), or (in the words of Mrs Gatty) as 'a manner so highly nervous and excitable, that it alters the tone of her voice at first, causing her to speak *shrilly* and to laugh more than natural' (Maxwell, 134). This no doubt made many social occasions a torture rather than a pleasure to her.

She remembered her period of 'young ladyhood' as marked by an intensification of the studies of history, botany and languages that had been going on since childhood, and by discussions of serious issues, mostly about morality and principles which they used literature and history to illustrate, with other young women of her own age. Another boon – thanks to the Kebles – was being present at gatherings where she could listen to serious subjects being discussed by cultivated and learned people. Interestingly, it seems that she had no shyness with older men. When she was in her forties she wrote of herself as: 'getting on easily with superiors, but stiff, shy, & disagreeable to others' (WDRO: Acc. No. 308: CMY to Anne Yonge, 24 October 1868). This seems borne out by what Lewis Carroll wrote of her in 1866: 'I was very much pleased with her cheerful and easy manner – the sort of person one knows in a few minutes as well as many in as many years' (Green, 243).

Furthermore, for the rest of her life, she called on these academic and clerical acquaintances to lend her the books she needed for her historical research, and to check her work for historical and theological accuracies. In 1867, for example, she asked her publisher Macmillan to procure a book for her because

'Dr Moberly's copy on which I reckoned proves to be packed up for leaving Winchester so as to be unobtainable' (BL: Add. 54920/172–173: CMY to A. Macmillan, 17 January 1867), and in 1889 wrote to W. J. Butler, formerly a curate for her friend Marianne Dyson's brother, but by then Dean of Lincoln, 'Please tell me if I am wrong in objecting to have the 1st Psalm set down wholly as Maccabeean?' (BUT: 2, 11 July 1889). Once she had some reputation she found it easy to spread her net of scholarly contacts even beyond the High-Church inner circle, and had no problems with posing questions and expecting answers from, for example, Francis Palgrave of the *Golden Treasury*, Frederick Furnival, who initiated plans for the OED, and the Oxford historian E. A. Freeman.

This was a kind of confidence in herself and her academic legitimacy that would only have developed much later, and might not have done so at all without the Keble connection. Thus if she had 'come out' into the less intellectual world provided by her own relatives, her experience might have been a good deal more painful, and could well have turned her into a rather different sort of novelist.

In 1893, in a letter of reminiscences about Keble, J. W. Butler commented:

> Also we owe to Mr Keble the absolute firmness of Miss Yonge. I mean her strong grasp of Church principles, in spite of many forces which might have drawn her into the 'femme forte' direction. (Butler, 239)

While we would certainly agree that Keble's influence ensured that Yonge never had much sympathy with the Women's Movement, we would also suggest that it was not because she imbibed from him a set of anti-feminist prejudices – indeed when Keble died in 1866 the movement had scarcely begun – but because, thanks to Keble, she encountered none of the opposition to her emotional and intellectual needs and desires that forced other women to become 'strong-minded'.

In 1847 one of the founders of the Women's Movement, Bessie Rayner Parkes, then aged eighteen, wrote to a friend:

> The worst situation for a noble continuation of labor is where all kinds of demands are made on time temper & spirits in a small domestic life, & among a heterogeneous mixture of people, & this is the case of most girls & women, & what makes hindrances to female improvements infinitely great. (GC: Parkes Papers, V, 2: BRP to BB, 1847)

But in the High-Church scale of values 'a noble continuation of labor' as long as it was as a 'handmaid to the Church', whether it was Sunday School teaching, raising money for foreign missions, or writing poetry and fiction with a religious message, took precedence over petty domestic and social concerns, always assuming that this did not involve rebelling against legitimate authorities like fathers and parish priests – who in Yonge's case were the ones inculcating these values. Her school-teaching and her writing fell into these categories.

The connection with Keble and the High-Church movement also saved her from the insecurity and secrecy that haunted the early stages of many literary women's careers. There seems to have been an almost seamless transition from the 'studies' of her late adolescent years to her career as a professional writer. Just as she had shared her literary and historical enthusiasms with the local High-Church circle, so, when she began writing her first novel, or rather 'tale', her whole circle were kept up to date with the progress of her ideas and contributed suggestions for the plot, and she received considerable encouragement if also stringent criticism from her father, the Kebles, the Dysons, the Moberlys and the Heathcotes. This unselfconscious chattering about her novels continued throughout her life. Elizabeth Wordsworth, the first principal of Lady Margaret Hall, was amazed and delighted at being regaled with her account of where her current novel, *The Pillars of the House* was heading, and being asked to suggest a suitable popular song for a particular incident (Romanes, 147).

But in the Keble circle it was assumed that talents should be harnessed to the service of the Church, and even before her first book was published, Charlotte Yonge was co-opted into the propaganda machine that can be seen as an outcome of Tractarian emphasis on the pastoral aspects of the religious obligation: the huge effort to get books promoting 'Church principles' into the elementary schools, a down-market continuation of the ideals of *Tracts for the Times*. Yonge's (and Keble's) friends Marianne and Charles Dyson had in 1842 begun publishing little stories suitable for village schoolchildren (see Blakeway). By 1844 Yonge was contributing to the journal they had started, *Magazine for the Young*, and her tale, 'Abbeychurch', was brought out by the publisher of the magazine, James Burns. The magazine then passed into the hands of the Mozley family of Derby, two brothers from which had attended Oriel College and come heavily under the influence of Newman (both of whose sisters married Mozleys), while two other brothers continued the family's publishing business in Derby. Yonge continued contributing stories of village life to the magazine, now edited by the publishers' sister, Anne Mozley, and they published her second novel, *Scenes and Characters*, in 1847.

The Mozleys were committed to the same propaganda effort as the Kebles and Dysons, and ended up publishing a range of High-Church journals addressed to different parts of the market.[1] In 1850 they had agreed to fill another niche by asking Yonge to edit a monthly addressed to young middle-class women. The outcome was the *Monthly Packet*, which she edited for the next forty years. Most of her major novels were serialized in it, and in the 1850s and 1860s she wrote several series of articles on history, the Bible, the Prayer-Book, art and natural history, the majority of which were republished by the Mozleys in a format designed for the middle-class schoolroom.

On the other hand her circle of friends seemed to feel that she should find a more prestigious publisher as her novels grew in power, and by the time *The Heir of Redclyffe*, her first and most spectacular success, was finished, Sir John Coleridge introduced her and her father to the firm of J. W. Parker (PCP: C0171, Box 29, Folder 7: CMY to W. Besant, 18 March 1879). She gave their reasons for abandoning the Mozleys to one of the early contributors to the *Monthly Packet*:

> I do not think country publishers have the opportunity of promoting the sale of their books to such an extent as London ones. I do not know how far you are committed to Masters, but I should say myself that J W Parker of the Strand is the publisher with whom I have had the most satisfactory dealings, and I think he commands a larger sale than either his namesake of Oxford or than Masters. (HL: HM 26133: CMY to E. Roberts, 21 January 1854)

Parker published her fiction 'on commission' (that is, she paid all the expenses and they took a percentage of the profits) until 1863, when the firm folded, and on the advice of Frederic Furnival she transferred these works to Macmillan and Company who remained her main publishers for the rest of her life.

Under Keble's influence, however, (and in part perhaps because of a belief that it was not 'genteel' for women to earn money), a large part of her early earnings were given to Church missionary efforts. She was evidently not absolutely committed to this practice – in 1869 she wrote to Macmillan that the proceeds of *The Chaplet of Pearls* would pay for her visit to France – but apparently one of her big disappointments when her brother got into financial difficulties in 1876 was that the money she had earmarked as an endowment for the new Otterbourne parish had to go on baling him out (Coleridge, 1903, p. 273). On the other hand, the fact that she did not rely on her earnings for her daily support meant that she was in a better position to strike a good bargain with her publishers than many of her contemporaries who were chronically short of money. She kept firm control of her financial affairs as her many surviving letters to both Alexander Macmillan and Arthur Innes (who took over the Mozley titles and periodicals) show.

\*\*\*

The authors of biographies of Charlotte Yonge have expressed a certain amount of horror at how 'quiet' and 'uneventful' her life was. The main events are clear. Her father died, her brother married, and she and her mother moved to a house nearby called Elderfield. Here she lived for the rest of her life, writing her novels and growing older, and, after her mother died, sharing her house with her sister-in-law's invalid sister. She played little part in London literary society, she only left England three times, and two of those were to go to Scotland and Ireland. What is overlooked in these accounts, but what a reading of her letters makes very clear, is that Charlotte Yonge was no recluse, though the world she lived in was not the one to which her novels would have provided an entrance, but the clerical world into which she had been introduced by Keble. In 1871, for example, she wrote the following to her fellow-novelist, Elizabeth Sewell, with whom she was collaborating on a book of history readings:

> Would you mind my changing the time of your proposed session to the later day you had fixed. I am asked to spend a day or two at Mr Portal's to meet the Bishop on the 10$^{th}$, and that is a thing I should like so much to do that I venture to ask you to change the day. The week after I go to Miss Dyson.
>
> I think you said at first Friday the 21$^{st}$. My only objection to a Friday is that I want to begin a class of freshly confirmed girls on Friday evenings (the confirmation is on the 1st and I think if I break it up so soon after the first start it will never come to good). (PCP: C0171 Box 29, Folder 6, CMY to E. Sewell, 3 March 1871)

What letters like this reveal is that Yonge had little time for travel or for allowing herself to be lionized by the literary world. She was a very busy professional woman, who, quite apart from producing a major novel a year, was active in three other areas, in each of which she had what could be seen as a full and successful professional career.

In the first place there were her responsibilities to the parish, informed by Keble's ideas of pastoral care. Quite apart from her involvements with wider Church activities organized by the Winchester diocese, such as the Mother's Union and the Girls' Friendly Society (GFS), she seems to have acted as unpaid education officer for the village. She performed many of the functions of headmistress to the village school (which was one of the reasons she sometimes gave for not leaving home during term-time), not only going every day to take a class, but supervising the pupil teachers and coaching them for their exams. Her concern and interest in them is clear in the letters she wrote to Christabel Coleridge in the 1870s:

> Our pupil teachers have both got 1$^{st}$ class in Scripture examinations. (CRC: 40, 13 February 1877)

> Our senior pupil teacher has just got the 1st prize from the local Cruelty to Animals Society for an essay on Beer – I did not know she was doing it. (CRC: 42, 3 August 1877)

> Our poor pupil teachers are in the final tug of preparation - They go to Salisbury the first Monday in July, and worked all through Whitsunweek enough to addle their brains. (CRC: 47, 17 June 1878)

She also oversaw the village lending library and seems to have played a major part in organising cultural events like harvest festivals, Mayday celebrations and penny readings (Yonge, 1887).

Secondly there was her educational and other non-fictional writing. The bibliography prepared by Marghanita Laski in the 1960s lists 207 separate items of which only about 90 are fiction. Even for a literary career lasting fifty-five years this is a substantial *oeuvre*, and there was no doubt a great deal of incidental journalism – for example, she reviewed books regularly for the *Guardian* (Coleridge, 341) – that has not been listed.

When writing to Macmillan she frequently stressed that this educational work was her *real* work, involving as it did considerable library research, and the difficult business of being both accurate and simple in presenting the ideas.

> I am going to spend September at my uncle's in Devonshire, and I do not look to being able to do settled work that takes much head till I come home. I should like to leave Bethlehem [a religious text, never published, that she was preparing for Macmillan] alone till then, and mean time clear out of its way the Dove in the Eagle's Nest, and all the small matters that if not done before hand take up and dissipate one's mind from the main matter in hand, as perhaps they have been doing now. (BL: Add. 54920/92–3, CMY to A. Macmillan, 6 June 1865)

And:

> Meantime the Chaplet of Pearls creeps on, but not very fast - it is rather play work, and winter is the best time for what is rather tougher. I have been asked to do an educational book for the middle class reading books put forth by the Clarendon press, and this is rather taking up the time for hard work. (BL: Add. 54920/132–3, CMY to A. Macmillan, Epiphany 1866)

Furthermore her correspondence with Macmillan makes it clear that she was part of a network involved in this sort of propaganda work, as her response when he asked her to edit a *Sunday Library* for him reveals:

> I should very much like Miss Keary's help in the Sunday Library. Mr Ashwell the Principal of the Training College at Durham is the gentleman I should most like to ask for help,...I only hope he (Mr A) may have time, but gentlemen are always so busy, and it is but a very select few who can hit off the exact medium between writing incomprehensibly to the young, and writing obtrusively *down* to them, especially on serious matters. Those who have the faculty write in perfection but it is a rare one! (BL: Add. 54920/142–3, CMY to A. Macmillan, 5 Febuary 1866)

> The only person to whom I have actually proposed the work is Miss Peard. In the 'Monthly Paper on Sunday Teaching' (Mozley) there are many good papers of hers signed FMP - as there are also of Mr Ashwell's signed ARA - rather tied down in both cases by being written for a lower class, but good specimens. She would be glad to undertake either the History of the Prayer Book or Bible Scenery,...I think Miss Wilbraham would do St Bernard and the Crusades beautifully . She got up the subject well, when about her 'Cheshire Pilgrims,' and though she writes a story heavily, yet on historical ground, she describes beautifully, and with all her heart. (BL: Add. 54920/144–7, CMY to A. Macmillan, 17 February 1866)

In the end Yonge declined editing the *Sunday Library*, and her various refusals to Macmillan demonstrate how the Keble influence operated. Her first response was very guarded:

> About the Editorship, I think I could manage it, if (I hate what I am going to say) I had full power of selection...I would gladly be on the staff of contributors, give all the help in my power, or else edit having full authority, but I am afraid of divided responsibilities. I know this has an unpleasant conceited sound, but it is brought to my knowledge again and again that my name is taken as a guarantee of an Anglican tone that is High and not Ultra high, and not at all Broad, that I do not feel as if it would be fair towards that class of readers to give that sort of sanction if I did not with my whole heart approve. If I did become in any way responsible, it must be with full authority. (BL: Add. 54920/134–5, CMY to A. Macmillan, 22 January 1866)

When finally refusing the editorship she wrote:

> I think I must lay aside that which I have hardly taken up the Sunday Library superintendence. I am sure that with my tone of principles, that the sort of responsibility would lead to questions & difficulty of

conscience that would hurt my health....As a fact I am afraid you must accept it that I am too High Church and too narrow for work not of that exclusive character, except at the expense of some harass - and that I find I am not equal to. (BL: Add. 54920/148–149, CMY to A. Macmillan, 19 March 1866)

The third of her professional careers was as educator and mentor to a group of young women, many of whom later joined the High-Church propaganda machine of which she was a leading figure. In 1859, encouraged by Mary Coleridge, one of the daughters of Keble's friend, Yonge started an essay society for a group of young women, the children of friends and relations, who were in need of more mental stimulation than the life of a Victorian daughter at home afforded them. To ward off accusations of pedantry and pretension they named themselves, self-deprecatingly, the Goslings, and Yonge was their Mother Goose. For all that, the intellectual ambitions of the society were quite serious. Each girl adopted a fancy pen-name such as 'Hedge Rose' or 'Shamrock'. Each wrote (at least at first) two essays a month for the society, and the best essays were circulated among them all. At the height of its prosperity, the society ran a delightful manuscript magazine, *The Barnacle*, which carried fiction, articles, drawings and translations by the members and their friends.[2] These girls were all being educated at home while their brothers, if they had any, went to schools and universities. Many were the daughters of rural clergymen or landowners and led isolated and monotonous lives. It must have been enormously encouraging for them to have a well-known woman writer and editor criticising their work and taking their intellectual aspirations seriously.

The foundation of the Gosling Society reflects the anxiety felt by many Victorians about the restricted educational opportunities for women. Its existence coincided with the dramatic expansion of schools and universities open to women. Although it does not seem that any of the Goslings benefited personally from these developments, they were, as Julia Courtney has argued, of the generation who helped to bring such schools and universities into being.[3] Yonge herself was not a wholehearted supporter of schools and universities for women. Although from the start she approved of the first of the educational initiatives of the pioneering Emily Davies, opening the Oxford and Cambridge 'local examinations' to girls (Yonge (1877), 33–4), she refused her support for another of Emily Davies' initiatives, Girton College, writing:

...as I have decided objections to bringing large masses of girls together, and think that home education under the inspection or encouragement of sensible fathers, or voluntarily continued by the girls themselves is far more valuable both intellectually and morally than any external education I am afraid I cannot assist you. (GC: GCRF, 9/1/22)

In fact the programme 'voluntarily continued' by the Goslings, with its twenty-four essays a year on topics ranging through history, theology, literary criticism and natural science, was at least as demanding as many of today's undergraduate courses in the humanities. It can have been no mean feat to research and compose two essays a month on such topics as 'The distinguished Christian characters of Milan' or 'What parallel stories does folklore in different countries present to the adventures of Ulysses in the Odyssey?' or 'The citizen of Athens', from the resources of Papa's library, for the inspection of eleven other young women and a famous novelist.

One of the Gosling Society's incidental functions was to introduce to Yonge a group of new contributors to her magazine, *The Monthly Packet*. Our work on Yonge's correspondence has enabled us to add to the list of members offered by Courtney in her work on the *Barnacle*, to see more clearly the connections between the members, and to see the extent to which they continued to play a part in Yonge's professional life for many years.[4] At any given moment there were twelve members of the society. It ran in all for about eighteen years, ending by mutual consent in September 1877. In that time it had at least 59 members (some of whom stayed only a short time). Of these two were slightly older, published writers (Frances Mary Peard and Florence Wilford) whom Yonge recruited in the mid-1860s to stiffen the standard of composition. Of the remainder, two, Christabel Coleridge and Mary Anderson Morshead, became stalwarts of the *Monthly Packet*, providing many features right to the very end of its existence. Coleridge eventually became its editor, and Anderson Morshead played a large part for many years in the management of the successive essay societies run under the aegis of the magazine under the names Arachne and her Spiders and Debateable Ground. Two, Mary Arnold (Mrs Humphry Ward) and Theodora Clarke (Mrs Bartle Teeling), though they did not last very long as members, and do not seem to have contributed to the *Monthly Packet*, went on to have long careers as professional writers. Phoebe Allen was another Gosling who graduated from working on the *Monthly Packet* to a career as a professional writer, publishing many works on natural history as well as fiction. Emily (Moberly) Awdry, the childless wife of a bishop, published a number of biographies. Long after the Gosling Society had ceased to exist, Yonge wrote to Florence Wilford:

> Going over our old brood...what a remarkable set they have been, for good, and alas! sometimes for the reverse,[5] but there are a good many that I am proud of. (Coleridge, 321)

These younger women, and others she came to know simply through their contributions to the *Monthly Packet*, turned to Yonge for guidance on how Keble would have viewed certain issues (Coleridge, 325), and continued the task of inculcating the 'Church principles' defined by the Oxford Movement. They also provided for Yonge in the latter part of her life the supportive interest, though not the stringent criticism, that had earlier come from her parents and the Keble circle.[6]

***

Keble's other major influence was on the values portrayed in Yonge's novels. There can be little doubt that Yonge would inevitably have become a novelist even if she had never met Keble, but the 'ethos' of the Oxford Movement pervaded her work, and had profound repercussions for her literary reputation. In 1896 Bessie Rayner Belloc wrote that 'justice has never been done her by the literary critics. Her books have been injured in literary circles, by her loyal devotion to her convictions in regard to the Anglican Church' (Belloc, 30). Even the revival of interest in women writers in the latter part of the twentieth century left her on the margins, primarily because, Nicola Diane Thompson argues, 'Yonge has fallen between both patriarchal/sexist and feminist critical agendas' (Thompson, 107). Those critics who have approached her have, as Alethea Hayter points out, been primarily concerned to uncover the less savoury elitist and misogynist implications of her high-minded principles or to explore 'the tension between Miss Yonge's natural creativity and the limitations imposed on it by dogma' (Hayter, 13).

The ethos of the novels does indeed outrage some readers, in particular those who find Jane Austen's Fanny Price or Barbara Pym's 'excellent women' intolerable. For them the most confronting and affronting aspect of Yonge's work is the extent to which she defines what came in the twentieth century to be seen as the legitimate pursuit of happiness as pride and selfishness, and what is regarded by some psychologists and psychoanalysts as almost wanton self-sacrifice and self-immolation as 'Christian submission', a devout bending to the will of God, accepting misfortune and traditional obligations as a 'cross' to be borne. Yet these views were not even specific to the Oxford Movement but accepted by her contemporary readers as the basic premises of their religion, propounded Sunday after Sunday in sermons and prayers. They were exposed to them from babyhood on, learning to sing, for example:

> There's not a child so small and weak,
> But has his little cross to take,
> His little work of love and praise
> That he may do for Jesus' sake. (Alexander 1850)

The 'role models' presented to them were missionaries and slum priests, to which could be added the 'noble women' celebrated in Girls' Annuals during the second half of the century: Joan of Arc, Grace Darling, Florence Nightingale and a host of lesser figures who devoted themselves to philanthropic activities (see Vicinus). Such nobility, they were taught, was only to be achieved through a training in self-control and self-sacrifice.

Part of Yonge's aim as a 'handmaid to the Church' was to breathe life into what were in danger of becoming conventional platitudes to which people paid unthinking lip service, by showing interesting and sympathetic characters acting out the dilemmas raised by such doctrines in social situations which the readers could recognize as 'true to life'. Thus in *The Daisy Chain* the heroine, Ethel May, gives up her classical studies, devoting her time to organising a school in a neglected hamlet, and her chances of marriage, in order to remain her father's companion. Similarly, in *The Pillars of the House*, Lance Underwood, perhaps the most attractive of all her male characters, abandons all thoughts of a singing career to help his brother in the business which supports the family of orphaned children.

There are, however, attitudes expressed in the novels that even those who can accept these characterizations as a genuine imaging of the *zeitgeist* of their period find disturbing, and these must be seen as having their origin in Keble's teaching. Even so sympathetic a critic as Alethea Hayter writes:

> It is not necessary to be an avowed feminist to be affronted by the degree of male chauvinism in Miss Yonge's novels. Even her most devoted admirers are shocked by the demands for womanly submission made throughout her works. Brothers as well as husbands and fathers are accorded the most despotic rights. (Hayter, 58)

Even here, however, it is necessary to put this submission into a broader context. There is no doubt that as her novels became more focused on female characters, and as the Women's Movement began proclaiming new 'rights', condemnation of female independence and self-sufficiency figured prominently in novels such as *The Clever Woman of the Family* (1865), *The Three Brides* (1876), and *Nuttie's Father* (1885). Nevertheless, as June Sturrock has pointed out, in all Yonge's books the same values are in fact applied to both male and female characters: the importance of family life, the temptations of competition, the need for self-sacrifice (Sturrock, 45, 99), and to this should be added willing, though not necessarily uncritical, submission to the Church and to those defined in its Catechism as one's 'governors, teachers, spiritual pastors and masters'. In the early novel *Dynevor Terrace* (1857), for example, most of the action is moved forward by the failure of two male characters in two different walks of life, Louis Fitzjocelyn, heir to a peerage, and his cousin James White, a schoolmaster, to pay proper respect to the wishes and advice of their father and uncle, the Earl of Ormersfield. In what Yonge believed to be a divinely ordained hierarchic world both men and women were, in her view, in a similar position to army officers, bound to obey their superiors, and to exact obedience from those beneath them. For women these superiors were more likely to be male, but they could, for both sexes, be female. Boys were, after all, expected to obey their mothers, nurses and governesses, and male servants their mistresses.

This same hierarchic view of submission is behind another of the characteristics that modern readers can find disturbing in the novels and thus in the ethos of the Oxford Movement: the paternalistic attitude to the working class and particularly the expectation of signs of respect (the curtsey, the tugged forelock) and the assumed right to deliver homilies on behaviour and financial management, not just to congregations and church groups, but to individuals. Even more disturbing for modern readers is the stern determination evidenced by Yonge's clerical and philanthropic characters to make access to schools and other charitable organizations dependent on membership of the Church of England, to exclude dissenters of all kinds, an attitude that seems even more outrageous when it relates to the leasing of farms and employing of farm labourers and servants.

It has to be accepted that this fierce sectarianism was very much a part of the Oxford Movement ethos, and one of the reasons why it is so frequently dubbed 'conservative'. Though adherents like Yonge were dedicated to educating all classes and promoting social mobility through education, to establishing charitable institutions – hospitals, orphanages, almshouses – more genial than the workhouse and to sponsoring community leisure activities, they held aloof from all the 'progressive' movements that did not come under the control of the Church of England. Though they had a vision of a welfare system providing for health, education, cultural enrichment and old age, it had to be a system sponsored by the Church, not the State. Thus whereas a moderate Anglican like Lady Knightley of Fawsley could be a long-time supporter of both the purely Anglican Girls' Friendly Society and the multi-denominational Society for Promoting the Employment of Women (Gordon), Yonge seems to have held back from such cooperation, particularly where education was concerned. The characters in Yonge's later books are, for example, dedicated to forestalling the 'godless education' of the Board Schools by raising money to establish Anglican elementary schools.

Yet the novels have strengths and charms that have ensured the continuing devotion of a substantial band of readers for a full hundred years since her death. Her characters are largely drawn through their brilliant, wryly humorous dialogue, and the richness of her world-building across linked novels rivals, if not surpasses, that of Trollope. Though she was modest about the construction of her plots, saying 'it is still my great deficiency,' she could hold the reader's interest over serial publications lasting years in length: her longest and perhaps most fascinating novel, *The Pillars of the House*, was serialized over the course of four years from 1870 to 1873. Her novels are also, as Margaret Maison has pointed out, 'quite untainted by any of the moralizing, sentimentality, or accounts of long-drawn-out agonies' that characterised so much religious fiction (Maison, 35).

Furthermore the novels have incomparable value as social history. Yonge was, it is generally agreed (see Strachey; Young), utterly trustworthy about the way things were, how people of various classes and religious affiliations behaved, their social and family relations, the attitudes they held, their enthusiasms. Furthermore her novels, covering as they do over half a century, allow one to see the changes taking place. Thus not only was Charlotte Yonge shaped by Keble, her books give a picture of his social philosophy and parochial practice, and of the philosophy and practice of his High-Church successors, that cannot be found in such rich detail anywhere else.

## Abbreviations

BL:     British Library
BUT:    Letters to Butler family in possession of Mrs Julia Birley.
CRC:    Letters to Christabel Coleridge in possession of Mrs Clare Roels.
GC:     Girton College Cambridge.
HL:     Huntington Library, California.
PCP:    Parrish Collection, Princeton University.
UIUC:   University of Illinois, Urbana Champaign.
WDRO:   West Devon Record Office

## Notes

[1] By the 1860s, as well as the *Magazine for the Young* they were publishing *Events of the Month*, called by Yonge 'a sort of school room Athenaeum' (BL: Add. 54920/28–29: CMY to A. Macmillan, 3 June 1864), a *Monthly Paper on Sunday Teaching* (edited by Yonge), and the quarterly *Christian Remembrancer* (to which over the years Yonge contributed half a dozen articles), addressed to the intellectual end of their clientele.

[2] The surviving volumes are in the library of Lady Margaret Hall, Oxford.

[3] Julia Courtney's paper is the only scholarly study of the group. One of Yonge's stories, *The Disturbing Element, or, Chronicles of the Bluebell Society* (1878) is about a middle-aged spinster who runs a reading group for a group of girls in a small resort in south Devon, and seems to draw on some of her experiences with the Goslings. There is also some discussion of essay societies in Yonge's regular column on 'Hints on Reading' in the *Monthly Packet* 30 (August 1865), 221–2.

4  A database of the known members of the Gosling Society is available on the web at www.cmyf.org. Any corrections and additions to this list are welcomed.

5  This is probably a reference to the later doings of Mildred Coleridge, daughter of Lord Coleridge and granddaughter of Keble's friend John Taylor Coleridge, for whom the society was originally founded, but whose marriage in 1885 came at the end of very public family row. It may also refer to Goslings like Mary (Arnold) Ward who later abandoned their 'Church principles'.

6  She cooperated with a group of them in writing two multiple-authored novels that Macmillan published: *The Miz Maze* (1883) and *Astray* (1886).

## Works Cited

Alexander, Cecil F., 'We are but little children weak', in *A Church School Hymn Book*, ed. Walter F. Hook, Leeds, 1850.

Belloc, B. R., *A Passing World*, London: Ward & Downey, 1897.

Blakeway, A., 'Towards a study of Marianne Dyson', London: Charlotte Yonge Society, 2002.

Butler, A. J., *Life and Letters of William John Butler, Late Dean of Lincoln and sometime Vicar of Wantage*, London: Macmillan, 1898.

Coleridge, C., *Charlotte Mary Yonge: Her Life and Letters*, London: Macmillan, 1903.

Courtney, J., 'The *Barnacle*, A manuscript magazine of the 1860s', *The Girl's Own: Cultural Histories of the Anglo-American Girl, 1830–1915*, Claudia Nelson and Lynne Vallone, eds, Athens, Georgia: University of Georgia Press, 1994, 70–97.

Dennis, B., *Charlotte Yonge (1823–1901), Novelist of the Oxford Movement: A Literature of Victorian Culture and Society*, Lampeter: Edwin Mellen, 1992.

Gordon, P., ed., *Politics and Society: The Journals of Lady Knightley of Fawsley 1885 to 1913*, Northampton: NRS, 1999.

Green, R. L., ed., *The Diaries of Lewis Carroll*, London: Cassell, 1953.

Hayter, A., *Charlotte Yonge*, London: Northcote House, 1996.

Keating, P., *The Haunted Study: A Social History of the English Novel 1875–1914*. London: Fontana, 1991.

Laski, M. and Tillotson, K., 'Bibliography', *A Chaplet for Charlotte Yonge*, G. Battiscombe and M. Laski, eds, London: Cresset Press, 1965.

Maison, M., *The Victorian Vision: Studies in the Religious Novel*, New York: Sheed and Ward, 1961.

Maxwell, C., *Mrs Gatty and Mrs Ewing*, London: Constable, 1949.

Moberly, C. A. E., *Dulce Domum: George Moberly, His Family and Friends*, London: John Murray, 1911.

Mozley, A., *Tales of Female Heroism*, London: James & Burns, 1846.

Romanes, E., *Charlotte Mary Yonge, An Appreciation*, London: Mowbray, 1908.

Strachey, R., *The Cause: A Short History of the Women's Movement in Great Britain*, London: Virago, 1928.

Sturrock, J., 'Heaven and Home': *Charlotte M. Yonge's Domestic Fiction and the Victorian Debate Over Women*, Victoria, Canada: University of Victoria, 1995.

Thompson, N. D., *Reviewing Sex: Gender and the Reception of Victorian Novels*, London: Macmillan, 1996.

Vicinus, M., 'Models for Public Life, Biographies of 'Noble Women' for Girls', *The Girl's Own: Cultural Histories of the Anglo-American Girl, 1830–1915*, C. Nelson and L. Vallone, eds, Athens, Georgia: University of Georgia Press, 1994.

Yonge, C. M., *Womankind*, London: Mozley and Smith, 1877.

—— *What Books to Lend and What to Give*, London: National Society's Depositary, 1887.

Young, G. M., *Victorian England: Portrait of an Age*, London: Oxford University Press, 1953.